FREAK SCENES

Music and the Moving Image

Series Editors
Kevin J. Donnelly, University of Southampton
Beth Carroll, University of Southampton

Titles in the series include:

Film's Musical Moments
by Ian Conrich and Estella Tincknell (eds)

Music, Sound and Multimedia
by Jamie Sexton (ed.)

Music Video and the Politics of Representation
by Diane Railton and Paul Watson

Contemporary Musical Film
by Kevin J. Donnelly and Beth Carroll (eds)

British Music Videos 1966–2016: Genre, Authenticity and Art
by Emily Caston

The Auditory Setting: Environmental Sounds in Film and Media Arts
by Budhaditya Chattopadhyay

Music in the Horror Films of Val Lewton
by Michael Lee

Freak Scenes: American Indie Cinema and Indie Music Cultures
by Jamie Sexton

www.edinburghuniversitypress.com/series/MAMI

FREAK SCENES

American Indie Cinema and Indie Music Cultures

Jamie Sexton

EDINBURGH
University Press

Edinburgh University Press is one of the leading university presses in the UK. We publish academic books and journals in our selected subject areas across the humanities and social sciences, combining cutting-edge scholarship with high editorial and production values to produce academic works of lasting importance. For more information visit our website: edinburghuniversitypress.com

© Jamie Sexton, 2023, 2024

Edinburgh University Press Ltd
The Tun – Holyrood Road
12(2f) Jackson's Entry
Edinburgh EH8 8PJ

First published in hardback by Edinburgh University Press 2023

Typeset in 10/12.5 Adobe Sabon by
IDSUK (DataConnection) Ltd, and
printed and bound by CPI Group (UK) Ltd,
Croydon, CR0 4YY

A CIP record for this book is available from the British Library

ISBN 978 1 4744 1406 7 (hardback)
ISBN 978 1 3995 1460 6 (paperback)
ISBN 978 1 4744 1407 4 (webready PDF)
ISBN 978 1 4744 1408 1 (epub)

The right of Jamie Sexton to be identified as the author of this work has been asserted in accordance with the Copyright, Designs and Patents Act 1988, and the Copyright and Related Rights Regulations 2003 (SI No. 2498).

CONTENTS

List of Figures		vi
Acknowledgements		viii
1	Introduction	1
2	A Brief History of Indie Music in American Indie Film	17
3	Sonic Authorship 1: Gregg Araki	35
4	Sonic Authorship 2: Sofia Coppola	57
5	Documenting Scenes and Performers 1: Punk, *Smithereens* and *Suburbia*	80
6	Documenting Scenes and Performers 2: Grunge and Riot Grrrl	104
7	Indie Music, Film and Race 1: *Medicine for Melancholy* and *Pariah*	131
8	Indie Music, Film and Race 2: *Sorry to Bother You*	155
9	Conclusion	176
Bibliography		182
Index		191

FIGURES

1.1	*Scott Pilgrim Versus the World*: the band rehearsing	2
2.1	*Repo Man*: Circle Jerks perform as a lounge band	22
2.2	*Ladies and Gentlemen, the Fabulous Stains*: Diane Lane as Corrine Burns	23
3.1	*The Living End*: Jon breakfasts with Luke in front of a prominent poster of The Smiths	40
3.2	*Mysterious Skin*: Neil listens to Ride on his headphones	53
4.1	*The Virgin Suicides*: fragments from the Lisbon sisters' personal items	64
4.2	*Lost in Translation*: Bob awakes jet-lagged in Tokyo	68
4.3	*Marie Antoinette*: Marie looks at the camera, accompanied on the soundtrack by Gang of Four	74
5.1	*Smithereens*: Wren plasters images of herself on a subway train	85
5.2	*Smithereens*: Wren places an image of Eric on a record over a poster of Eric	86
5.3	*Suburbia*: D.I. perform 'Richard Hung Himself' in concert	93
5.4	Frontal shot of the gang in *Suburbia* which references *A Clockwork Orange*	95
5.5	Frontal shot of the gang in *A Clockwork Orange*	95

FIGURES

6.1	*Slaves to the Underground*: Shelly and Suzie performing on stage with their band No Exits	110
6.2	*Slaves to the Underground*: Jimmy discusses independent media in a direct-to-camera monologue	114
6.3	*Down and Out with the Dolls*: Fauna performs for the first time with The Paper Dolls in a private garden	121
6.4	*The Itty Bitty Titty Committee*: Sadie graffities a wall as part of a Super 8 montage	126
7.1	*Medicine for Melancholy*: Micah and Jo dance intimately in the nightclub	138
7.2	*Pariah*: Alike feels conflicted as she rides home on the bus, prior to changing her clothes	146
7.3	*Pariah*: Bina puts on a Honeychild Coleman record for Alike	149
8.1	*Sorry to Bother You*: Worryfree's billboard advertisement becomes transformed through the Left Eye Group's adbusting	164
8.2	*Sorry to Bother You*: Worryfree's billboard advertisement becomes transformed through the Left Eye Group's adbusting	164
8.3	*Sorry to Bother You*: Cassius celebrates his telesales successes	169
8.4	*Dope*: a list of 'white shit'	172

ACKNOWLEDGEMENTS

Many people have aided in the development of this book, either directly through discussions and comments on work, or indirectly.

Firstly, I would like to thank Gillian Leslie at Edinburgh University Press. Gillian has been *very* patient with a slow writer who should have submitted his manuscript earlier and has helped in alleviating further stress and guilt. Sam Johnson has also been very helpful answering several questions and helping in various ways. I'd also like to thank others at EUP who have aided me, including Fiona Conn, Aidan Cross, Caitlin Murphy and Richard Strachan.

Kevin Donnelly and Beth Carroll, as editors for the *Music and the Moving Image* series, have been supportive of the book and have provided some helpful comments. Elsewhere, I'd like to thank Lori Burns, Geoff King and Holly Rogers for inviting me to publish on indie film and music in previous edited books. Thanks also to Kate Egan, Nessa Johnston, Elodie Roy and Cecilia Stenbom.

Parts of the Introduction and Chapter 1 have previously appeared in Sexton (2017), 'Independent Intersections: Indie Music Cultures and Independent Cinema' in Geoff King (ed.), *A Companion to American Independent Film* (Malden: Wiley Blackwell).

Significant parts of Chapter 7 have appeared in Sexton (2022), '"Everything About Being Indie is All Tied to Not Being Black": Indie Music, Race and Identity in *Medicine for Melancholy* and *Pariah*', in *Music, Sound and the Moving Image* 16.2, published by Liverpool University Press. My thanks to Liverpool University Press for permission to republish these sections.

1 INTRODUCTION

Released in 2010, *Scott Pilgrim Versus the World* (Wright) illustrates how indie music can be used in a film to both aid marketing and strengthen a film's indie credentials. Based on a Canadian indie comic, the film included characters playing in an indie-rock band, performing songs written by Beck, with a soundtrack featuring an extensive amount of indie-rock music by bands such as Broken Social Scene, Beachwood Sparks and Black Lips.[1] These elements were used to promote the film to its target youth demographic, and the existing appeal of both indie music and the indie comics it adapted were considered hooks which might encourage audiences to see the film. *Scott Pilgrim Versus the World* points to both the risks and potential benefits of such a strategy. Its aim of targeting existing indie music and comic fans was supplemented by social media advertising, where it was hoped that younger social media users would share content to further promote the film. Its initial box-office performance was, however, disappointing. Although the film was discussed and shared heavily across social media sites, some marketers thought that it was being shared by a limited community and creating, according to marketing agent David Berkowitz, an 'echo chamber effect' (Friedman 2010). Since its release, though, it has continued to generate cult interest and further revenue, with its soundtrack a prime factor in its continued relevance (a tenth anniversary soundtrack edition was released in 2020 in variant-coloured discs). As such, it points to how targeting indie fans in this manner can be risky for larger-budgeted films if they do not appeal beyond their core target demographic. The continued interest in the film, however, also emphasises how a

Figure 1.1 *Scott Pilgrim Versus the World*: the band rehearsing

niche fanbase might sustain interest in specific films and spread awareness of them to newer generations.

Scott Pilgrim Versus the World connects to several issues that will be examined in this book, including the licensing of indie music within indie films and the representation of both indie performers and indie music scenes. Yet, as a film which cost around $60 million and which was produced and distributed by Universal, it also represents the more commercialised realm of 'indie' filmmaking, a realm that some would not consider authentically 'indie'. The growing commercialisation of both indie film and music sectors, within which so-called 'indie' music and films are released through corporate-controlled entities, is another crucial issue informing this book. Such issues, I argue, should not be overstated as they have long existed, but they have certainly accelerated since the millennium.

Although an extensive body of work on popular music and film now exists, not a great deal of attention has been paid to the intersections between indie music and indie film.[2] It is perhaps surprising that there has not been more work investigating the many relations between the spheres of indie music and film, particularly considering Newman's (2011: 4) argument that 'indie' was first used within music cultures before being applied to other cultural areas, including film. In this book I examine a number of films that license indie music and represent indie music scenes, as well as commission indie musicians to create scores and other music. The work is informed by history; as both indie music and American independent film were seen to enter new, distinctive phases in the 1980s, my focus spans the early 1980s up until today, and

I outline some very broad historical developments in Chapter 2. It is important to be aware of some historical shifts across both film and music culture because dominant conceptions of indie can change over time. The following sections will outline broad connotations of the term indie within music and film, indicating some important historical developments that will be covered further in Chapter 2. As the concept first developed in music, I will scrutinise this area in some detail before noting similarities between indie music and American indie film.

A Brief Overview of Indie Music

Frequent use of the term indie occurred initially within the UK independent music scene in the 1980s. At first it was merely an abbreviation of 'independent', but over time it began to accrue other connotations, such as generic qualities and ethical positions. Yet because these connotations developed piecemeal, were subject to historical shifts, and never fully agreed upon, the term indie remains quite broad and difficult to fully pin down in a straightforward sense; it is, as Maria Raha (2005: xi) has argued, a 'loosely structured' category. This is also the case for many other genres; Simon Frith (1996: 77) has argued that features attributed to musical genres 'have never been clear or consistent. Genre maps change according to who they're for.' Historically, indie has referred largely to a predominantly white mode of guitar-based music that emerged from the punk rock explosion and is often associated with intelligence and rebellion in comparison to the more 'manufactured' pop music associated with the mainstream (Hesmondhalgh 1999: 38). Beyond these distinctions, many different subgenres can exist within indie, such as chillwave, grunge, industrial, jangle-pop and shoegaze, to name a few examples. As such, the term indie exists as a kind of generic umbrella term. But it also operates in other ways: it still, for example, often connotes independence more generally, and in this sense can be used as an adverbial modifier of other genres. When employed in this way, the term can also refer to types of music that fall outside its more dominant connotations: for example, indie hip-hop, or indie R&B (I will return to question the contours of indie sketched here in the final two chapters, which focus on race and indie).

Ryan Hibbett (2005: 59) has argued that definitions of indie can subjectively differ from person to person:

> Depending on which bands one comes to associate with the genre – through which portal one enters the indie 'scene' – specific conventions are likely to be recognized and anticipated. That is to say, particular notions of 'what is indie' are closely bound to personal experience, as well as age and social class.

In this book I want to draw on some of the more dominant ways that indie has been used within the music world but also acknowledge other, sometimes more marginal, ways it has been employed culturally. This necessitates recognition of its historical and subjective variability, and acknowledgement that some users of the term will stress different factors: for some it is primarily a loose generic term, for others it is more of an industrial term that does not necessarily denote any musical style and is primarily an ethical choice.

As indie first emerged as a shorthand for independent, it is necessary to outline what 'independent' connotes within the music industry. Initially, independent music referred to any music released outside of the major record companies, who have long dominated the record market. While independent record labels have a longer history, it was in the 1980s that 'independent music' started to become a much-discussed topic following the emergence of punk and the explosion of a new cadre of independent labels. These new independent labels were forming when the major record companies had increased their control of the global music industry. By the late 1970s the music industry was dominated by six transnational companies: EMI, CBS, PolyGram, WEA, RCA and Decca.[3] The late 1970s and 1980s were crucial stages in the growth of the independent music business, when 'independent' – sometimes (and increasingly) shortened to indie – became associated with a set of values as well as styles of music.

Core values emerging from participants within the independent music sector – many of which are still important within indie cultures – included a commitment to DIY ('do-it-yourself') and a rejection of industry standards. One of the key dimensions of punk and post-punk music was that professionalism could be bypassed; one did not have to release a record on a major label – a difficult process for a new act – or even be a competent musician. Signing to a major label often required a standard of musical proficiency and an ability to produce music of a 'professional' standard, which was costly. Many punk and post-punk musicians perceived such standards as stifling musical creativity and participation. Dave Laing (2015: 27) has noted how many independent record companies existed prior to the emergence of punk in the UK, but the sheer number of such labels, their often regional base (many being housed outside of London) and the associated ethos of non-professionalism and DIY marked a new stage in musical independence. These anti-mainstream currents would influence subsequent independent music scenes within and outside of the UK. It is for this reason that I begin the historical development of indie music's inclusion in film with punk, whose importance is also signalled by its influence on large swathes of subsequent indie music.

While independently produced music containing a discernible antimainstream ethos and a concomitant commitment to DIY principles developed in the United States as well, many critics have considered the UK indie music scene as influential on American independent music. Holly Kruse (2003: 38) has noted how the development of an independent music distribution network in the United States was influenced by the Cartel in Britain, a cooperative established by numerous independent record companies to distribute independent records nationwide more effectively. Michael Azerrad (2001: 5–6) has also claimed that many American independent labels were inspired by British indie labels such as Stiff and Chiswick in the late 1970s. While the term indie did tend to be used more frequently in the UK in the 1980s than in the US, it has been employed increasingly in the US since the 1990s. Hibbett (2005: 58) claims that the huge success of Nirvana and subsequent mainstream status of much grunge music was a key moment marking the increased use of indie within the US because 'alternative' had become too associated with commercialism and co-optation.[4] If indie has since become a more dominant term than 'college rock' and 'alternative' within the US, it should be noted that 'alternative' is still often used in similar ways to indie, both in the US and UK (college rock doesn't get used so much in the current climate), and I will often use the terms 'alternative' and 'indie' synonymously. It is worth noting some core differences between the UK and the US here, as independent and college rock referred to different ways of conceptualising music dissemination. In the US, college rock referred to a broad range of rock music playing on college stations, which specialised in playing music not often aired on more mainstream stations. In terms of specialist charts, the UK has had an official independent singles and album chart since 1980; in the US only a comparable independent albums chart exists – and this only since 2000 – while the most similar singles chart is 'Alternative Singles'[5], based on radio plays as opposed to the UK independent singles chart, which is based on music sales (and, since 2014, music streaming data). The story of the independent charts in the UK points to overlaps between independent (and its abbreviation indie) as a term referring to a production process on the one hand, and as a broad generic identifier on the other. The UK independent charts referred originally only to the companies producing and distributing the music and not to any musical style, but by the mid-1980s independent and its abbreviation indie were being used to refer to styles of music, most commonly guitar-based 'pop-rock' that emerged from punk.[6] There was, of course, a range of music released on independent labels that lay outside of such sonic parameters, but this was the most dominant type of music associated with indie at this stage. The C86 cassette released by *New Musical Express* magazine was a key moment when indie began to function as a genre-like term, and at this point in the UK it often referred to jangle-pop, a mode of pop-rock that harked back to 1960s harmonic rock and featured chiming, 'jangly' guitars as a chief sonic ingredient (often on 12-string guitars).[7] The Byrds are probably the most influential band on the jangle-pop sound, and in the UK The Smiths were its most popular proponents. Jangle-pop also made its presence felt in the US indie/college rock scene in the 1980s, with R.E.M. the biggest act associated with the sound.

The rising generic connotations of indie would also have been influenced by the nature of other specialist charts in the UK at this point. Outside the main singles and albums charts, specialist charts existed that were all, bar the independent chart, classified according to musical genre, including rock and metal, R&B and dance music. This positioning amongst generic charts would have undoubtedly influenced some to connect the independent/indie charts with a style – or at least *styles* – of music. From around the mid- to the late-1980s indie music was often differentiated from other charts and so partly gained meaning negatively: firstly, it was often considered different from mainstream music; secondly, it was also distinct from other specialist forms of music with dedicated charts. Due to the ways that independent companies were differentiated from the majors, distinction from the mainstream was important, which is why music released by independent labels was also dubbed alternative in some circles. As a range of independent music around this time was grounded in pop structures – though there were other, more experimental forms – *pop* was not necessarily the core factor used to differentiate indie from the mainstream. Rather, mainstream pop and indie-pop in the late 1980s were often distinguished through production values and an associated attitude: many mainstream pop stars built music around synthetic sounds and would promote themselves via a carefully constructed public persona, which was often visually-oriented; 'indie pop' at this stage was more nostalgic in harking back to 1960s guitar-based pop music, often used lo-fi production, was less committed to ideas of professionalism, and tended to shun the new visually-oriented era, in particular the music video (many indie acts did not even make music videos; those who did would often produce extremely low-budget videos). And yet while indie was often distinguished from the mainstream and more specialist genre chart music, there were occasional overlaps: independent records did sometimes sell enough units to enter the mainstream Top 40, while other independently released records would appear in the dance, or metal and rock, charts. One particularly notable overlap between the mainstream and independent charts was the case of British production team SAW (Stock, Aitken and Waterman), who despite releasing records on an independent label (PWL) were firmly catering to mainstream tastes. They had a slew of number one hits with artists such as Rick Astley, Jason Donovan and Kylie Minogue in the 1980s which, due to their mainstream, hi-NRG sound and huge sales (the records were distributed by major companies), were rejected by many within the indie community. While the records were released on an independent label, they were still othered by many in the independent music world due to their indistinguishability from mainstream music. They were nevertheless included in the independent charts.

The connection between independent/indie music and specific music styles would continue into the early 1990s, when a large range of dance music was regularly listed on the independent charts. According to David Hesmondhalgh (1999: 51), this was a period when many industry insiders started to campaign for the independent charts to be based more firmly around musical values due to the increased overlaps between the indie charts and other charts, and because the existing criteria for eligibility for the independent charts was starting to be undermined by major labels. Major record companies could produce and distribute records that would be eligible for the independent charts if they set up a small offshoot label and distributed records through existing independent means (usually via the independent network, the Cartel); an example is Virgin Records subsidiary Hut, which released records by bands such as Moose and The Verve that reached the independent charts. Such issues point to how the term independent is rarely straightforward: dominant types of music considered part of, or anathema to, independent music can change over time, as can distinctions and relations between major and independent companies.

As noted, the situation in the US was slightly different, though there were many connections between independent music cultures in these respective countries. While *indie* was not used as frequently in the US, independent record companies did also emerge in large numbers there during the 1980s. As in the UK, much of this was kickstarted by punk, which became the most dominant type of independent music discussed, alongside other independently released rock music. As Holly Kruse (2003: 8) has noted, there were a large range of other types of music also released independently – e.g. blues, rap, bluegrass, folk – 'but the word "indie" is perhaps most commonly used to describe independent rock and pop labels'. Some iconic American independent labels that appeared during the late 1970s and early 1980s include Twin/Tone (1977), SST (1978) and Alternative Tentacles (1979), followed by more in the 1980s, such as Wax Trax! (1980), Touch and Go (1981), K Records (1982), Taaang! (1984) and Sub Pop (1986).

The values associated with independent music cultures tend to highlight, most prominently, a belief in the superiority of independent production for several reasons, though the most common is that independent production affords greater artistic autonomy and less of a need to compromise commercially. If the major record companies represent a world in which commercial and professional values are paramount, then independent companies offer a space in which music artists can potentially work free from huge commercial pressures. As signing with a major company often entails extensive promotional duties and attention paid to how a band markets itself, working with independents sometimes enables musicians to at least avoid excessive promotional work. Consequently, independent artists have tended to be considered more authentic than mainstream pop stars because they are often seen as spending more time on things that really matter, such as making music, as opposed to expending too much effort on promoting themselves and/or working on their public image.[8]

These are, admittedly, broad examples of *perceived* differences between the majors and the independents frequently reproduced in discourses; they do not reflect the complex differences existing across both independent and major labels. Independent record labels, for example, can vary greatly in terms of size and operational scale. At the smaller-scale end of independent record companies are micro-labels, which Robert Strachan (2007: 247) describes as 'small scale operations usually run from private addresses by one or two individuals who undertake all the tasks necessary for the commercial release of a recording themselves (from making contractual arrangements with musicians to organizing finances, from designing and packaging to promotional activities and the organization of distribution)'. There are many larger independent companies, however, who have formed alliances with major labels: examples include the American label I.R.S. Records, often referred to as an independent, which maintained distribution deals with larger companies throughout its existence, including A&M, MCA and EMI; British independent label Creation was partly taken over by Sony in the early 1990s, who purchased a 50 per cent stake in the company. While some independent companies are formed and continue as very small-scale operations, those which expand often face problems if they wish to retain their independence. Expansion without any corporate involvement can be difficult to achieve and precarious (hence the collapse of other iconic British independent labels Factory and Rough Trade in the early 1990s);[9] not expanding might be considered detrimental to the artists on the label, and it also often entails running the label on a shoestring budget without generating enough income for those involved to earn a living. As such, compromise is often necessary within the world of independent record companies. While some may consider such processes examples of co-option by the mainstream, David Hesmondhalgh has persuasively argued how independent record labels can still maintain distinctive identities even if they have deals with, or are partly owned by, major companies 'by forming a protective shield':

> whereby corporate finance and corporate culture are kept at 'arm's length' distance from musicians and staff who share tastes and political backgrounds. A purist's position which sees professionalization as 'co-option' implies a way of living which is difficult for many people to sustain: a constant existence on an impoverished margin. The choice to set up more permanent positions and careers, while despised by so many enthusiasts, is often based on a genuinely idealistic commitment

to fostering talent, and to providing an alternative. (Hesmondhalgh 1999: 440–1)

Owners of independent companies might have to compromise, but they can still maintain a vision that is separate from companies who maintain influence over them.

One reason for the major labels' growing involvement in the independent sector is that they have often viewed it as a kind of testing ground; if a music artist starts to sell significant units and/or gain a substantial following, then a major label might sign the artist and attempt to take their career to the next level (something which independent labels might not have the resources to bring about). This has historically led to debates around independent artists 'selling out' by signing to major companies versus remaining locked within a safe, independent ghetto. Some bands who are signed to, and who make their reputation on, an independent label may have no interest in retaining independence and consider this a temporary stage before signing to a major. Other bands might be more strongly attached to an independent, anti-corporate ethos. If, on many occasions, acclaimed artists are accused of weakening their sound when releasing music on a major, others can still maintain credibility: examples include American artists who have moved from releasing independent records to the majors such as The Flaming Lips and the now-defunct Sonic Youth, who, because they were seen to still exert a certain level of artistic control and integrity, often maintained an indie status.

Generically, indie music today still often connotes white guitar pop-rock music differentiated from mainstream music, but it has undergone change over time. One notable development is that, since the emergence and spread of digital technologies, electronic sounds are increasingly incorporated within indie music, which has expanded the types of music frequently classified as such, leading to further definitional problems. Very broadly, indie music is often considered a mode of production that tends to fall somewhere between the experimental and avant-garde on one hand, and the commercial mainstream on the other (much like indie cinema). A significant amount of music classified as indie tends to employ reasonably conventional pop structures, but still retains a veneer of *difference*, either sonically (through moderate experimentation within conventional forms) or through the attitude of musical artists (such as being committed to independent production and rejecting industry norms). However, due to the escalating commercial co-option of independent music – through releasing 'indie' music via major labels or through majors buying interests in independent labels – there is usually a closer relationship to, and dependence on, the music industry than more marginal forms of independent music production. In the current climate, indie music is often linked to a smaller-scale engagement with consumer capitalism rather that an outright rejection of it. As Keir Keightley has argued in his discussion of indie-rock (the most privileged mode of indie music):

> Indie rock is defined by its concern for the scale of consumer capitalism, rather than by its radical rejection of an economic system. This concern with reduced scale may also be glimpsed in indie culture's investment in the miniature: in boutique record stores, 45 rpm singles, small runs of home-made cassettes, or the reverent recreation of miniature models of past eras or albums. (Keightley 2001: 336)

American Independent/Indie Cinema

There are many similarities between indie music and (American) indie cinema. Like independent music in both the US and UK, American independent cinema entered a new phase in the 1980s, even though there is a longer history of independent filmmaking in the US preceding this era.[10] Over time, developments in American independent filmmaking from the 1980s have become a core part of histories and accounts of modern independent cinema in the US (King 2005; Tzioumakis 2011b). And, like independent music, American independent cinema would often be termed *indie* by critics and audiences over time. Within both music and film cultures, the term indie was originally used as a shorthand for independent but would subsequently take on a range of further connotations, encompassing aesthetics, modes of production and distribution, institutions and audiences (i.e. niche audiences who tend to favour music or films outside of the mainstream). Aesthetically, the indie film is a film that is different from Hollywood in form and/or content, though the parameters of such differences can vary. As a mode of production, it is relationally contrasted to Hollywood (which it nonetheless may be connected to) as a sector allowing greater opportunity for filmmakers to enjoy creative freedom. It is also a label that can be used by both marketers and audiences: promotional materials may highlight a film's indie values, and these may influence embracers of this mode of production to see it. Institutionally, both indie film and music tend be promoted and discussed in specialist critical magazines and ezines and disseminated via various specialist venues (film festivals and smaller, independent cinemas in the case of film, smaller venues in the case of music). Discussing indie film, Sherry B. Ortner (2013: 92) claims that an indie 'scene' – which she defines as 'a positively shared social and cultural world' – 'consists in part of an infrastructure with a range of institutions: production companies, professional organizations, festivals, film schools, magazines, and so forth'.

Both indie film and indie music are difficult to define in any precise manner because they connote a range of different types and styles of film and music. As such, both indie music and indie film cannot really be considered singular entities, as argued by Michael Newman (2017: 25), who writes that 'indie is a type of movie, a mode of production and distribution, a community of practice, a cultural ideal, and a shorthand for something people too easily celebrate or deride. Actually, it is not one type, mode, community, ideal, and shorthand, but several.' Newman's emphasis on indie as a multivalent concept indicates the complexity of a term which spans different cultural processes. Indie often refers to different types of production outside of Hollywood (film) or the major companies (music), but it can also include examples that have been produced and/ or distributed by major corporations. The pattern of independent record labels being purchased by majors in the 1990s was mirrored in the film industry, with some notable independent film businesses being acquired by Hollywood companies: examples include Disney's acquisition of Miramax in 1993, Turner Broadcasting System's acquisition of New Line in 1994, and Universal's purchase of majority stakes in October Films in 1997.[11] The increasingly commercialised climate of the independent film industry also led to the establishment of studio specialty divisions – resembling the establishment of 'indie' subsidiaries by majors within the record industry – such as Sony Pictures Classics (1992), Fox Searchlight Pictures (1994) and Universal's Focus Features (2002). Because these companies often made films that were aesthetically closer to independent films than traditional mainstream Hollywood fare, and targeted them at more niche demographics, many such films were positioned – in promotion and critical reception – as indie films. Since the late 1990s at least, 'indie' has often referred to both fully independent productions *and* some studio-based productions. As is the case with music, indie cinema can exist in different forms: from extremely low-budget, DIY productions that are independently distributed, to mid-level productions which gain larger distribution deals with Hollywood companies. Beyond these modes of production, indie cinema can also span different genres (such as drama, comedy, horror) and aesthetic forms.

As indie music and indie film share similarities, with many people committed to investing time and effort in indie cultures, then the interconnections between them are worthy of study. As such, this book is a contribution towards a growing tendency within studies of American indie film to locate it within a broader media environment. Tzioumakis (2011b: 332) has noted this trend but also emphasised how much more work needs to be done:

> In today's age of media convergence, of global entertainment industries and transnational media economies, it becomes increasingly important to locate the study of one particular media form and institution – in this case American independent cinema – within a wider context in order to account for the wealth of influences, associations, trends and tendencies that characterise it. Given that this work has appeared only in very recent years, there is still great potential for a rigorous examination of independent filmmaking within several wider contexts.

This book is not an exhaustive attempt at documenting the intersections between these cultural industries: the deepening histories of their respective spheres and the huge wealth of media content that has been – controversially or not – considered indie, render such an attempt questionable. I largely focus on the licensing of indie music across various indie films and the representation of indie music scenes and performers, while also discussing some examples of indie musicians who have scored indie films. There are many other intersections, including indie musicians either acting or undertaking other filmmaking roles, including direction; indie film directors making music videos for indie acts; indie music being an increasingly central component of many independent film festivals; independent music companies becoming involved in film production (such as JagJaguwar). Some of these will be touched on in this book, but they all are worthy of further research. I should also mention that a huge number of documentaries on various indie music artists and scenes have also been made; while I do refer to some of these in the book, I mostly focus on the fiction film.

Scope and Focus

The selection of films/music to focus on has been a difficult task due to the huge number of films and musical selections that can be termed indie. Before discussing my reasons for exploring specific films and issues, I will outline how I will be using indie myself, starting with music. I have largely adopted a discursive approach to indie music; that is, I have focused on music which has frequently been positioned as indie by critics, though there are further aspects to establish. Firstly, I have mostly focused on a more dominant mode of indie music, indie pop-rock, and in particular a range of guitar-based music that emerged from punk. But as indie originally referred to independent, and is still used in this manner on occasion, I've also included some other forms of independent music in the coverage, such as industrial and electronic music; in Chapters 7 and 8 I question some of the more dominant understandings of indie music through an exploration of race. As indie music is often considered a very white mode of music, I question to what extent dominant, largely generic conceptions of indie music are racist. Though much of the music covered in the book has been released by independent labels, there is some discussion of music that was released on major labels, particularly if the artists have been frequently discussed by critics as providing some kind of alternative to the mainstream; once again, punk provides an example in that some punk music was released by major labels, but was perceived frequently as providing an alternative to the mainstream, mainly through aggressive sounds and anti-social attitudes.

My approach to music is from a broadly cultural, as opposed to a musicological, angle. I am interested in the ways that indie music connotes broader meanings and values, and some of the reasons it appeals to its audiences. Consequently, core values which circulate around indie music (and indie film) are explored within sections of the book. One of these is the idea of *alternative*: indie music has often been perceived as providing alternatives to mainstream music, and as such has tended to appeal to people who themselves might feel alienated from and/or dissatisfied with the societies within which they find themselves. Yet because many forms of indie music adopted existing pop-rock structures, such differences were often modest rather than radical, which ultimately made it – or at least its more conventional examples – ripe for commercial co-option. The case is similar for indie filmmaking. One issue I explore in various pages is the complicated ways that ideas of alternative, and of independence, can be mobilised within a highly commercialised media environment. David Hesmondhalgh and Leslie M. Meier (2015: 100) have argued that by the turn of the century 'even the most committed fans would be hard pressed to argue that indie and alternative musical culture was in any meaningful sense "independent" of, or "alternative" to, anything much'. Yet many audiences committed to indie/alternative forms of culture *do* often still consider certain 'indie' media as offering an alternative to more mainstream products; even if these judgements are increasingly likely to involve aesthetic, as opposed to political, distinctions, and might partly be driven by maintaining elitist distinctions between themselves and less discerning consumers, they are still important factors to explore.

Despite much indie film and music existing as part of a highly commercialised, capitalist culture, issues such as 'selling out' and the concept of authenticity remain strong. Consequently, this book will engage with some of these debates, particularly the concept of authenticity. Michael Newman (2011: 224–6) has previously discussed the importance of authenticity as a concept within indie film cultures, arguing that it continues to be an important way of judging films despite the increased commercialisation of the indie sphere. He claims the concept operates in two main ways: (1) pertaining to the *sincerity* and *commitment* of an artist; (2) as a way of judging distinctions between authentic and inauthentic. In the first category, the concept acts as a way of measuring the genuine authorship of a film: this can happen within studio-backed films if there is a perception that an artist (director) has managed to avoid making too many commercial concessions. In the second category, there can exist debates over whether a film is a 'true' indie picture: once again, this might not depend on the institutional basis of the film, but on judgements around its aesthetics, whether it is considered as offering a genuine alternative to the mainstream. Newman contends that, following the commercialisation of the indie sphere, which includes 'indie' pictures being released by studios, there have been increased discussions over whether films can be considered 'true' or 'fake' indie pictures, though he also adds that no straightforward criteria can be used to assess such judgements, that they arise from 'a matter for interpretation and discursive positioning' (226).

These ideas of authenticity are important, and will be drawn on within this book, but I also explore authenticity through the representation of music scenes. This is a slightly different way of judging the authenticity of films, for it does not rely so squarely on authorial integrity – though this can be an important factor – but is more concerned with judging the 'reality effect' of certain films. Such issues are particularly important in the discussion of films which depict indie music scenes and/or feature music performances. As I will demonstrate, many films that feature indie music performances and scenes are grounded in documentary research of and/or participation within the scenes depicted, and often include other markers of authenticity, such as featuring real indie bands in the production of, and appearance in, filmed music performances. Balancing the twin demands of fictional entertainment and documentary-style representation can be quite a difficult balancing act for filmmakers. Whether such films are received by critics and wider audiences as authentic can then depend on the extent of a viewers' knowledge of, and participation within, such music scenes, and how viewers estimate the credibility of the depicted events.

The concept of 'selling out', meanwhile, is another crucial issue that informs this study. The idea of selling out within indie music cultures has been constant over its history; Klein et al. (2016: 13) argue that while such debates are not as pressing as they once were, they do still inform discussions over artistic integrity and credibility, though have become more 'nuanced' and 'contradictory'. Questions of selling out became a core theme of many 1990s indie films representing indie music scenes; following the commercial breakthrough of grunge music and the rising status of 'alternative rock', the difficulties of remaining independent within an increasingly commercialised environment became addressed frequently. Some of these, including *Slaves to the Underground* (Peterson, 1997) and *Down and Out with the Dolls* (Voss, 2001), are covered in Chapter 6.

The coverage of the book is informed by several factors. Firstly, I have attempted to include a range of music and films from the early 1980s up until the present day. Secondly, I have explored race and gender issues within indie music and examined how these have been addressed in some films. As there has been frequent discussion of sexism within indie music cultures, Chapter 6 investigates representations of women in indie-rock, and links this to the impact of riot grrrl culture that emerged in the early 1990s. The whiteness of indie music is also addressed in Chapters 7 and 8, which look at how indie is often opposed to blackness: these chapters examine the ways indie-rock can play an important role within the construction of eccentric black characters in two films – *Medicine for Melancholy* (Jenkins, 2008) and *Pariah* (Rees, 2011) – but also seek to question existing understandings of indie, probing whether there can exist less racially prejudiced conceptions of indie music. Thirdly, I explore some of the ways that authorship can be related to indie music. The idea of musical choices feeding into a broader authorial profile is a topic that has gained increasing attention in recent years, so I have closely examined how two directors – Gregg Araki and Sofia Coppola – have used indie music within many of their films and explored how this informs their filmmaking more broadly.

The book takes, as mentioned, a largely cultural approach; that is, I am interested in the ways that indie music – both generally and in more specific instances – tends to connote certain values, which can themselves inform the meanings of films that they are embedded in. When placed on a film's soundtrack, music can create intertextual associations – whether this is related to a specific song, the artist who performed it, or a broader scene it might be connected to – and create additional meaning. In these cases, music points to a world outside of the film, often commenting on some of the issues being played out in the film's diegesis. Yet music is also often a core component of a film's diegesis: in many films covered here, music is discussed and listened to by characters within the film, and sometimes played by characters; music can therefore contribute to a sense of realism (music as part of the fabric of many people's everyday lives) as well as link to character construction (such as when a character's musical tastes may indicate something about their personality).

The commercial elements of music will also be touched on frequently. In particular, the ways that the use of music on a film's soundtrack, as well as the representation of music cultures, might appeal to potential audiences. The commercial exploitation of a range of indie music has grown over the years; it became particularly notable following the breakout success of grunge music in the early 1990s, while since the 2000s a number of larger profile indie films – such as *Garden State* (Braff, 2004), *Juno* (Reitman, 2007), *500 Days of Summer* (Webb, 2009) and the previously mentioned *Scott Pilgrim Versus the World* – have used indie music prominently as part of their overall 'indie aesthetic' and have often signalled its presence through advertising and spin-off soundtrack albums (the soundtracks for these films all sold well).

In the next chapter I provide a very broad overview of some historical developments in the licensing of indie music within American independent (and other) films, as well as noting some appearances in independent films by punk and indie musicians. I commence with an overview of the representation of punk cultures and the licensing of punk music, before charting the increased commercial appeal of indie music throughout the 1990s and since the 2000s, noting some factors that have led to such changes. This will provide a broad framework for the subsequent chapters which focus on specific filmmakers, films and issues.

Notes

1. The film also had links to video games: it incorporates a video game aesthetic, and a video game of the film was also produced.
2. There have been some articles and books which look at indie music within the films of specific directors, some of which I draw on within this book, but not much work addressing how indie music both informs and is employed in indie film. The closest work I have encountered to my study is the thesis by Matthew William Nicholls (2011) on the use of popular music in independent American cinema. Like Nicholls, I am focusing on American independent cinema, but he looked at music more broadly (even though he does examine some indie music).
3. Today the music industry is dominated by three large conglomerates: Sony, UMG and Warner Music Group.
4. 'Indie', nevertheless, became quickly commercialised in a similar manner.
5. It was launched in 1988 as 'Modern Rock Tracks' and was an alternative to the Mainstream Rock Tracks chart. It was named 'Alternative Songs' in 2009.
6. I am adopting 'pop-rock' from Motti Regev (2013).
7. The tape was available for readers to buy via mail order. *NME* had previously released an independent compilation in 1981 – *C81* – which was musically more eclectic (though C86 was not entirely homogeneous in sound even though it featured a good deal of jangle-pop music).
8. Rachel Lifter has noted that there was more interaction between indie styles and the fashion industry from the 1990s onwards, but that even when indie bands became more engaged in fashion and appearance, they would still tend to downplay the importance of fashion: 'For musicians, who were styled for media coverage, adhering to the values of rock meant eschewing a too obvious engagement with appearance, often considered costume' (Lifter 2020: 54).
9. Rough Trade was revived as a record label in 2000.
10. Work on American independent cinema far outweighs work on other national independent cinemas, which is one of the prime reasons why I am focusing on American independent filmmaking. Certainly, there is – and always has been – a range of independent productions outside of the US, but there is not a recognised indie sector in any other country on such a scale.
11. Turner Broadcasting System merged with TimeWarner in 1996.

2 A BRIEF HISTORY OF INDIE MUSIC IN AMERICAN INDIE FILM

Charting a broad overview of historical developments relating to the inclusion of indie music in American indie film is important in terms of establishing indie music's increased screen value, commercial clout and cultural status. While I am focusing on film/music relations, the use of indie music has risen in screen-based media generally, not just film, including – most prominently – television, advertising and video games. As such, I will refer to other media industries on occasion, specifically television, as many personnel work across film and television (another trend which has become more common due to the heightened convergence between these two industries in more recent times). I will begin this historical sketch in the late 1970s, a 'pre-indie' phase that was nonetheless so crucial to the emergent concept of indie that it warrants further discussion.

As mentioned in Chapter 1, punk and post-punk are often linked with the beginnings of a new era for independent music. While some artists had previously released music independently – whether on labels run as small companies or through the private pressing of records – the independent music sector in the late 1970s and early 1980s became particularly important in terms of its scale and its impact on the broader, mainstream industry. Punk and post-punk music was also used in several American films during this period, the majority of which were independent productions, including very low-budget 'punk' films as well as more genre-based fare from larger independent companies. Lower budgeted films were being made on a regular basis in this period by small crews: the commitment to rough, unpolished and DIY principles in film mirrored, to a certain extent, similar attitudes amongst some punk musicians.

Links between the two forms were strengthened by the fact that punk musicians and music often featured in these films. Ivan Král and Amos Poe's *The Blank Generation* (1976), for instance, is a documentary snapshot, without synchronised sound, of music being performed at CGBGs as the punk and new wave movements took off (Blondie, The Ramones, Talking Heads and Patti Smith are among the artists appearing). Amos Poe's next films were narrative features but still included punk musicians on-screen, including Debbie Harry in both *Unmade Beds* (1976) and *The Foreigner*, as well as punk bands The Cramps and The Erasers appearing in *The Foreigner* (1978), while John Lurie and Lydia Lunch both appeared in *Subway Riders* (1981).

Punk fed into several independent productions in four main ways. Firstly, the DIY approach to music making and culture typifying punk was also paralleled in filmmaking. Many filmmakers without any formal training made very low-budget films – mostly shorts, though some features were also made – without significant distribution deals. Like punk musicians, filmmakers would often distribute films on a very small-scale basis, often through screening informally at clubs or galleries, or by gaining distribution deals with organisations devoted to promoting experimental and underground films.[1] Secondly, and undoubtedly influenced by the DIY approach which opened up cultural production as a valid activity for all (not just the professionally or traditionally skilled), there were many overlaps between music and film spheres: punk and post-punk musicians acted in and directed films; filmmakers also made music (in addition, people often engaged in other artistic practices including literature, fine art and performance). Thirdly, punk and post-punk cultures were often represented in independent films, with punks constituting prominent filmic characters. Fourthly, many independent films included punk or post-punk music on their soundtracks.

Within the ultra-low-budget/underground filmmaking sphere many films, in addition to Amos Poe's work, also intersected with punk and post-punk music, including *Blank Generation* (Lommel, 1980), *The Decline of Western Civilization* (Spheeris, 1981), *Smithereens* (Seidelman, 1982), *Variety* (Gordon, 1983) and *Stranger than Paradise* (Jarmusch, 1984). *Blank Generation*, a different film from Poe's *The Blank Generation* (1976), was directed by German filmmaker Ulli Lommel, who had acted in some Fassbinder films in addition to forging a directorial career. Unlike Poe's film, this was a narrative feature and Lommel's second feature made in the US, following *Cocaine Cowboys* (1979). Both these features focused on music scenes – the rock scene in *Cocaine Cowboys* and the punk scene in *Blank Generation* – and featured appearances by Andy Warhol. *Blank Generation* centres around a punk character and subculture as well as featuring punk music. Starring Richard Hell (of Richard Hell and the Voidoids, formerly a member of Television) as a punk singer, it also features performances from Hell and the Voidoids (Hell also appeared in and contributed to the soundtrack for Susan Seidelman's *Smithereens*, covered in detail in Chapter 5). *Variety*, meanwhile, does not feature punk music extensively or punk musicians, but it is an ultra-low-budget film largely made by and featuring non-professionals, while the soundtrack was provided by John Lurie, who was a member of the post-punk 'fake jazz' combo The Lounge Lizards. Lurie himself also made a no-budget short film – *Men in Orbit* (1979) – as well as appearing in several films as an actor and composing film soundtracks. These included, as an actor, *Rome '78* (Nares, 1978), *Red Italy* (Mitchell, 1979), *Underground USA* (Mitchell, 1980), *Subway Riders* and, as soundtrack composer, *Permanent Vacation* (Jarmusch, 1980) and *Subway Riders*. Out of these filmic contributions it is Lurie's work with Jim Jarmusch that he is best known for, as Jarmusch – while emerging from the punk and post-punk New York underground – broke through to a wider audience with *Stranger Than Paradise* and then became a more notable filmmaker associated with a new wave of American independent filmmaking in the 1980s.

Jarmusch had already directed one feature, *Permanent Vacation*, prior to the release of *Stranger Than Paradise*. *Permanent Vacation* did not, like its successor, gain extensive theatrical distribution but it did play at some venues internationally. The film was, like others already mentioned, linked to punk and post-punk music. While it did not feature music that sounded punk or no wave, its soundtrack – heavily indebted to Gamelan music – was composed by Lurie, who also briefly appeared in the film as a street musician playing the saxophone. Jarmusch himself also had links to music as he was a member of the post-punk band The Del-Byzanteens. Jarmusch's next feature, *Stranger Than Paradise*, extended such connections to the post-punk underground through featuring Lurie and musician Richard Edson in two main acting roles. Edson was previously a drummer in now-iconic band Sonic Youth (who emerged from the post-punk, no wave movement) and, at the time, was a member of post-punk band KONK. Lurie once again composed the soundtrack to the film, which is extremely sombre in tone and more redolent of classical composer Béla Bartók than punk or post-punk music. Lurie also composed the music for Jarmusch's *Down by Law* (1986) and *Mystery Train* (1989).

While the use of punk and post-punk music featured most heavily in underground independents, it also featured in several commercially-oriented independent films. One of the first commercial-independent films to use punk music was *Rock 'n' Roll High School* (Akrush, 1979), produced by Roger Corman's New World Pictures and featuring The Ramones. The Ramones were, of course, one of the most notable acts to emerge from the American punk explosion in the late 1970s. While at this point their records had not sold huge amounts, they were critically acclaimed and had a large cult following. They also had one of the more cartoonish profiles amongst punk acts, personae suited to an equally goofy film that combined the menace of punk with comic-strip levity.

The band had already started to move in a slightly more commercial direction with their fourth album, *Road to Ruins* (1978), and their appearance in *Rock 'n' Roll High School* should be considered an attempt to extend their fan base through exposure; fittingly, a soundtrack album was also released, which featured Ramones tracks as well as some other songs featured in the film by artists such as Brian Eno, Devo and Alice Cooper.

Rock 'n' Roll High School mimics the nature of a number of 50s rock'n'roll films in its generally light approach to its subject matter and through a thematic focus on generational tension. Roger Corman's former employers, American International Pictures, had been involved in several rock music films such as *Shake, Rattle and Rock* (Cahn, 1956) and *Rock All Night* (Corman, 1957), and in the later 1960s were involved with more serious (though sometimes kitschy) countercultural films such as *The Wild Angels* (Corman, 1966), *Wild in the Streets* (Sheer, 1968) and *Psych-Out* (Rush, 1968). *Rock 'n' Roll High School* harks back to Corman's 1950s rock'n'roll films through its tone and use of music. This could be considered fitting in the sense that punk often harked back to rock'n'roll as a more primitive and superior alternative to the kinds of music – sophisticated singer-songwriters and progressive rock in particular – it was reacting to. Yet there was a more practical element to this decision: executive producer Roger Corman wanted to make a film that nostalgically evoked those 50s films with a more modern soundtrack. He didn't initially envisage the music as punk and had intended Todd Rundgren or Cheap Trick to star in the film, but due to their prior commitments had to find an alternative; The Ramones were suggested by Paul Bartel.

If *Rock 'n' Roll High School* marked the point where some punk bands were becoming more popular and/or mainstream in sound, then a very different New World Pictures film – *Suburbia* (Spheeris, 1983) – would represent the next phase of American punk, hardcore (and will be discussed in more detail in Chapter 5). Hardcore punk was less associated with New York and, while emerging in different regions, was particularly strong in Los Angeles. At the end of the 1970s the first wave of punk was undergoing transformation, with artists such as Blondie and Talking Heads breaking through to the mainstream and others – such as The Ramones – attempting to. It is also important to note that the first wave of punk, associated particularly with New York and the CBGB scene, had undergone transformation in terms of record label ownership and distribution. Some bands had moved from independent labels to major labels, while many bands – including The Ramones, Talking Heads and Richard Hell and the Voidoids – were signed to Sire, which had itself ceased to be an independent label in 1978 when it was acquired by Warner Records (for the previous year Sire had a distribution deal with Warner Bros.).

Hardcore punk was also a feature of *Repo Man* (Cox, 1984), a film distributed by Universal. However, it was produced by an independent company

(Edge City), was relatively low-budget (approximately $1.5 million) and was given a limited release. It was also referred to as both an 'independent' and an 'indie' at the time of its release within trade publication *Variety* (Anon 1984: 43). The film's primary protagonist, Otto (Emilio Estevez), is a young punk rocker who hangs around with other punks listening to music and drinking, but who subsequently becomes a repo man and is drawn into an increasingly bizarre conspiracy plot. The film features songs from Californian hardcore bands such as Black Flag, Circle Jerks, The Plugz and Suicidal Tendencies, while Iggy Pop created a new track for the credits sequence.

The music in *Repo Man* links to both personal preferences of the director, to the film's characters and narrative, as well as to industrial ploys targeting young audiences, particularly those passionate about punk music. The film is redolent of the types of cult films that had become popular on the midnight movie circuit in the 1970s. Combining subcultural appeal with a quirky narrative that melds disparate generic influences – including sci-fi and the road movie – *Repo Man* did eventually become a cult film and its punk soundtrack and attitude undoubtedly contributed to this status. Where it differed from many previous punk films, however, was that it avoided the more straightforward documentation of a punk subculture – as in *Smithereens* or *Suburbia* – as well as the musical-style format of *Rock 'n' Roll High School*. Though the film starts as a more typical punk film, it moves in a different direction as Otto, the main character, loses touch with his punk entourage. In line with Otto's trajectory, the music in *Repo Man* becomes less overtly punk in sound even when performed by punk bands: thus, when the Circle Jerks appear in the film performing in a bar, they play a lounge-style, acoustic cover of their own 'When the Shit Hits the Fan'. The gradual shift away from punk sounds reflects Otto's move away from a punk lifestyle, though a punk spirit continues to infuse his activities as a morally dubious repo man. His repo partner Bud (Harry Dean Stanton) imbibes and shares amphetamines with Otto, while proclaiming his devotion to living an 'intense' lifestyle and a distaste for ordinariness (most notably summed up when he says to Otto, 'ordinary fucking people, I hate 'em'). Neither the punks nor the repo men are straightforwardly sympathetic: the former are depicted as rather stupid and violent, while the repo men are venal creatures who prey on the vulnerable. The film presents exaggerated characters in a washed-out, hyperreal Los Angeles, a landscape whose general greed and stupidity reflects the Reagan era; this anti-consumerist undercurrent is most visibly apparent in all grocery products being labelled with the most basic, generic information and design, a slyly resistant dig at the process of product placement in films.

Punk music was also integral to two other low-budget films produced in the early 1980s: *Times Square* (Moyle, 1980) and *Ladies and Gentlemen, The Fabulous Stains* (Adler, 1982). The former was a low-budget yet

Figure 2.1 *Repo Man*: Circle Jerks perform as a lounge band

commercially-oriented independent produced by the Robert Stigwood Organization, a record company which had become involved in filmmaking and had been behind huge music film hits *Saturday Night Fever* (Badham, 1977) and *Grease* (Kleiser, 1978). *Ladies and Gentlemen, The Fabulous Stains* was a low-budget, niche production from Paramount (again, likely to be termed an indie in today's media environment), obviously geared to cash-in on the punk phenomenon and the midnight movie crowd; Adler the director had already produced some midnight hits, most notably *The Rocky Horror Picture Show* (Sharman, 1975), and been involved in music as the founder of Orde Records. The midnight movie scene was starting to wane in the 1980s, however, which may have been a reason behind Paramount sitting on *The Fabulous Stains*: though finished in 1980 it was not released until 1982, and then only had an extremely limited run before being released on video.

Times Square and *The Fabulous Stains* both centre on female punk protagonists, a trait the films share with Seidelman's *Smithereens*. The female leads of these films may have been a factor fuelling the production companies' reluctance to release them. *Times Square* wasn't shelved in the manner that *Fabulous Stains* was, but it was subject to interference: Moyle was fired towards the end of the project, many cuts were made and music selections changed. Such manoeuvres reflected a general unease about how to market such films and whether there was a sufficient audience for them. On the one hand, they were symptomatic of a growing involvement of women in punk and post-punk music, and rock more generally. On the other hand, there was an uncertainty (informed undoubtedly, whether consciously or subconsciously, by sexist attitudes) about the audience for such films, as punk and rock were still assumed to interest a largely male constituency. In the case of *Times Square* this led to a softening of some of its rougher edges, including the removal of lesbian scenes and an avoidance of its punk credentials (the word punk is not mentioned in the film, for example, while some punk music originally planned for soundtrack inclusion was eventually replaced by more mainstream rock tracks).

Times Square contained a soundtrack that ultimately led to its general perception as a diluted approach to punk. While it contained The Cure, The Ramones and Talking Heads, it also featured more mainstream songs from Suzi Quatro, The Cars and Joe Jackson. *The Fabulous Stains* opted to use mostly newly written songs to be performed diegetically by the fictional bands The Stains and The Looters: the latter featured ex-Sex Pistols members Paul Cook and Steve Jones, who wrote songs for both the film's fictional bands. Both films, though particularly *Ladies and Gentlemen, the Fabulous Stains*, have gained a cult status following their inauspicious initial releases. *Stains*, for example, has been embraced by female punks, with members of Bratmobile and Bikini Kill having cited their admiration for the film.

In the later 1980s, Allison Anders, Dean Lent and Kurt Voss's *Border Radio* (1987) was a low-budget feature that included performances from, as well as music by, figures associated with hardcore punk. A story about two musicians and a roadie who flee to Mexico after stealing money, it starred John Doe and Chris D. from the punk band The Flesh Eaters and Dave Alvin of The Blasters

Figure 2.2 *Ladies and Gentlemen, the Fabulous Stains*: Diane Lane as Corrine Burns

(whose 1982 track 'Border Radio' provided the film's title). It also featured a music soundtrack of notable punk and alternative music, including The Flesh Eaters, X (also featuring Doe), The Divine Horsemen (also featuring D.) and Green on Red (whose 1985 album *Gas Food Lodging* would provide the title of Anders's next film, her breakout feature). Both Anders and Voss would go on to co-direct two further features based around L.A. musicians: *Sugar Town* (1999), which covered the L.A. rock scene, and the crowdfunded feature *Strutter* (2012). Voss also directed *Down and Out with the Dolls* (2001), which covered an all-female band in Portland, and which is covered in more detail in Chapter 6.

Several other 1980s American films also included punk and a variety of post-punk music. These include independently made genre films as well as studio-backed films. Punk music featured heavily on the soundtrack of low-budget horror film *Fear No Evil* (LaLoggia, 1981); teen comedy *Batchelor Party* (Isreal, 1984) included many acts signed to the IRS label including R.E.M.; and *Party Animal* (Beaird, 1984) also included R.E.M. alongside punk act The Flesh Eaters. Most prominently, several John Hughes films employed a range of music including some British indie selections. *Pretty in Pink* (Deutch, 1986) and *Some Kind of Wonderful* (Deutch, 1987), for example, featured many tracks by British bands linked to indie music, including Echo and the Bunnymen, The Jesus and Mary Chain, New Order and The Smiths.[2] While the use of alternative and indie-rock within films was still rather modest overall, it was beginning to increase as the decade wore on, in line with the rising profile of such music. This trend would accelerate into the 1990s, particularly following the rise of grunge and the growing awareness of alternative rock/indie-rock as a significant commercial concern.

The 1990s

The 1990s marks an important era for American independent cinema and indie music. 'Indie' began to appeal to more audiences both across film and music, which led to the increasing commercialisation of these respective industries. Miramax has often been considered a prime agent in the escalating commercial development of American indie film as a niche-oriented, 'quality' signifier. Alisa Perren (2012: 4) argues that the companies' tactics were influential on the major industry, noting that by the beginning of the millennium 'each major studio had developed at least one division modeled largely on Miramax's production and distribution strategies'. Miramax started the decade as an independent, but following successes such as *sex, lies and videotape* (Soderberg, 1989), it was struggling to survive within a marketplace it had helped to create, as prices had been driven up. The company was purchased by Disney in 1992, which helped it to expand budgets on productions as well as bolster finances to aid acquisitions and its marketing of films. As Yannis Tzioumakis (2012: 8) points out, studio involvement in niche films was not new – there had been several studio specialty divisions operating in the 1980s such as Universal Classics – but studio subdivisions and involvement in niche filmmaking did expand. Such filmmaking also started to differ from its 1980s forebears: independent films were now more likely to be commercially-oriented, hence the rise of more recognisable stars, the use of stronger generic frameworks, an emphasis on well-defined niche audiences and an increased deployment of authorship in promotion.

As mentioned in Chapter 1, many larger record companies also attempted to incorporate indie music to an extent through buying out or buying a stake in independent companies, or through setting up their own specialty subdivisions (as well as continuing to sign artists from independent labels). Within the US, though, there was a very specific moment that emphasised the commercial appeal of alternative/indie music, which was the breakout success of Nirvana. Formerly signed to indie label Sub Pop, Nirvana signed to Geffen Records subsidiary DGC Records in 1991; while they did not change their sound in a radical sense, their debut major album *Nevermind* (1991) was a more polished affair than their previous releases. The album represented a watershed moment for the crossover success of indie/alternative rock and was also connected to a growing audience for such music, reflected in MTV slots devoted to alternative music (most notably *The Cutting Edge* (1983–87) and *120 Minutes* (1986–2000)), a sharp increase in independent rock bands being signed to major labels, and the beginning of popular alternative music festival Lollapalooza in 1991.

Following the accelerated commercialisation of both the indie music and film sectors, the licensing of indie music within all types of filmmaking grew, especially within indie filmmaking. The indie film sector saw a huge growth in production and – at the upper, studio-involved end – an increase in budgets. The growth in production was a factor leading to a greater demand for music, with indie and alternative music a prominent beneficiary. Other factors include an increasing awareness of, and attempts to cater to, niche cultures (particularly important within indie filmmaking); the growing importance of music supervisors; corporate convergence, in which many music and film concerns were housed under one conglomerate, and which aided cross-licensing and cross-marketing opportunities; and directorial preferences. The latter refers to the fact that many directors – and this would have been particularly the case in indie filmmaking where directors tended to have more creative freedom – would have themselves been fans of such music. A final important factor was the huge expansion of television channels during the 1990s, which increased the demand for music content and increased the exposure of indie music.

Within alternative/indie music circles, grunge arguably had the greatest popular cachet in the early 1990s (even though many bands did not like the term).

Denoting a blend of punk and metal influences, grunge was heavily associated with Seattle and the Sub Pop label in the late 1980s, though it would spread to other areas (the impact and aftermath of grunge is covered in more detail in Chapter 6). A prominent example of grunge being used in an indie film is Kevin Smith's *Clerks* (1994), which is worth further discussion as it highlights how grunge music could be used to promote a low-budget indie film. *Clerks* received significant media coverage, and much of this focused on its production details: it was made by Smith at a convenience store he worked at, with shooting taking place after hours. Many articles noted how the film was produced for only $27,575, with Smith raising the money himself from loans and grants. The more planned, commercial aspects of the film were mostly overlooked, however – including its final budget of around $230,000 – probably because they would not have fitted neatly into the romantic stories about an underdog producing a successful film against all odds. When the film was screened at Sundance, it only featured two songs on its soundtrack. After being purchased by Miramax, Jeffrey Kimball was hired to oversee music supervision (Evans 1994) and Benjie Gordan appointed as chief music supervisor for the film.

Benjie Gordan was involved in selecting the songs for the film as well as shaping a coherent soundtrack. He has claimed that he wanted to 'assemble a low-budget, punk-rock soundtrack that would be a significant musical milestone for my generation in the '90s – like Valley Girl or Repo Man was in the '80s' (Atwood 1994: 32). Love Among Freaks had provided tracks for the cut of *Clerks* that previewed at the Sundance film festival in January 1994. A decision was then made to include more commercial acts alongside lesser-known acts. This strategy, when successful, uses the more well-known 'alternative' artists as ways to draw attention to the soundtrack and film, while lesser-known acts might be discovered through listening to the film or soundtrack. Alice in Chains and Soul Asylum were the more commercial bands on the soundtrack and, while their sounds are not really 'punk rock', they did fit reasonably comfortably into a broad grunge/punk-oriented soundtrack. The soundtrack was tailored towards a younger demographic, particularly college students, as indicated by Gordan's remarks about wanting to create a soundtrack that would appeal to a generation. However, as Gen Xers were often perceived as resistant to being sold things in an overt manner, this marketing component of the film was subtle: music was, in one sense, harnessed to act as a hook which might generate further interest in the film (a film that was released selectively and gradually, indicating it was hoped that the film could build viewers over time, with the soundtrack creating buzz and anticipation).

Not many people commented on the plainly commercial musical package of *Clerks* even though two rather commercially successful grunge acts – Alice in Chains and Soul Asylum – featured on the soundtrack to bolster its promotional appeal, and Kevin Smith directed a *Clerks*-themed music video for Soul

Asylum's 'Can't Even Tell'. Emphasising the more commercial elements would have detracted from the prevailing narrative of the film as an authentic, low-budget creation from a new director. Although the music licensing was quite costly, the soundtrack album sold well, and the inclusion of Alice in Chains' 1992 track 'Got Me Wrong', which had previously been released, led to the track being reissued due to renewed interest, thus illustrating the power of films to promote music. The ways in which its commercial aspects were played down exemplifies Michael Newman's argument that the term 'indie' can sometimes function as a 'mystification of the more straightforward category "independent." . . . This mystification diminishes or makes vague the significance of economic distinctions and injects added connotations of a distinguishing style or sensibility and of a social identity' (Newman 2011: 4). In the case of *Clerks*, its broad acceptance as an 'authentic' and genuine indie text meant that the more calculating, commercial considerations that informed it were either played down or not considered important. This is undoubtedly partially related to how the film *appears* gritty and low-budget, but in this case appearances are slightly misleading.

The awareness of indie as an important music category which could appeal to specific niche cultures spread during the 1990s. Films depicting youthful disaffection and anger, in particular, often featured indie-heavy soundtracks. This trend started to occur prior to the explosion of grunge but accelerated following Nirvana's commercial success. Examples include *A Matter of Degrees* (Morgan, 1990), *Pump Up the Volume* (Moyle, 1990), *Guncrazy* (Davis, 1992) – which featured the first use of a Nirvana track in a major feature, 'Lovebuzz' – *S.F.W.* (Levy, 1994), *Love and a .45* (Talkington, 1994) and *Mad Love* (Milne, 1995). The grittier, and controversial, *Kids* (Clark, 1995) also employed some indie music on its soundtrack, including songs by Daniel Johnston and Sebadoh. By the mid-90s there was a growing interest from marketers and financiers in the commercial appeal of indie-rock music, which became a tool in promoting a film.

In a 1994 article for *Billboard*, there was discussion of how independent filmmaking was an important area through which music could be promoted:

> Several major labels are turning to the cutting edge of independent cinema to expose new and established alternative acts. Although indie films gain only limited exposure, their soundtracks can help shape the images of modern rock artists and, more importantly, help sell records. (Atwood 1994: 8)

The rising profile of indie and alternative music, its relatively modest licensing costs in comparison to more mainstream music, and inbuilt appeal to niche audiences, led it to become an increasingly important component of independent filmmaking, which could benefit music artists by helping them gain more exposure on the one hand, and provide films with promotional benefits on the other.

Marketing and promotional concerns do not, however, exhaust the functions of indie music within films, even in cases where this may be an overriding concern. Music will often be chosen for other purposes, most notably for its role within the film itself (that is, music which is considered to reflect, or perhaps complicate, aspects of the narrative, mood and/or character) and/or because of its value to the director. The late 1980s and 1990s was a time when some directors who were themselves music lovers, and whose tastes included indie music, emerged, a topic that will be covered in more detail in Chapters 3 and 4.

The 2000s and Beyond

Following the 1990s, the 2000s saw both an extension of previous trends as well as some significant new developments. In terms of its commercial value, indie music's stock rose further and was licensed for use in more films than in the previous decade, particularly within indie films. The rising value of indie music as a resource to be used in films was noted regularly in both the film and music trade press. Further, many film festivals and events started to incorporate music activities and panels into their schedules. In 1998, for example, the Los Angeles Independent Film Festival featured extensive music-related events which included a music video series and, most relevantly, an indie music night including an evening concert featuring emerging artists on indie labels (Klady 1998: 4). In the same year, the IFC Channel announced an 'Indie Rocks' weekend which included screenings of many indie films featuring notable rock soundtracks; while this was not centred exclusively on indie music as such, some films featuring indie music – including the aforementioned *Clerks* – were included (Katz 1998: 20). Generally, indie-oriented film festivals started to increase their music provision from this point onwards, while many music festivals would also incorporate film screenings on a regular basis.

Another symptom of indie music's growing screen value was the emergence of specialist companies geared towards providing custom soundtracks. An example is MasterSource, a music library created in 1993 by ex-rock guitarist Marc Ferrari. As soundtracks were often designed around particular genres, MasterSource created music for use across film genres but specialised in creating 'indie' style music for indie films (Crisafulli 2003). The increasing commercial significance of indie music is a factor in the growth of MasterSource, which was eventually purchased by Universal Music Group in 2007. The 2000s would see more music companies emerging to produce custom-made soundtracks, with indie-rock being a prominent generic area. An example is Shockoe Noise, LCC, which was founded by David Lowery, who had been in indie bands Camper Van Beethoven and Cracker, and who specialised in creating 'indie-sounding' music for films, television and advertising (Crisafulli 2007). Another notable indie-oriented music production library is Jingle Punks, formed in 2008 and still active.

By 2010 indie music was being regularly discussed as an important genre in its own right – for it was now largely being used as a genre term (though not *always*) – that was starting to yield greater commercial rewards. As such, it was used in all types of media, not just indie media, although it has retained a crucial link with indie film. This was an era when music streaming was becoming the preferred mode for consuming music, with a concomitant impact upon record sales (sales were falling following digital music piracy and digital downloads). Record labels were now beginning to take a more active role in pushing their newer artists for licensing placements in response to this shifting environment (Butler 2009). While fewer soundtracks were being released physically, some could still make significant profits. An example is the *Juno* soundtrack, which was of course very indie-focused and alerted some to the potentially lucrative nature of releasing indie-based soundtracks. However, attempts to exploit such trends could also fail: the soundtrack for *Nick and Norah's Infinite Playlist* (Sollett, 2008), which like *Juno* was a slightly twee indie romantic comedy, disappointed hugely on its release. Overall, there was a slight reduction in the material release of film music soundtracks, but film continued to play a crucial role in exposing music to audiences even in the absence of an official soundtrack release. Spotify, for example, hosts numerous playlists based around film directors or related to specific films; even when these soundtracks have gained official releases, unofficial Spotify playlists can still be important in linking to a greater range of music included within a film (because many soundtrack releases will only feature selections, often due to licensing issues). New digital apps such as Shazam also help audiences to identify music played within films that they might be unaware of; in line with increased information on soundtracks disseminated via the web – including, though far from limited to, IMDb listing songs featuring in a film – such processes enhance film's capacity to function, in one sense, in ways similar to an audio-visual radio broadcast.

Taste Cultures and Promotional Culture

The growing commercialisation of indie music (and indie film) can be linked to notions of taste cultures and promotional culture. While indie music can feature within and help promote films, indie musicians are also increasingly targeting films – alongside other media such as television and video games – as a way of promoting their music and gaining extra revenue for their work. In a 2009 article for *Music Week*, Susan Butler (2009: 12) noted that 'Movies are attracting more attention from the music industry, and those trying to break into the music industry, than ever before'. Butler was discussing music in general here, not just indie music, but the latter has been noted frequently as a type of music which can be attached to films for commercial purposes, while also aligning the film with certain sensibilities. In 2010 Justin Shady reported on how indie music is increasingly being used in film trailers. While he does mention its use in mainstream films, he largely focuses on how indie music is an attractive option for indie filmmakers and that it can imbue such films with an air of 'alt rock sensibility' and 'credibility'.

The rise of promotional culture has led to increased attention paid to how music artists now brand themselves. Promotional culture refers to how promotional activities have become embedded within daily life to an increasing degree, 'as ordinary individuals, in their day-to-day experiences, have both grown accustomed to a promotion-rich society and come to internalize and reproduce basic promotional practices' (Davis 2013: 3). Davis (2013: 103) also notes that promotional culture feeds into cultural production, which has seen a rise in numbers of 'promotional intermediaries' working on cultural products to effectively target relevant audiences. The rise of promotional culture has impacted on the music industry in particular ways. As Klein et al. have noted (2016), this has resulted – in conjunction with the reduction of money earned from record sales – in music artists being aware of themselves as brands, as well as seeking additional revenues through licensing their music for use in other media:

> In response to this changing landscape, the popular music industries have generally become much more adroit at marketing popular music to a range of constituents through a variety of channels. . . . Well- and lesser-known musicians are increasingly pressured to think about, if not actively strategize, the development of coherent, relatable brand identities that will traverse permeable media boundaries. (Klein et al. (237))

Klein et al. (233–4) argue that contemporary indie artists are not as concerned with 'selling out' as 1980s and 90s indie acts were, but that ideas of cultural autonomy and integrity are still important. Rather than being focused on, as they once were, selling music per se, such arguments are now more likely to revolve around the *types* of companies and products that artists affiliate with. Indie artists, they note – echoing Keightley's points outlined in Chapter 1 – have historically been more concerned with the scale of commercialism rather than an outright rejection of it. Often, they will favour smaller companies over large corporations, though in today's environment many indie artists will still associate with corporate entities; even in such cases, they may still actively choose to associate with products they value and attempt to demonstrate discernment in licensing music, to ward off criticisms about lack of integrity. Acts can, however, still be subject to accusations of selling out if they are considered to license indiscriminately and/or if they license to entities considered at odds with their reputation.

Films, too, can use indie music as a broader way of indicating their indie identity. In her analysis of marketing and independent film, Finola Kerrigan (2017: 186) argues that 'signals of "indie" are made through a combination of brand elements that collectively indicate the indie nature of the film'. While she largely discusses factors such as directors, actors and scriptwriters as examples, music can also act as such a 'brand element'. Significant indie-related music on the soundtrack of a film can, in some instances, act as a form of branding while not announcing itself as such. In many instances, indie films will not wear their commercial credentials on their sleeves, which again links to Michael Newman's argument that indie can in one sense be considered a *mystification* of 'independent'.

Music Supervisors

The growth in indie music as a crucial component of independent filmmaking occurred in conjunction with the rising profile of music supervisors. While music supervisors still maintain a generally low profile in the industry, they are becoming more recognised as creative figures. In 2011, the Guild of Music Supervisors was established and now has an annual awards ceremony to highlight music supervisors' contributions to film, as well as television and video games. Within academic work on film music, the music supervisor is also often overlooked. In an article on music supervision written in 2001, Jeff Smith wrote that the music supervisor is 'woefully neglected in academic work on film and music' (126). In more recent years, some music supervisors have gained a modest status and there has been some further academic writing on their contributions (e.g. Lewandowski 2010; Anderson 2013b).

Tim Anderson has noted the growth in the status of music supervisors and indicates some causal factors, which include the increased importance of film and television in exposing new music, the explosion of cable channels, the rising significance of niche markets and a heightened focus on branding strategies within media industries. The first of these factors has already been noted and relates to the dwindling opportunities for radio play. Anderson quotes music supervisor Joel C. High, who argues that films are now a better channel through which to expose new music: 'Now if you put something to good use in a big motion picture, more people are going to hear that song than if it's played on a few stations in some sort of rotation. And those people will then go to a Web site to find that music, thanks to the rise of the Internet' (quoted in Anderson 2013b: 376). Within such a climate, Anderson argues that music supervisors' importance as cultural intermediaries and as tastemakers has risen (Ibid.). The explosion of cable channels is noted as another factor, with increased media content feeding a growing need for music; while not noted by Anderson, the increase in film production over the last twenty years is a further cause influencing a rising demand for musical content. The significance of niche markets within media industries also links to the music supervisor's rise in status and is a topic covered elsewhere in this book. Anderson argues that the importance of branding also involves the expertise of music supervisors, and that independent music labels will often package their music to offer to television and film companies.

> In this climate, independent music labels have taken advantage of the multiple branding demands of those who simply cannot afford major label talents or catalogs. Because independent labels tend to operate with smaller staffs whose members are part of distinct musical niches, they can mobilize their resources to engage emerging trends in popular music and business operations much faster than the majors. (Anderson 2013b: 383–4)

This trend also connects to independent filmmaking as well, as independent filmmakers – particularly those working with lower budgets – will not be able to afford bigger music acts due to prohibitive licensing costs. Anderson adds that television and film can 'leverage [independent] music's ideological investment in "authenticity" as a source for product differentiation' (Anderson 2013a: 384).

The work of a music supervisor may vary from project to project, but typical duties include suggesting music placements that can be afforded, clearing music licenses and creating music packages around particular films. They will often be involved in creative, legal and marketing duties (Lewandowski 2010: 867), though their creative contributions may depend on the director they are working with. Some film directors will have clear ideas about what types of music they want within their films and how such music will be used: in such situations, the music supervisor might offer suggestions on types and uses of music, but such suggestions are often driven by the film director's overall vision. In other cases, the director might want a music supervisor to play a freer role in providing music suggestions and/or how such music is used within the film. Natalie Lewandowski has argued:

> Involvement in all types of music within the film often allows a degree of creativity for the music supervisor in music choice. However, this collaborative creativity varies from project to project, with some directors being very specific as to the choice of music and others allowing the music supervisor greater creative freedom. (Lewandowski 2010: 868)

Whilst filmmakers might sometimes choose music selections based on their own musical tastes, they must also think more practically about what types of music are relevant for use in specific scenes. These aesthetic-practical considerations are accompanied by other recurrent issues such as not being able to license selected music, which leads to a need for replacement tracks.

Since the 2000s a few music supervisors have become critically regarded, many of whom have been linked to an increase in licensing indie tracks. One of the first music supervisors to gain a profile for licensing a significant amount of indie music – though this was initially for television – was Alexandra Patsavas. Alyx Vesey (2009) has claimed that Patsavas is 'largely responsible for the commercialization of indie rock during the 2000s, almost single-handedly catapulting bands like Death Cab for Cutie into mainstream success'. For *The O.C.* (2003–7) and *Grey's Anatomy* (2005–) she licensed numerous indie tracks, and continued to do so for her film work across very different films, such as the hugely successful *Twilight* (Hardwicke, 2008) and the indie teen film *The Perks of Being a Wallflower* (Chbosky, 2011). Patsavas also owns her own record company, Chop Chop Records, through which she releases recordings by indie bands as well as film and television compilations that she has worked on. In addition to Patsavas, other music supervisors who have been linked to indie-heavy soundtrack selections include Linda Cohen, Tracy McKnight, Randall Poster and Brian Reitzell. Poster was involved in indie-oriented soundtracks at an earlier date: he was co-writer and producer of *A Matter of Degrees* (1990), which featured tracks by Pixies, Throwing Muses and The Lemonheads, and has gone on to supervise music for directors including Wes Anderson, Larry Clarke, Harmony Korine and Richard Linklater. McKnight, meanwhile, has worked on many films and with notable indie directors including Gregg Araki, Lisa Cholodenko, Hal Hartley and Greg Mottola. Like Patsavas, McKnight also created a record label; with Walter Yetnikoff, former president and CEO of CBS Records, she established Commotion Records, which specialised in soundtracks for 'indie movies' (Gallo 2003: 18).

While the music supervisor is not scrutinised in detail within this book, there will be the occasional reference to specific supervisors, and it is necessary to establish their importance within the creation of music soundtracks. The next two chapters will focus on connections between authorship and indie music, and it should be emphasised that music supervisors play an important role in contributing to a director's musical needs.

Notes

1. Of course, a DIY approach to filmmaking was already in existence – notably in the realm of underground film – but it is arguable that punk influenced many more people to engage with low-budget productions. Jim Jarmusch, for example, has

discussed how the DIY approach evident across a range of punk music influenced him: 'you didn't have to be a virtuoso musician to form a rock band. Instead, the spirit was more important than any kind of expertise on the instrument' (Jarmusch quoted in Belsito 2001: 27).
2. The Jesus and Mary Chain and Echo and the Bunnymen's tracks were released on major labels, but both bands were frequently positioned as alternative rock acts and often categorised as indie within critical discourse.

3 SONIC AUTHORSHIP 1: GREGG ARAKI

Authorship is a long-standing, albeit often controversial, lens through which films can be approached and read, as well as a concept that aids in the marketing and promotion of some films. The author figure tends to be more overtly present in various discourses related to American independent cinema – such as criticism, theory, promotion – than it does in Hollywood cinema. This is not to argue that authorship is ignored within Hollywood cinema but that, relatively speaking, it is more prominent within the sphere of American indie cinema. Michael Z. Newman (2017: 28–9), for example, has argued that independent cinema is often distinguished from Hollywood cinema through discourses that stress the greater autonomy of the former in contrast to the latter, and that the figure of the auteur is a prominent filter through which such autonomy is constructed. For Newman, this does not necessarily reflect the actual, material differences between independent and Hollywood production (spheres that can often overlap), instead referring to the ways in which distinctions between these spheres are imagined.

Authorship has traditionally focused on visual style rather than the soundtrack. While some of the more radical approaches to the soundtrack have previously gained attention due to their links with director-authors – including Eisenstein and Godard – attention towards how auteurs use music distinctively is a relatively recent development. A key piece in establishing this line of study is Claudia Gorbman's 'Auteur Music', in which she argued that some directors' use of music can constitute part of their directorial style: 'music participates forcefully in what used to be called, in the simpler days of auteursim, the director's worldview' (Gorbman 2007: 150). This article was symptomatic of a burgeoning interest in auteurism and music, which stimulated further such investigations (e.g. Wierzbicki 2012, Ashby 2013). Gorbman calls directors with a distinctive musical style *mélomanes* ('music lovers') and argues that this is a relatively recent trend (beginning around the 1960s). While she admits that directors who started making films earlier – such as John Ford and Alfred Hitchcock – often used music in interesting ways, she sees the beginning of a new kind of music-obsessed director emerging in the work of directors such as Stanley Kubrick and Jean-Luc Godard. Several articles and chapters devoted to the exploration of music in the work of specific auteurs now exist, yet much work remains to be done in this regard.

Several indie auteurs incorporated forms of indie music into their filmmaking regularly in the 1990s. The increased use of indie music within films in this decade has already been noted, though an additional factor is that in this era many directors emerged who were passionate fans of such music. While Allison Anders co-directed her first feature in 1987 – the previously mentioned *Border Radio* – she became a more recognised figure with her next feature, *Gas, Food, Lodging* (1992). While this film did not focus on musicians, it did feature some indie music on its soundtrack, including tracks by Nick Cave and the Bad Seeds, The Velvet Monkeys and Swedish indie band Easy. It was also named after an album by Green on Red, and was scored by J. Mascis, the leader of indie-rock band Dinosaur Jr. Anders has gone on to make several films based around musicians and the music industry; while these have not always focused on indie music, she has continued to license numerous indie tracks for her films.

Richard Linklater does not use indie music across all his work but has used such music notably in some of his films, including his breakout feature *Slacker* (1991). Linklater had already filmed a short 16mm film called *Woodshock* (1985), which documents the 1985 Texas music festival of the same name, and features Daniel Johnston. A range of independent music appeared on the soundtrack of *Slacker*, including tracks by the Texan acts Butthole Surfers, Glass Eye and Daniel Johnston. These tracks are not employed in a particularly intrusive manner in the film but rather provide, for the most part, a sonic backdrop that bolsters an authentic depiction of a specific cultural milieu. In one sense, *Slacker* uses local independent music to contribute to a realistic depiction of a vibrant, regional DIY culture; it both reflects, and plays a part in the production of, an Austin scene (punk and indie music scenes are examined in more detail in Chapters 5 and 6). Linklater's fourth feature, *SubUrbia* (1996), also contains an indie-heavy soundtrack, including tracks by Butthole Surfers, Meat Puppets, Sonic Youth and Superchunk, with Sonic Youth members Lee Ranaldo and Steve Shelley contributing to its score.

Hal Hartley is another director who became acclaimed in the early 1990s and used indie music on quite a consistent basis, particularly within his earlier films, sometimes in unusual ways. A much-noted scene from *Simple Men* (1992) presents an elaborate, quirky dance to Sonic Youth's 'Kool Thing', following a discussion on Madonna; while his American Playhouse television film *Surviving Desire* (1992) includes an equally quirky scene set to indie-rock: as Jude (Martin Donovan) and Henry (Matt Malloy) walk down the street and converse, their dialogue is drowned out by indie-rock band The Great Outdoors, who are performing their song 'Gonna Miss You' in the street. Both scenes stand out for their prominent and offbeat use of indie music: the former scene is a non-realist interruption into the narrative of an incongruous, and playful, musical scene; the latter is odd because there is no seeming logic for the band playing electrified in the street in this manner, and because the music drowns out the dialogue, again toying with conventions and expectations. Hartley used indie music frequently in his first four features and his early shorts, including numerous songs by Yo La Tengo. His own soundtrack work – under the name of Ned Rifle – has also demonstrated an indie-rock influence, while P. J. Harvey featured in his short *Book of Life* (1998), which also included a cameo from Yo La Tengo as a Salvation Army band.

Many other indie directors who emerged in the 1990s have also included indie music in their films frequently, including Lisa Cholodenko, Nicole Holofcener and Steve Hanft. Many such directors, however, tend to use indie music in some of their films, but not in an entirely consistent manner. This is unsurprising, as music will often be selected in accordance with the requirements of the film, which does not always call for extensive indie music. Linklater's output points to such trends; while he does use indie music in many of his films, this is not always the case. After *Slacker*, he made *Dazed and Confused* (1993), which, because it was set in a 1970s high school, utilised classic 1970s popular rock songs; licensing such music was also made possible by the higher budget he worked with on *Dazed and Confused*.

This chapter focuses on one director who has used indie music in more consistent ways than most – Greg Araki – while the following chapter scrutinises an auteur whose early films featured a range of different modes of indie music, Sofia Coppola. Most of Araki's films feature indie music, particularly shoegaze music, though his earlier films also employed industrial music. While I have not scrutinised the role that music supervisors have played in these case studies, it should be noted that directors do often work with music supervisors. Consequently, the attribution of sonic authorship needs to acknowledge the collaborative nature of film music, even if the director is most responsible for decisions regarding licensing. And while sonic authorship has tended to focus on the selection and placement of pre-existing music, a director's choice of and collaborative work with composers on scores is also an important consideration, and I will make some mention of scores in the next two chapters.

Gregg Araki: *The Living End*

Araki first came to prominence with his third feature film, the low budget *The Living End* (1992), which was considered a key example of 'New Queer Cinema' by B. Ruby Rich (1992) in her pioneering article for *Sight and Sound*. New Queer Cinema (NQC) was a term that indicated a new wave of queer productions which challenged prominent representations of gay characters. Rejecting negative stereotypes but also refusing to portray queerness in a wholly positive manner, NQC was typified by an unashamed and undiluted – sometimes aggressive – depiction of queer characters. Although not all the films initially mentioned by Rich were American, a number were low-budget American independent productions: alongside *The Living End* Rich also mentioned *Poison* (Haynes, 1991) and *Swoon* (Kalin, 1992). Rich (2013: 92) has called Araki 'the bad boy of New Queer Cinema' due to his aggressive and often nihilistic approach to filmmaking. Yet it should be mentioned that while there are many continuities running through Araki's oeuvre, there have been occasional changes in style and tone. His earlier features were shot guerrilla-style (without permits) on shoestring budgets, resulting in a rough, lo-fi aesthetic. His fifth feature, *The Doom Generation* (1995), changed direction somewhat. While he was still focusing on young people and sexuality, he moved into a more hyperreal style as he started to work with higher budgets. His characters tend to be young, good-looking and sexually adventurous, while his influences merge disparate sources including exploitation cinema, art cinema, soap operas and MTV. But there are a few films that diverge from his predominant style, including his stoner comedy *Smiley Face* (2007) and his darker, adapted melodramas *Mysterious Skin* (2004) and *White Bird in A Blizzard* (2014).

The Living End (1992) – Araki's third feature film but first to receive widespread distribution[1] – centres on hustler Luke (Mike Dytri) and depressive film critic Jon (Craig Gilmore), both HIV positive, who become lovers and outlaws on the road. Musically the film is dominated by industrial music, but all the music used in *The Living End* was sourced from independent labels and can be considered indie in this regard. The emergence of industrial music is usually dated to the mid-1970s, specifically to the Industrial Records label, founded in England in 1976 by the group Throbbing Gristle, but it wasn't until the 1980s that 'industrial' was used frequently as a generic term. Earlier industrial music was very much rooted in avant-garde aesthetics, taking inspiration as it did from artists and movements such as William Burroughs and Futurism and interrogating the nature of an increasingly technological environment, focusing on issues such as control and manipulation. S. Alexander Reed (2013) states that industrial music was anti-hegemonic and anti-capitalist, as well as obsessed with transgression and extremism. The extremist elements of industrial music have proven controversial and have led some critics to associate it with fascism, but Reed claims that this is a result of its flirtation with extreme imagery and its ambiguous nature (acts associated with it rarely engaged in straightforward political sloganeering). Much industrial music 'revels in shocking, transgressive subject matter' because 'where there is transgression, there is law, and where we reveal law, we reveal external control' (Reed 2013: 10). While early industrial music was particularly experimental – utilising noise, electronics and samples – over time it splintered into different forms, such as industrial dance music and industrial metal; in the process many forms became more accessible (though more experimental variants have continued to exist). Araki draws on industrial music's transgressive associations within *The Living End*, heightening the confrontational aesthetic of the film. Industrial music is also connected to queerness: Yetta Howard (2017: 36) has noted how its transgressive tendencies often 'placed industrial within shared subcultural contexts associated with gay, fetish, and BDSM (bondage and discipline, domination and submission, sadism and masochism) sexual cultures'.[2]

The Living End draws on different types of industrial music, including post-Throbbing Gristle acts Chris & Cosey, Coil and Psychic TV, but the musical soundtrack is largely dominated by acts who were on Chicago's independent Wax Trax! Records, which had by 1989 'become the most visible and successfully branded of any industrial record company' (Reed 2013: 242) and was key in spreading the genre beyond the underground. In his analysis of music in *The Living End*, Jack Curtis Dubowsky (2014) claims that the film's limited budget would have partly influenced the music selections in this film: lower budgets result in difficulties affording the licensing rights to tracks that one might want to use. Hence, in *The Living End* a lot of music is indicated through dialogue or posters: Joy Division, The Jesus and Mary Chain (whose 1985 track 'The Living End' provides the film's title), The Smiths and Echo and the Bunnymen are mentioned but their music does not appear on the soundtrack. As these were all at this time esteemed and canonical British indie bands, their music would not have been affordable. Araki instead licensed a range of more arcane artists, many of whom still had devoted fan followings and subcultural cachet, and which also linked to his own tastes and experiences. Araki used to visit queer industrial nightclubs in L.A. and was an avid music consumer: music was, and has remained, an important component of his filmmaking. For example, he has claimed in his commentary for *The Living End* that 'music has always been a really big influence on me . . . It's really super inspired by a lot of the post punk music I was listening to at the time . . . That whole period I was very, I am still very much influenced by my CD collection' (Araki quoted in Dubowsky 2014: 45).

Figure 3.1 *The Living End*: Jon breakfasts with Luke in front of a prominent poster of The Smiths

While Dubowsky astutely picks apart the ways in which music on *The Living End* functions in term of its cachet – aligning subcultural audiences with the film – his comments on how it informs narrative, mood and character overlook some important nuances. He argues that the music in the film works well only in two respects – 'bridging transitions and representing subculture' – but claims 'in moments of real high drama' it 'fails' and, narratologically, is 'ineffective' (Dubowsky 2014: 40). But Dubowsky here judges the music in *The Living End* by normative standards when the film is anti-normative in several respects: it was deliberately anti-mainstream not just stylistically but also in its depiction of gay characters, who are distinguished from straight culture *and* more mainstream aspects of gay culture (with industrial music representing their double otherness in this regard). Likewise, it distanced itself not only from Hollywood cinema but also from more established, and larger budgeted, strands of independent cinema; this is most explicitly announced when Luke, who is a hustler, shoots two homophobes who are wearing T-shirts respectively adorned with the film titles *sex, lies and videotape* and *Drugstore Cowboy*.

The above moment indicates the extent to which *The Living End* trades in symbolic warfare, with music constituting a core component of Araki's arsenal.

At its broadest level, music in the film denotes untamed queer desires. Opposing stereotypes of gay taste, music in the film is indicative of a more aggressive and *transgressive* gay subculture. Rather than attempting to assimilate, the gay characters in this film – particularly Luke – are unapologetically queer; Luke himself, a rather nihilistic character, is more concerned with the destruction of normative culture than he is with fitting in. Much of the music features beat-driven electronics, distorted vocals and metallic guitar punctuations, representing dance- and metal-influenced subgenres of industrial music. Such sounds often function as symbols of rage, indicative of the filmmaker's and the two main protagonists' sensibilities.

Music does also occasionally relate to narrative and character in *The Living End*. At times it functions to heighten mood and accentuate crucial narrative moments. For example, when Luke takes over driving responsibilities from Jon early into their road trip, he replaces a cassette of Chris & Cosey with 16volt; the musical shift relates to Luke's more reckless nature, which leads the action to move from uneventful into more exciting yet dangerous territory, and expresses the emotional turmoil that Jon often experiences when he is with Luke (leading to Jon becoming increasingly disillusioned as the road trip progresses). Music in the film sometimes contributes to the ratcheting up of narrative tension, primarily in relation to Luke's escalating violence and Jon's correspondingly fraught mental state. So, for example, in the above scene as well as in a later scene when Luke flips out and shoots an ATM, music reflects how the two are facing danger following a transgression. In the ATM scene, Luke's gunshot, sounds of impact, an alarm and the car engine roaring as they drive away are all amplified high in the mix and produce a quite cacophonic section of organised noise, which eventually merges briefly – as their car accelerates away – with a flurry of beats and a sampled guitar riff excerpted from Chemlab's 'Blunt Force Trauma'. The rather dissonant quality of these sounds indicate Jon's growing agitation at Luke's recklessness, which leads him to self-consciously denounce how this 'romantic road fantasy has come to an end' soon afterwards. For Jon, reality intrudes into this road-based escapist venture, which was perhaps inevitable considering that his status as a doomed romantic has already been established. For Luke, boundaries separating reality from fantasy seem to have been demolished as he attempts to live recklessly moment-to-moment. While conventional film narratives are based around goals and progression, the narrative of *The Living End* is shaped by the death-drive (unsurprising, as it was made during a period when many people died from AIDS). Araki is more concerned with symbolic gestures than carefully plotted narrative coherence.

Music in *The Living End* both connects the characters and also signals their differences. As music selected by Luke and Jon largely falls into the industrial music category, this broad genre indicates how they both share common tastes and are outsider characters. But these two characters are also very different in other respects, traits emphasised by music *and* dialogue about music. Jon is more of a music lover than Luke, indicated by his dialogue, his clothing and the posters in his apartment. So, when we are first introduced to Jon, he is driving and listening to music in his car (barely discernible at this point as it is low in the mix and underpins Jon's voiceover). His obsession with music is announced to us at the same time as he mentions that he had his first AIDS test – 'bought the new Dead Can Dance CD, got the results for my first AIDS test' – which turns out to be positive. Music accompanies both Luke and Jon at various moments throughout the film, but it is Jon who discusses music with greater frequency. Luke barely mentions it unless he is expressing distaste, such as when he steals a lesbian couple's car and complains about their tapes (dismissing the singer-songwriters k.d. lang and Michelle Shocked). In the previously mentioned scene when Luke puts on 16volt, he replaces Chris & Cosey's darkly atmospheric 'Cords of Love' (chosen by Jon) with the hard and fast industrial track 'Hang Your Head'. Before he does so, he states 'Man, that stuff is putting me to sleep', to which Jon sarcastically replies 'Thanks for the nice relaxing nap music'. These reactions to music indicate differences between Jon and Luke to an extent: Jon's choice of driving music is more romantic than Luke's, whose choice is more relentlessly visceral and aggressive. Jon is presented as a cultured, intellectual and sensitive character, in contrast to Luke's more physical, spontaneous and impulsive personality. Such differences between the characters are symbolically denoted by music and reinforced by other characteristics: Jon, for example, is a film critic and Luke a hustler; Jon is more rooted in a sedentary lifestyle than drifter Luke, so he initially considers the road trip to be an exciting, romantic adventure.

The relations between music and character in American independent cinema have been analysed fruitfully by Jennifer O'Meara (2015), who highlights the importance of characters selecting music within films, a process which 'can . . . establish individuality through music' (134). She also states that characters talking about music is a further means by which characters can display their tastes; in conjunction with musical selections, musical affiliations can enable audiences to form ideas about characters and potentially engender allegiances between audiences and specific characters. Of course, the actual ways an individual audio-viewer reacts to characters selecting and discussing music will vary depending on their knowledge of, and attitudes towards, the music being played or discussed, and in line with how they perceive characters more broadly. O'Meara's arguments are relevant to *The Living End*, as most of the music in the film is selected by characters, while discussion of music (as well as other references to music) is prevalent throughout the film. Jon's greater interest in music is communicated by his continual references to music culture, the posters on his apartment wall, as well as T-shirts he wears of Joy Division and

Morrissey. His musical interests are mostly – as indicated by his conversational reference points – related to British indie music of the 1980s, much of which is associated with angst. The centrality of music to his personality is emphasised when Jon's best friend, Darcy, tells her partner Peter that she is worried about him. This is followed by:

> Darcy: He's acting as though everything's okay but [pauses] I've never seen him so lost before.
> Peter: Darcy, it's hardly like he's the most well-adjusted person in the world to start with.
> Darcy: What's that supposed to mean?
> Peter: We're talking about a guy who went into severe depression for two weeks when Echo and the Bunnymen broke up.
> Darcy: So? [pauses] It was only a week and a half.

This sardonic discussion stresses Jon's obsessive interest in music (and how it affects him emotionally), as well as his sensitive, depressive nature. It further links these characteristics to forms of music that were seen to appeal to such personality types. In this sense, audio-viewers who themselves are fans of some of the music mentioned by Jon might themselves sympathise and align with him.

Araki's tendency to link musical taste to character types is evident throughout his filmography and is highlighted through one of his directing techniques: providing actors with compilation tapes and lyric sheets to inhabit their characters. On the director commentary for the 2008 DVD region 1 release of *The Living End*, he notes how he did this for Craig Gilmore – who played Jon – because 'music was so important to his character' (Araki 2008). Much of the music that Jon likes is indicated via dialogue or display (posters, T-shirts) as opposed to actually being played by him, largely because such music, as mentioned, would have been too expensive to license, but it isn't the only reason; talk about music is nearly always a crucial aspect of Araki's films. Dubowksy (2014: 46) criticised the film's tendency to use music 'as a wallpaper backdrop for dialogue and action' at the expense of fulfilling narrative functions, but I would stress that the pervasive use of music is important within Araki's films (as well as in numerous other films). Rather than use music in the foreground constantly as a requisite means to underpin dramatic moments, Araki's films are saturated with music on many levels. When music plays under a conversation or is played at a nightclub, Araki is stressing just how important music is to his characters and the environments they inhabit; it is worth noting that most of his films are peopled by teenagers or young adults, a period in life when music's emotional and affective weight is arguably at its zenith, and when music is a particularly crucial resource for identity construction. Araki has himself discussed how he likes to depict teenagers because of the intensity of emotions they feel, claiming that 'There's something monumental and heightened about their hormone-mad lives . . . They live and die ten times a day' (Moran 1996: 25). In *The Living End* and in most of Araki's subsequent films, music acts as a backdrop against which young people live out their lives. Music often accompanies their everyday experiences – in bedrooms, clubs and cars, for example – and at certain moments comes to the fore. It functions to delineate identities and it also connects individuals socially: bonds are forged through musical similarities in conjunction with other resemblances (outsiderness, queerness), broadly symbolising alternative lifestyles and personalities.

TOTALLY FUCKED UP

The social dimension of music is emphasised more prominently in *Totally Fucked Up* (1993), Araki's follow-up to *The Living End*, which is unsurprising as the film is more of an ensemble piece than its predecessor and is presented as a series of sixteen fragments (Araki here references Godard, whom he has claimed as a big influence, specifically *Vivre sa Vie* (1962), which was structured in twelve 'tableaux'). *Totally Fucked Up* focuses on a group of queer friends who, between numerous video diary segments, discuss music regularly and listen to it in a variety of situations. Like *The Living End*, *Totally Fucked Up* was a low-budget film shot guerrilla-style on 16mm, which was blown up to 35mm for projection; it also addresses homophobia, refers to AIDS and explores the alienation of its characters.

The amount of music featured in *Totally Fucked Up* again indicates Araki's obsessive interest in music and how it plays an important role in the lives of many of his filmic characters: music is frequently discussed, emblazoned on T-shirts and posters, while dialogue and titles often incorporate song lyrics or titles. Music is the core unifying thread that unites the disparate young gay characters in *TFU*. As a symbol of a broader subcultural network, it also largely connotes a generalised disaffection with mainstream culture and again consists of indie/alternative tracks. As with *The Living End*, there is a definite taste for industrial music, but the soundtrack consists of a broader range of music and includes a substantial amount of music licensed from iconic British independent label 4AD (by bands such as His Name is Alive, Pale Saints, Red House Painters, This Mortal Coil and The Wolfgang Press), as well as The Jesus and Mary Chain, who are an important reference point for Araki. While The Jesus and Mary Chain provided the title of his previous film, they are not only used on the soundtrack of *Totally Fucked Up* but are also name-checked in a conversation and have extracts from their lyrics displayed on two of the frequent title cards that Araki uses throughout the film: the first is 'your screaming automatic pain', which appears at approximately 64 minutes, the second is 'feels like God in Heaven's gone insane', appearing at approximately

69 minutes. These lyrics are from the respective tracks 'Blues from a Gun' and 'Coast to Coast' which, like 'Head On' – which is included on the soundtrack – appear on *Automatic*, the band's third studio album released in 1989.

As in *The Living End*, music is discussed in both positive and negative terms. In that film, it was mostly Luke who voiced his musical dislikes through direct commentary. In *TFU* discussions about music are increased; this signifies the characters' passion for music but doesn't mean they are always appreciative listeners. Because Araki's characters spend their lives immersed in music, the film acknowledges the variability of music listening pleasure, which can fluctuate according to mood and sometimes disappoint. Less positive responses to music in *TFU* are notable, particularly in discussions featuring Andy (James Duvall), who amongst the ensemble cast is the most prominent character. In an early scene in the film, when Andy and his friend Deric (Lance May) are at a nightclub at which industrial music is playing (16volt's 'Motorskill'), Andy says 'This music sucks' and Deric replies, 'So what else is new?' Such dialogue could indicate an authorial and/or a character's dismissal of a form of music, but we know that the first of these is not true through Araki's own statements about music, while we also know that Andy is into some forms of industrial music as we see him wearing a Ministry T-shirt later in the film. It seems that this scene, and others like it, reflects not so much musical distaste as it does characters' mood at certain moments. This is more clearly implied when a group of friends idly talk, playing a board game called 'Heartthrobs', while industrial music plays low down in the mix. When the record ends, Patricia moves towards the off-screen record player to put on a different record. 'What are you putting on?' asks Andy, who has been slouching and looking bored. 'Cocteau Twins', she replies, to which he responds 'Shit no, I'm sleepy enough as it is'. The record eventually put on is Unrest's 'Angel, I'll Walk You Home', though whether this is because of Andy's negative reaction to the suggestion of Cocteau Twins is open to conjecture.[3] Nevertheless, it seems once again that Andy's reaction is more to do with his current mood than a dislike of Cocteau Twins, considering how highly Araki rates the band. (It may be argued that Araki's tastes cannot be conflated with that of his characters, but he does often align his characters' tastes with his own, as I will mention further on.) Music is an important ontological crotch for the young people in Araki's films, but their existential ennui can often still block their enjoyment of it.

At other times in the film, music aurally signifies more blissful emotions. It is in such scenes that Araki's preference for many 4AD acts becomes particularly important. As noted, he starts to include more delicate pop and rock music, particularly shoegaze and dream pop. These two music categories are usually interrelated and refer to music that emphasises ethereality through textured soundscapes (guitars are often treated with various effects such as flange and delay). 'Dream pop' is usually attributed to A. R. Kane's Alex Ayuli in the late 1980s, though Cocteau Twins are often considered to be the band that pioneered the sound avant la lettre. Shoegaze is arguably a descendant of dream pop and has become more frequently used as a generic concept, which is somewhat odd considering that it was originally used as a term of abuse (in a *Melody Maker* live review of the band Moose, it was used to describe a wave of post-My Bloody Valentine bands who would often stare at the floor when performing). Shoegaze tends to denote, like dream pop, music which emphasises texture and atmosphere over driven riffs and more extrovert rock sounds, evoking introversion and mental escape. It was often considered neo-psychedelic because of the careful attention paid to sound effects and for the ways the music tended to indicate the cosmic via swirling vortices of guitars; its marriage of the inner and outer in this sense also hinted at drugs and altered states. Vocals in shoegaze music are often mixed to further emphasise texture, as another element in the mix rather than the dominant focus, sometimes featuring a blurred, androgynous mix of male and female vocals. Araki uses dream pop/shoegaze music in ways that are congruent with typical associations of bliss and escape, including sexual pleasure.

THE DOOM GENERATION AND NOWHERE

Following *Totally Fucked Up*, Araki's filmmaking style shifted somewhat; due to higher budgets he was able to produce with permits, on 35mm and with more recognisable actors (usually up and coming young actors who had appeared on television). Many continuities do exist, though, between his first few features and his films beginning with *The Doom Generation*. *Totally Fucked Up*, *The Doom Generation* and *Nowhere* (1997), for example, constitute a 'teen apocalypse trilogy' and all feature James Duvall. An obsession with good-looking but often disaffected teens and young adults runs through most of his films, while his preference for forms of indie music to flesh out such characters and provide a broader subcultural milieu has also largely remained. If Araki's first four features are distinguished by their gritty look, then his subsequent films are more strikingly glossy in presentation: there is movement from an underground aesthetic towards a more mainstream style, though Araki tends to toy with mainstream conventions and subtly subvert them. Hart (2003: 33) argues that Araki's films 'play with the conventions of various genres in order to make them serve new and radical purposes', drawing on familiar film genres/cycles such as juvenile delinquent films, buddy movies and road movies. *The Doom Generation* certainly conforms to such an approach: whereas Araki labelled his previous films 'homo' movies, this film is announced as a 'hetero' movie, but this is no straightforward move away from a depiction of gay characters: Araki will often frame male torsos in a homoerotic manner and imply male-on-male attraction by lingering on eye contact between male characters (Hart 2003: 33). In *The Doom Generation* we are presented with a heterosexual couple at the beginning – Amy (Rose McGowan) and Jordan (James Duvall) – but their romantic hetero coupling is complicated by Xavier's (Johnathon Schaech) arrival and turns into a love triangle marked by homosexual and heterosexual attraction.

Music is a core means through which Araki has achieved some form of continuity across differently budgeted films, with rising budgets leading him to develop an aesthetic marked by bold colours and somewhat fragmented, deliberately anti-realist narratives. *The Doom Generation*, for example, is a metaphorical fantasy grounded in very real subject matter. Metaphorically, the film takes place in Hell, as indicated at the very beginning of the film when 'Welcome to Hell' appears in fiery lettering in a nightclub, while on the soundtrack Trent Reznor sings the same line (from the Nine Inch Nails song 'Heresy') as Jordan and Amy dance frenetically. While this was the second film in the teen apocalypse trilogy, it is more directly centred around an apocalyptic theme than *Totally Fucked Up*, stressed by the predominance of red lighting throughout the film as well as the recurring motif of 666 (most goods purchased in the film, for example, cost $6.66). If the grittiness of *Totally Fucked Up* grounded that film's diegesis in stark reality, then the gaudy production design and metaphorical narrative of *The Doom Generation* nudges the film into a more fantastical realm. This fantastical aspect of the film, however, is itself rooted in realities of the time: of teenage angst and the ways in which teenage life is filtered through media content. The metaphor of Hell and apocalypse relates not only to teenage experience but also to how teenagers – or at least a sizeable section of teenagers – were being perceived by some social commentators.

Media itself has often been considered a pernicious influence that can incite negative behaviour; at the time of the film's production and release, great concern was being expressed about media violence and its impact on youth. For right-wing ideologues, particularly those of a Christian bent, this generation troubled them because of its supposed lack of morals and interest in all things considered degenerate, particularly certain forms of music and film, as well as video games. Such worries had manifested themselves particularly forcefully within the area of media censorship: in music, for example, there were fears in the 1980s over the Satanic influence of heavy metal music, as well as concerns over the violent imagery propounded within hip-hop, especially when combined with anti-authority views (perhaps the most egregious example being N.W.A's 1988 track 'Fuck tha Police'), fears which would continue into the 1990s and beyond. The Parents Music Resource Center (PMRC) was established in 1985 to address the issue of protecting children from explicit content (mainly sex, violence and drugs, but also themes such as Satanism), and their efforts eventually led to the Recording Industry Association of America (RIAA) accepting that 'Parental Advisory: Explicit Lyrics' stickers be placed on records that contained potentially offensive lyrics from 1990. Controversy over such issues did not, however, disappear and many music releases were denied airplay over the next few years. Film was another medium that was under attack because of unacceptable levels of violence and other content considered to be morally unsavoury. In 1992, conservative film critic Michael Medved published *Hollywood Vs. America: Popular Culture and the War on Traditional Values*, in which he argued that Hollywood was producing films that were increasingly violent and disrespectful of traditional values, in the process negatively influencing young minds. He made similar arguments about the negative impact of other media, particularly rock music.

Within this context, *The Doom Generation* should be considered a somewhat parodic take on the idea of satanic forces using the media to corrupt young minds. The young minds in this film – Amy, Jordan and Xavier (whose surnames are Blue, White and Red, another nod to Godard) – have already been tainted by the evils of the world, particularly in the sense that their lives are absolutely saturated by media, most prominently music but also films, television and video games. After the opening scene in the club, Amy and Jordan drive to a disused drive-in lot to have sex for the first time (Amy mentions they are virgins), but their sexual activity is interrupted by violence erupting outside of the car and the arrival of Xavier. Explanations about the causes of these violent scenes is elided, though their unfolding against a backdrop of a blank cinema screen does hint satirically towards fears of the pernicious influence of media. Xavier, meanwhile, can be considered an almost devilish character who arrives just as they are about to 'sin', and who aids their descent further into Hell; their music influences and drug ingestion have already nudged them along this pathway, with sex and violence following. In a further nod to media debates, Araki includes several shots of violent video games being played and a scene where Xavier watches a news report announcing that the murder they were involved in was committed by Satanists.

Music in *The Doom Generation* continues Araki's tendency to associate characters with music and to stress how it is a crucially important, albeit sometimes mundane, companion to the lives of young teens. In this film, however, it also takes on another layer of meaning through its perceived role in corrupting young people. The generational nature of these tensions is also emphasised by the lack of parental figures in the teens' lives, bar a brief phone call between Jordan and his mother (though, importantly, we only see and hear *him* speaking in this scene). Beyond its more satirical function, music in *The Doom Generation* does conform to many ways that Araki had used music in his previous films. For example, the range of music licensed shares similarities with *Totally Fucked Up*: many tracks are shoegaze, dream pop and industrial music, though Araki's use of Aphex Twin begins a tendency to supplement such sounds with electronic music. Music is also largely diegetic: it is important that this music is mostly selected by characters within the film, and that it is nearly always listened to – sometimes attentively, often as backdrop – with friends and/or others (as when music plays in a nightclub). In Araki films, music emanates from car radios, nightclub speakers, portable stereos and record players, but we rarely see characters listen to music on personal stereos. *The Doom Generation* does contain one very small exception to the socially connected modes of listening that Araki focuses on, albeit extremely briefly. This is when Jordan, who is waiting in the car while Amy and Xavier have sex in the motel room, is smoking, listening to and getting lost in The Verve's 'Already There'. This nod to the pleasures of listening to music by oneself is soon swept aside, however, as Xavier comes out and joins Jordan; their conversation unfolds against the same Verve track, which now slips into the background.

Music is used similarly in the third of Araki's teen apocalypse trilogy, *Nowhere*, which also continues the aesthetic style of *The Doom Generation*, particularly its colourful, exaggerated mise-en-scene and shoegaze-heavy soundtrack. In *Nowhere*, diegetic music is even more pervasive than in previous Araki films. A string of almost uninterrupted, but constantly changing, music tracks dominates almost the whole of the first twenty minutes of the film, a pattern that only very gradually lessens as it progresses. Once again, music on the soundtrack shares many similarities with Araki's previous films, though a wider range of indie music is employed, including some acts linked to 'Britpop' such as Elastica and Blur, and further inclusion of electronic dance music (such as Daft Punk). Again, music tends to blare from speakers in bedrooms and public spaces, often underpinning conversations and sometimes coming to the fore in more striking ways. Araki continues to position music as particularly important to his filmic characters (and to himself as well as potential audiences), so that it permeates the lives of all protagonists; two of the characters – Cowboy (Guillermo Diaz) and his drug-addicted drummer-partner Bart (Jeremy Jordan) – are even in a band.

While The *Living End* included an intellectual character in Jon, and *Totally Fucked Up* featured people discussing various ideas in their video diary segments, *The Doom Generation* and *Nowhere* seem less cerebral in tone. Along with the shift in budget and style, Araki seems to have adopted a slightly more distanced relation to characters than previously. Distanciation was a characteristic of his earlier films, certainly, hence his exaggerated character types in *The Living End*, and is a key component of many of his films (the twin influences of Godard on the one hand, and of camp underground films on the other, seem most relevant to such an aesthetic). From *The Doom Generation* onwards, however, increased budgets enabled him to create a greater sense of camp excess, while references to more mainstream aspects of popular culture are heightened. *The Doom Generation* and *Nowhere*, for example, nod towards other types of teen movies, but the music, sex, drugs and meta-aesthetic details move it beyond the films of, say, John Hughes. *Nowhere* in particular also draws inspiration from trashy television, including soaps, comedies and dramas, most evident in its casting Jason Simmons from *Baywatch* to play the role of 'teen idol'. The adult characters in the film, meanwhile – though largely peripheral – are all people known from television and film comedy, including Beverley D'Angelo (as Dark's mother) and Christopher Knight and Eva Plumb from *The Brady Bunch* (as Brad's parents). Like *The Doom Generation*, Araki mixes these conventional elements into a rather strange brew through campy excess and deviation. Beyond sex, drugs and indie music, we also witness the eruption of sci-fi elements and the apocalyptic narrative: in this film, it is indicated that it is Armageddon, and we witness the aftermath of two teenage suicides, one of which follows a violent sexual assault (by the teen idol). In short, what Araki seems to be doing with these two films is recreating conventions associated with clean teen dramas and undermining them through various means to reveal their dark underbelly and portray the types of teenage behaviours that lead to generational concern. Moving on from his 'homo' movies, he starts to queer the 'hetero' movie. While the majority of relationships in *Nowhere* are heterosexual, attraction between Dark and Montgomery (Nathan Bexton) forms a core part of the film narrative, while other same sex relationships are also included (e.g. between Cowboy and Bart, while Dark's romantic interest, Mel (Rachel True), is bisexual). The heterosexual relationships, meanwhile, are generally deviant – such as the sadomasochistic sex between Alyssa (Jordan Ladd) and Elvis (Thyme Lewis), the intense sex games acted out by Shad (Ryan Phillippe) and Lilith (Heather Graham), or the actual rape inflicted on Egg (Sarah Lassez).

In both *The Doom Generation* and *Nowhere*, while some characters are marked as more intelligent than others, most nevertheless have difficulties expressing their feelings. For some characters, this can be linked to the limited nature of their intelligence: Jordan in *The Doom Generation*, for example, is good-natured but not particularly bright, which is indicated at various points in the film where he attempts, not very successfully, to grapple verbally with life's complexities. Other characters are presented as brighter, but even the more intelligent protagonists sometimes have difficulties articulating their feelings, probably because Araki constructs them as subject to a whirlwind of hormonal emotions. As a result, characters in his films tend to not only have difficulty finding meaning in the external world (hence the pervasive nihilistic attitudes), but also struggle to understand their own desires and motivations. In this sense, the extensive use of music in these films partially expresses emotions that the characters themselves might not be able to articulate and, in *Nowhere* in particular, works to further distance the film from more conventional teen-based media.

Mysterious Skin and Beyond

Mysterious Skin signalled another shift in Araki's style. In contrast to the gaudy, camp excess of *The Doom Generation*, *Nowhere* and *Splendor* (1999), *Mysterious Skin* – Araki's first adaptation – is reasonably restrained by comparison and treats its characters with less ironic distance. This imbues the film with a weightier emotional heft; it approaches the themes of child abuse and its lingering aftereffects in a straight, serious manner. This shift was noted in many reviews of the film, which is Araki's most acclaimed film to date. The more serious tone of the film was often stressed in reviews, with Michael Koresky (2005) writing that it was more mainstream than Araki's previous films and his 'most accomplished, emotionally gripping work'; while Marjorie Baumgarten (2005) wrote that with *Mysterious Skin*, Araki 'crosses over from the fringes to make his most mature and penetrating drama to date'. Despite this evident aesthetic shift, the film nevertheless contains several elements that Araki had become noted for. It concerns troubled teenagers, includes frequent gay sex, and includes fantastical elements (though in this film the fantastical elements are rationalised, which lends the film a more realistic tone than his previous three features). One other continuity is the music on the soundtrack, which is again marked by the sounds of dream pop and shoegaze. There is, however, a slight difference in the ways that music is produced and employed on *Mysterious Skin* in contrast to his previous films. The film features a more extensive score than his previous films; while *The Doom Generation* and *Splendor* were also scored (by Dan Gatto and Daniel Licht respectively), they were not used as much and were outweighed by licensed tracks. In *Mysterious Skin* there is a greater balance between the score and the licensed tracks, and less diegetic music than is typically common in Araki's films. While many Araki films feature characters listening to music frequently – and often discussing music – there are only a few scenes in *Mysterious Skin* where music is diegetic. The reduction of licensed music, the sparing use of diegetic music and a more prominent score contribute to a more conventional use of music in this film by Araki.

While most of the music in *Mysterious Skin* is non-diegetic, it is nevertheless quite consistent in style: the score by Robin Guthrie and Harold Budd has some similarities to much of the licensed songs. Guthrie was, of course, a member of Cocteau Twins, a band whose music Araki had previously used in his films and displayed great admiration for. Their sound is often considered to have established the 'dream pop' sound: characterised by Guthrie's heavily reverbed, layered guitar, Elizabeth Fraser's soaring vocals, which often eschewed recognisable language, and often underpinned by Simon Raymonde's bass, they have frequently been referred to as 'ethereal' and 'dreamy'. Budd, meanwhile, is an ambient pianist who had previously collaborated with Fraser, Guthrie and Raymonde on a 1986 album *The Moon and the Melodies*. This album was less song-based than most Cocteau Twins records – with only some tracks featuring vocals by Fraser – and its instrumentals act as a broad template for *Mysterious Skin*'s score. The score features some of Guthrie's characteristic shimmering, reverbed guitar patterns, but these tend to be more muted than on the majority of Cocteau Twins recordings, while Budd's delicate, 'soft pedal' piano style intertwines with Guthrie's guitars to create deeply atmospheric, spacious pieces. Due largely to Guthrie's distinctive guitar sounds, the score also dovetails with much of the licensed music employed. Though the score tends to be more minimal than most other music on the soundtrack, both it and the licensed tracks share ethereal qualities. Araki uses songs from Curve, Slowdive, Sigur Rós and Ride and mostly selects instrumental sections characterised by either swirling guitars or repeated piano motifs, both of which feature on the score.

The dream-like qualities of the music in *Mysterious Skin* might seem an odd choice to accompany a film about child abuse, but the music relates to Neil's (Joseph Gordon-Levitt) subjective feelings of happiness when he was with Coach (Bill Sage), even though he was being taken advantage of; while it often connects to Brian's (Brady Corbet) need to escape and blot out the realities of his life. Both the score and numerous licensed tracks are used to denote subjective states on many occasions. The film opens with credits against a very pale, pinkish background and abstract, indefinable blobs of different colours (mostly green, red, orange) raining down the screen intermittently. This is accompanied by the opening section of Slowdive's cover of Syd Barrett's 'Golden Hair', which consists of atmospheric guitar treatments and Rachel Goswell's airy, indistinct, drawn-out vocals. When the title of the film appears on the credits, there is a sonic cut to a later segment of the song – more dynamic and centred around epic guitar patterns and feedback – which is accompanied by a speeding up of the image, so that the abstract blobs rain down the screen more rapidly. Gradually, as the camera lowers and the top of a young boy's head appears at the bottom of the frame, there is a slight focal change which enables us to see that these abstract shapes are fruit loops pouring over the boy, whose closed eyes and partially open, upturned mouth indicate a moment of bliss. This connects to a slightly later scene (approximately eleven minutes into the film) when Coach invites Neil around to his house and, after chucking cereal around, proceeds to molest him. While the scene is horrific, it isn't set up this way, because we are invited to share Neil's subjectivity: Coach's attention to him and his offer of cereal that his parents will not let him have, in conjunction with his less-than-ideal family life (his mother continually brings men to his home), offer him happiness that he struggles to otherwise find. So, rather than presenting his time with Coach in a deliberately sinister fashion, the film instead downplays the full horror of the events, which again matches the subjectivity of Neil, who has not fully faced up to what happened to him when we move to a later period in his and Brian's lives (the majority of the film takes place in 1991, with the earlier scenes set in 1981).[4] Brian, meanwhile, whose story is told in parallel with Neil's, is trying to make sense of the blackouts he experienced as a child; he believes that he was abducted by aliens. The score often reflects his subjective need to escape the stresses of his life: in reality, he has an unloving father and is recovering from a traumatic incident – sexual abuse at the hands of Coach – that he cannot access. While the score does sometimes indicate blissful escape – as when an airy drone and soft, reverbed piano sounds accompany his fake memory of watching a UFO with his mother and sister – the music that accompanies Brian tends to be slightly darker and gloomier than music accompanying Neil. This is fitting regarding their respective mental states later in life: Neil's memories are coloured by his happy times with Coach, which blocks him from really understanding what happened; while Brian is haunted by an event that he cannot fully comprehend.

The reality of what happened to Brian is eventually revealed by Neil after Brian tracks him down. The parallel narrative structure points towards connections between the two from the outset, and this connection is occasionally emphasised by music. In one of the few scenes in the film that does feature diegetic music, we first see Brian with Neil's friend Eric in Eric's attic bedroom, which occurs after Brian has attempted to track Neil down. In the bedroom they get drunk and listen to Ride's 'Drive Blind'; there is then a cut to Neil listening to the same song on headphones in New York (a rare moment in an

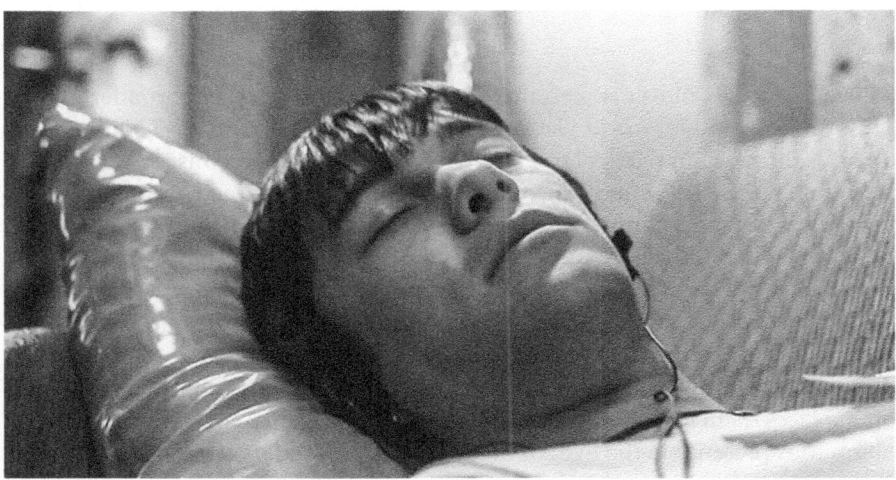

Figure 3.2 *Mysterious Skin*: Neil listens to Ride on his headphones

Araki film of someone listening to music on headphones). Araki perhaps used less diegetic music in this film to create a more conventional film by his standards, though another possibility is that this choice emphasises the isolation of the two characters; as argued, he often creates connections between characters via music, and in this film the traumatic childhood experiences of the two main characters make it hard for them to forge genuine connections with others. When 'Drive Blind' does highlight connections between Neil and Brian about seventy minutes into the film, it emphasises how they are inextricably connected and that they might be able to emotionally develop when they both confront their past.

Since *Mysterious Skin*, Araki has continued to license a large amount of indie music, particularly from UK artists. He has also employed Robin Guthrie to score two more of his films: *Kaboom* (2010, with Ulrich Schnauss, Mark Peters and Vivek Maddala) and *White Bird in a Blizzard* (2014, with Harold Budd), soundtracks again characterised by shimmering, dream pop textures. One of the outliers in his filmography is *Smiley Face*, which was a stoner comedy in the vein of a Cheech and Chong movie, and which also lent less heavily on indie music than his other soundtracks. Since *Smiley Face* (2007), he has reprised the campy teen film with *Kaboom*, and with *White Bird in a Blizzard* he returned to the more sombre aesthetic of *Mysterious Skin* (these two more sombre entries in his oeuvre are his only two adaptations). Additionally, Araki has made a television pilot for a series that was not commissioned and a television series: both *This is How the World Ends* (MTV, 2000) and his most recent series, *Now Apocalypse* (Starz, 2019, also scored by Guthrie), are teen-oriented dramas which contain typical Araki obsessions such as sex and death.

Conclusion

Music in Araki's films can certainly be considered part of his broader authorial profile, even his 'world view'. In a 2011 *Guardian* article (O'Neill 2011), music – shoegaze in particular – is singled out as the most consistent aspect of his filmmaking. The importance of music is further outlined through discussion of how Araki's filmmaking is influenced by his love of music, and details how much effort he will expend trying to obtain licensing rights for tracks he wants to use. The article also points to how Araki's films can provide viewers of his films with a 'crash course' in shoegaze, which illustrates how Araki has assumed the role of a musical tastemaker in certain quarters.

Araki transforms most of his filmic characters into music lovers as well, and often places them in environments where music plays, therefore stressing music's ubiquitous presence in the lives of many youths. Beyond its function as an ambient presence, music can also denote character traits, forge connections between characters and link to broader symbolic meanings. The ubiquity of music is emphasised further through characters wearing T-shirts of music artists, having posters of bands in their living spaces, and through many characters discussing music. Music lyrics are also sometimes used as intertitles or within dialogue – as when a character in *Splendor* intones 'Pearly Dewdrops Drops', referencing the title of a Cocteau Twins song – while some of Araki's films are named after music tracks/albums: *The Living End*, as mentioned, is named after a Jesus and Mary Chain song, while the film *Nowhere* was named after a Ride LP.

Music in Araki's films also indicates subjective states, with music expressing aspects of the characters that they might not be fully in touch with, and/or may be unable to express. The nature of music – an abstract art that nevertheless has emotional and cultural resonance, with lyrics providing occasionally more concrete expression – is well suited to such a task. Within films marked by a quite distanced aesthetic, peopled by characters who are not always particularly sympathetic, music also invites audiences to partially connect with specific characters. The actual ways in which any viewer reacts to characters can depend, of course, on a variety of different factors, but Araki himself likes the music he includes and often uses it to connect personally to his characters. He has noted, for example, how he often will create characters who have similar music tastes to himself as a way of identifying with them (Abraham 2015). This is a process he was still using on his 2014 feature, *White Bird in a Blizzard* (2014), an adaptation of a novel by Laura Kasischke. Discussing some of the changes he made to the novel, one of the most important was altering the music that the characters listened to:

> In the book Kat meets Phil and they begin their puppy love affair dancing to Journey, or something terrible like that, but in the movie I relocated it from a high school dance to a goth club and had Siouxsie and the Banshees playing. That's the look and the world that I was in – it allowed me to relate so much more to the characters. (Araki quoted in Abraham 2015)

While Araki notes that the main reason for such changes are so that *he* can relate to the characters, one can surmise that this works similarly for some audiences. His own immersion in alternative/indie music cultures as a young person and beyond has influenced how he relates to his own characters, and how many audio-viewers may also do so. In discussing film characters and emotional identification within a cognitive framework, Torben Grodal has argued that it is rare that audiences will fully identify with film characters to the extent that they will become totally immersed in them. Rather, he notes that in real life we often hold conflicting opinions of others and ourselves: 'Identification does not exclude a certain distance, just as we do not "fully identify with ourselves": normally we are not totally obsessed by ourselves, but are able to look at our own emotions with varying degrees of distance' (Grodal 1997: 85). Murray Smith (1992: 82–4) has also questioned prevalent ideas of identification as a 'singular process', arguing that there are different levels of engagement in processes of identification. He builds a model of identification based on three broad processes: recognition (how the spectator recognises and constructs a character), alignment (how a spectator is invited to share the actions, thoughts and feelings of characters) and allegiance (how the spectator may morally evaluate characters). In this way, Smith counters ideas that identification is an unthinking process in which spectators become absorbed and enraptured by characters they identify with. In Gregg Araki's films, which in many ways are typified by distanciation, music is a core aspect in which audience identification with characters might occur: it offers alignment and, if a spectator is a fan of such music, could also spur allegiance (though such allegiance can be disrupted by other actions and speech by specific characters).

Music not only links to Araki's authorial profile and to characters, but also to his films' broader appeal. That is, the styles of alternative indie-rock that he often uses might appeal to audiences with similar tastes (this seemed to be the case when *Totally Fucked Up* was shown at the Lollapalooza music festival; this programming was a demonstrable attempt to link music fans with certain tastes to an independent film). His films, then, exemplify the different functions that music – in this case indie music – can fulfil within filmmaking, both at the level of production, as an integral textual component that informs narrative, character and tone, and on the level of reception, to the point that his films have often been promoted at music festivals as well as within niche music publications.

Notes

1. Araki's first two features – *Three Bewildered People in the Night* (1987) and *The Long Weekend (O'Despair)* (1989) – are currently difficult to obtain, largely because of music licensing issues (the music Araki used in these films has not been cleared). *Three Bewildered People in the Night* was available as a bootleg VHS rip on YouTube at the time of writing.
2. It should also be noted that Wax Trax!, the label which provided much of the film's music, was established by two gay men, while other gay people were involved in industrial music, such as Peter Christopherson (Throbbing Gristle and Coil) and Jhonn Balance (Psychic TV and Coil).
3. It may be the case that Araki wanted to play Cocteau Twins at this juncture but couldn't get permissions to do so. While he thanks Ivo Watts-Russell (co-founder of 4AD, the record company that Cocteau Twins were on for most of their recording career) in the end credits, none of the acts he licensed music from had the profile of Cocteau Twins.
4. There are also brief sections set in 1983 and 1987.

4 SONIC AUTHORSHIP 2: SOFIA COPPOLA

Sofia Coppola is a female auteur who has managed to create a distinctive oeuvre over the course of her career. Disputes about Coppola's privileged position in the industry – she is of course the daughter of Francis Ford Coppola – have tended to overshadow her actual achievements. Such negative dismissals of her advantaged position stem from sexist assumptions about worthiness; many male directors, for example, take advantage of certain privileges but these are rarely scrutinised in the same negative manner as Coppola's have been. Her films have also been dismissed by some critics for their emptiness; for lingering on pretty images, for example, without any apparent 'substance'. But as many defenders of Coppola have argued, her films are anything but empty, and have been perceived as comments 'upon postfeminist concerns about consumption as a "feminine" ideal, and attempts to mirror and reverse macho tropes from the 1960s and 1970s male auteur movement, which includes her father' (Kennedy 2010: 37). Pam Cook (2009: 36) has noted how her first three features focus on the female rite-of-passage, while Belinda Smaill (2013: 50) has stressed how Coppola tends to examine characters, both male and female, who are in stages of transition. Coppola's films also tend to linger on experiential moments: while encased within narrative frameworks, they are less concerned with narrative drive than capturing subjective moods in a somewhat impressionistic manner. Her emphasis on mood and emotion is often linked to her visual style: her careful use of colours, framing, location and costume, and inspiration from photography and other visual arts have been noted frequently. In this chapter, however, I want to look at Coppola's

57

use of music, in particular her use of various indie/alternative music and how this informs her overall aesthetic.

Smaill (151) has drawn attention to Coppola's 'strong ties with the independent music scene': she has directed music videos for acts such as The Flaming Lips and The White Stripes, is married to Thomas Mars, vocalist for French group Phoenix, and uses independent music frequently within her films. Smaill mentions how Coppola's connections with, and use of, independent music imbues her films with subcultural appeal and contributes to the mood and tone of scenes. Yet Smaill does not have the space in her article to explore these issues in too much depth; in this chapter I want to extend the analysis of music both aesthetically and culturally, prioritising a focus on music that can be considered independent or alternative. While referencing other films, I will look mainly at her first three features – *The Virgin Suicides* (1999), *Lost in Translation* (2003) and *Marie Antoinette* (2006) – and the short film *Lick the Star* (1998), as these films utilise indie music to a greater extent than Coppola's other films.

By the time Coppola directed her second short – *Lick the Star*, which followed her debut short *Bed, Bath and Beyond* (1996) – she had already directed music videos for alt-rock bands Walt Mink ('Shine', 1996) and The Flaming Lips ('This Here Giraffe', 1996). While at the time both bands were signed to major record labels, they are still bands who have been termed 'indie' through their sound (as noted in Chapter 1, indie has increasingly replaced alt-rock as a very broad kind of generic category). Other links with indie/alt-rock included a friendship with Sonic Youth's Thurston Moore, who recommended to Coppola the novel *The Virgin Suicides*, which she would adapt as her first feature. Brian Reitzell, who was Coppola's music supervisor on her first three features as well as her fifth feature, *The Bling Ring* (2013), also has links with indie music, having formerly been a drummer for Redd Kross, as well as a member of indie synthpop band TV Eyes.

Lick the Star

In her short *Lick the Star*, Coppola makes extensive use of indie rock music, more specifically female-led guitar rock from bands including Free Kitten and The Amps. As Tim Anderson (2013a: 69) has noted, these bands were creating punk-influenced music that was associated with masculinity. Anderson also notes a link with riot grrrl bands as members of Free Kitten and The Amps – such as Kim Gordon and Kim Deal – were often considered inspirational figures for many riot grrrl bands and certainly can be connected to this feminist movement. One of the other bands on the soundtrack, The Go-Go's, were also considered inspirational by many female musicians involved in rock music in the 1990s. Even though their sound is poppier than either The Amps or Free

Kitten, they emerged from the L.A. punk scene and were important in being the first all-female band who both wrote songs and played all their instruments to top the Billboard charts with their 1981 debut album *Beauty and the Beat*. Only one music selection on the soundtrack, 'Heidi Cakes' by Land of the Loops, is made by a male-fronted act, but the track features quite childlike vocals by Simone Ashby, resulting in probably the least 'masculine' sounding track in the film (if, that is, we buy into stereotypical gendered assumptions). The selections themselves, even disregarding the ways that they are yoked to filmic images, indicate saliently the importance of gender on the one hand, and of gender reversals on the other; the film is, after all, about female school students, one of whom – Chloe (Audrey Kelly) – acts in a manner that comes across as 'masculine' in the sense that she exudes confidence and is rather aggressive.

Tim Anderson (69–70) argues that the aggressive music of The Amps and Free Kitten denotes the confidence and cool of Chloe.[1] This is correct, but it is also important to note that the film is framed by Kate (Christina Turley), and that Chloe's confidence and cool are bestowed upon her by her classmates. This has been argued by Smaill (2013: 42–3), who stresses how *Lick the Star* concerns Chloe's objectification by seeing her as others see her, and how Chloe's identity is forged by the perceptions and expectations of others. The snarling female hard rock sounds also act to highlight the ways in which the short film both utilises a familiar cinematic scenario but also deviates from it: the high school rites-of-passage film is, of course, a familiar component of cinema (and television) history, but Coppola avoids the common focus on males. Certainly, there have been numerous female-focused high-school films – for example, *Clueless* (1995) predates *Lick the Star* – but Coppola avoids typical 'girly' concerns of such films and presents a slightly rougher portrait of female students. The music of The Amps and Free Kitten, likewise, draws on a set of conventions and historical traditions largely associated with men, but inflects such music with a gendered perspective, therefore strengthening the idea of tough femininity.

Such manoeuvres were made more explicit and political in the riot grrrl movement, which drew on the sounds and DIY tenets of punk but rejected its often masculinist, sexist dimensions. Riot grrrl will be discussed in more detail in Chapter 6, but some of the criticism these performers received is pertinent to mention, namely the ways in which they were seen as occupying 'masculine' positions, which has been a recurrent criticism of other women in rock. As Gottlieb and Wald elaborate: 'Women performers go through complicated contortions as they both appropriate and repudiate a traditionally masculine rock performance position which is itself premised on the repression of femininity, while they simultaneously contend with a feminine performance position defined primarily as the erotic object-to-be-looked-at' (1994:

260). These complex positions are addressed in *Lick the Star*: at first, Chloe is a strong female who nevertheless takes on the role of bully more traditionally associated with boys and in a manner that directly challenges her fellow male students. Not only does she slap and reprimand Craig, who mocks her underpants, she then hatches a plan to poison boys at the school. Although the other girls ostensibly shun her due to a misunderstanding around a comment she makes, resulting in her being tagged a racist, a more implicit explanation is that she has transgressed gendered boundaries and therefore must be punished. Alone in a field by the end of the film following a suicide attempt, she is clutching Jean Stein's biography of Edie Sedgwick, a nod to her new status as a troubled, damaged woman. The rapidity of this shift from bullying cynosure to isolated outcast links to the pressure on females who assume roles of power within patriarchal culture and emphasises the fragility of such positions.

The Virgin Suicides

For her first feature, Coppola turned to a very different type of music nevertheless associated with the broad alternative/indie sphere of music culture. *The Virgin Suicides* was scored by French electronic duo Air, with additional contributions from music supervisor Brian Reitzell (who played drums and had formerly played drums on tour with Air). The actual score is distinct from the diegetic music selections, which are largely popular hits from the period in which the film was set (the late 1970s). While these diegetic tracks link to thematic and narrative aspects of the film, they are also employed in a more functional manner: that is, they reflect music that would have been played frequently during the period on commercial radio. In addition to the score and diegetic selections, the film also included a few tracks from the Canadian indie band Sloan, whose power pop sounds were retro enough to comfortably fit into the overall soundtrack design. The film is a framed narrative in which a narrator (Giovanni Ribisi) looks back at his younger days, when he and his friends were obsessed with the Lisbon sisters – Bonny (Chelse Swain), Cecilia (Hannah Hall), Lux (Kirsten Dunst), Mary (A. J. Cook) and Therese (Leslie Hayman) – who lived nearby in a suburban area of Detroit.

A French duo producing predominantly electronic music, Air became big on the indie/alternative circuit following the release of their debut 1998 album *Moon Safari*. This was a period when the broad realm of indie/alternative music was starting to include some newer sounds, particularly from electronic music. At least as far back as the early 1990s and the explosion of club music, elements of dance and electronic music – particularly the more ambient modes – were garnering interest within indie and alternative circles, as evidenced by coverage in music publications such as *Spin* in the US and *New Musical Express* in the UK. Air themselves were not only an electronic act but also were linked to the rise of retro-pop trends that had risen to prominence in niche circles around the mid-90s. British indie-rock outfit Stereolab had been prominent in the revival of interest in lounge music and 'space-age pop' (linked to artists such as Esquivel and Perrey & Kingsley, who utilised modern production techniques and electronics to create futuristic effects in the late 1950s and 60s). This led to numerous space age pop compilations being released in the 1990s, such as the *Space Age Pop* series (RCA, 1995). Stereolab's musical palette increasingly incorporated electronic sounds, particularly vintage analogue instruments, including Moog synthesisers and Farfisa organs. While Air's music was less grounded in traditions of indie-rock than Stereolab's, they nevertheless shared that group's interest in vintage electronics and space-age pop (they even included a guest appearance from Jean-Jacques Perrey on *Moon Safari*).

Air's 'electronic retro-futurism' (Jones 2004) is a fitting soundtrack for a film which not only reconstructs the recent past, but also foregrounds the memorial construction of that past from the perspective of a present-day narrator reminiscing. In her analysis of the film, Anna Backman-Rogers (2019: 28) claims that it enacts a 'feminist hauntology'. She elaborates in the following passage:

> *The Virgin Suicides* is a film that slips between regimes of the image since it both demonstrates the powerful drive for a narrative that would reclaim the lost object – and thus meaning – and the impossibility of creating a coherent, abiding trajectory that serves to contain and expound on the female body, since the female body always exceeds any attempt to delimit it. *The Virgin Suicides* actively works to accentuate lack, void, ruptures and lacunae. It also demonstrates how every narrative is predicated on what it excludes and that it is this structuring absence that can never be fully eradicated, despite its nonrepresentability and nonarticulability. (Backman-Rogers 2019: 40)

The Virgin Suicides is not merely about the recent past (around twenty years ago from the point of narration), but actively foregrounds the reconstruction of the past by male subjects looking back at a moment in their lives that has lingered persistently in their memories. It therefore can be linked to hauntology in the sense that it foregrounds the mediated processes through which the past is activated and filtered. As Backman-Rogers (2019: 39–44) has stressed, this hauntology is inflected by gender concerns as it actively frames the story of a group of teenage girls through the eyes of males, reflecting a patriarchal regime through which female bodies and experiences are reduced and imprisoned.

Not only is the narrative of the Lisbon girls filtered through male memories, but these memories are at times filtered through specific media: the most important of these being the photos that the boys find from the Lisbon family's discarded belongings. Media not only trigger memories in the film's narrative, however; at times obviously false memories are presented, such as when the boys appear to remember times spent with the Lisbon girls on a boat following their reading of a passage in Cecilia's diary. These shots are captured by a Super 8mm film camera, a gauge that has historically been closely linked to home movies. By presenting us with such a conspicuously false series of images, Coppola emphasises the unreliability of the boys' memories and hence the entire framing narrative. These memories are, Coppola would seem to suggest, partial, subjectively inflected attempts to revivify and thus to control such past events. Consequently, media which help to feed imaginative memorisation – whether the diary itself or photographs of the girls – assume the role of fetishistic totems within the boys' lives.

Discussing *Lick the Star* and *The Virgin Suicides*, Todd Kennedy argues how these films 'serve as a prolonged exploration of the degree to which female characters are idealized, objectified, and defined by the image that the film – and their society – imposes upon them' (2010: 44). As a result, while many of the images in *The Virgin Suicides* are 'luminous' (Handyside 2017: 43), signs of decay are often apparent and therefore draw attention to the fragility of alluring surfaces. Hence, we are presented with a very typical scenario of bourgeois domestic tranquillity at the beginning of the film, but this is immediately undercut by the notice placed on the tree outside of the Lisbons' home – a notice of removal due to Dutch Elm Disease – and then of Cecilia's suicide attempt. The theme of idyllic domestic surfaces dissimulating a more unpleasant reality is a common trope in many films, going back to at least *A Shadow of a Doubt* (Hitchcock, 1943), through to *Blue Velvet* (Lynch, 1984) and a film released not long before *The Virgin Suicides* – *American Beauty* (Mendes, 1999). *The Virgin Suicides*, however, links this trope to memory and control in a manner which renders it more complex than many such films. The fragility of idyllic surfaces is hinted at further in the ways in which the images themselves often seem poised on the verge of decay. Towards the end of the film, the narrator mentions how an algae infestation (resulting from an industrial accident) stank out the suburbs and led to an insect infiltration. Likewise, the media images within the film – the Super 8mm false footage and the still photographic images of the boys posing in various global locations with the Lisbon sisters – evidence signs of decay yet are strangely alluring. Images of decaying beauty are also representative of the narrative processes of the film: these boys are trying to recapture the girls via memory recall, but such images are fading away; they nevertheless retain their allure for the boys, whose obsession with the sisters has persisted over a twenty-year period.

It is within these broader themes of decay (both memorial and more general) that Air's soundtrack can be positioned. The retro-nature of the band is certainly one factor which feeds into the overall film itself: the ways that Air draw on past musical sources – both in terms of being influenced by former musical sounds and utilising vintage synthesizers – meshes with the film's nested narrative, of presenting the past framed through the present. Further, Air's music is dreamy and often tinged with melancholy, an emotional resonance which would have also fitted into Coppola's vision. The score represents the more languid aspects of Air's music and the influence of other film soundtrack music is detectable, including the soft psychedelia of early Pink Floyd soundtracks such as *More* (Schroeder, 1969) and *La Vallée/Obscured by Clouds* (Schroeder, 1971), Serge Gainsbourg's soundtrack work with composers such as Michel Colombier and Jean-Claude Vannier, as well as the more soulful, symphonic tracks from blaxploitation soundtracks. The musical soundtrack establishes the tone of the film from the beginning: the opening – a montage of picturesque shots of the suburbs – is accompanied by a moderately paced bass line overlaid with an atmospheric, steady two-note synth line which eventually segues into a delicate piano melody underpinned by gentle drumming. As the piano melody and drums kick in, however, a siren sound can be heard, which continues after the music track – 'Playground Love' – suddenly cuts out. The montage of sun-kissed images is itself interrupted by a shot of a bathroom windowsill whose colour palette, dominated as it is by cold blues, boldly contrasts with the more natural colours and sunlight from the previous shots, while the soundtrack now only consists of the siren (from an approaching ambulance) and the dripping sounds of water. At this point voice-over narration is heard for the first time, with the narrator stating 'Cecilia was the first to go', followed by shots of Cecilia being taken out of the bathtub and into an ambulance after she has cut her wrists. The abrupt termination of the music track here clearly introduces us to the film's processes of undercutting idyllic, dreamy nostalgia with the starkness of actuality. Air's soundtrack, for the most part, evokes the former more than the latter – appropriately meshing with the framing narrative as drawn from memory – though its melancholic undercurrent also hints towards the cold realities nestling amongst such reminiscences.

Air's soundtrack does not vary a great deal throughout the film: it is largely consistent in its use of languid, vintage timbres. Many of the tracks used in the film are marked by moderately paced drum and bass rhythms overlaid by atmospheric synthesizer lines: the rhythms ground the music while the synthesiser melodies are much more ethereal, a dynamic appropriate to a film about past events which have become distant and increasingly exotic via time and memory. The synth sounds used are often quite delicate, which again fits the ways in which ghostliness runs through the film. Yet, unlike some forms of music that came to be referred to as hauntological around the mid-2000s (see Fisher 2014; Sexton 2012), Air's soundtrack does not include prominent signs of ageing (such as re-recording on analogue formats to produce a 'worn', degraded sound, or through using worn vinyl sounds such as crackle to signify temporal decay), or – like some later hauntological music (though not all) – produce dark, eerie music. There is one exception: 'Dark Memories', which begins playing after a sequence in which the boys sift through the girls' magazines, is a darker and more overtly 'ghostly' track which is shorn of rhythm, built from backward loops and heavily reverbed vibraphone. It is introduced to accompany the narration at a point when the narrator stresses that the girls were slipping away from their memories. Only briefly heard for around twenty seconds, this piece hints at the amorphous fading of memory. More particularly, as the darkest piece on the soundtrack, it denotes the terror of the narrator losing his memories of the girls. Contrastingly, the warmer – albeit melancholic – sounds that predominate are used to denote how such memories offer the boys comfort and solace.

Much of the soundtrack music is used quite sparingly. The film only utilised around twenty per cent of the tracks produced by Air, and their music rarely plays on the soundtrack for more than a minute at a time (except for the end credits). While the use of snippets from recorded soundtrack production is not unusual, such usage does work to reinforce how the *fragment* is an important motif of the film. The boys, for example, can only access fragments of their past via memory, while they only possess isolated scraps from the Lisbons' belongings, so that the partiality and incompleteness of their narrative is signalled. The soundtrack in one sense mirrors these mental processes: falling in and out of the sound mix for brief moments, sometimes segueing into other,

Figure 4.1 *The Virgin Suicides*: fragments from the Lisbon sisters' personal items

often diegetic, sounds or emerging seamlessly out of a different sound mix, the soundtrack works as an ambient underscore for the most part but very occasionally takes a dominant, albeit transient, position in the overall sound mix.

Beyond its textual functions, Air's score also was significant on an extratextual level. This was Coppola's debut feature, so the soundtrack by a prominent 'indie' act would have helped in promoting the film. As argued by Anahid Kassabian (2001: 49), films 'are only partly discrete entities; they exist within a web of textuality that includes experiences of sound, music and visuals that begins long before a specific film experience and continues long thereafter'. The soundtrack to an album, particularly if produced by artists who already have a following, is a crucial segment of a film that also exists as a separate artefact. On a commercial level, Air's musical contribution acted to cross-promote the film; as a separately released commercial artefact, the score exists both as a standalone musical collection by Air as well as a companion to the film. In the former sense, the released soundtrack would have been purchased by some fans of Air – it was the follow-up to *Moon Safari* and was eagerly anticipated by many – who consequently might have become aware of and possibly seen the film. Of course, the cross-marketing potential of this works the other way as well: that is, people who went to see the film could be exposed to the music of Air and might have sought out the soundtrack (as well as other music by the band). Further, beyond the promotional and economic benefits of such cross-promotion, there is also a sense in which the film and soundtrack lend each other credibility, perhaps strengthening an indie/alternative identity of both film and music. As mentioned in Chapter 2, indie films can use indie music to strengthen their own indie 'identity' through such processes and, to quote from Joseph Tompkins, 'aim to solicit a coveted audience through deliberate audiovisual strategies, thereby demonstrating textual compatibility with perceived tastes, attitudes, and consumption habits' (2009: 72–3). Tomkins is discussing the close connections between horror films and metal music here, but indie films and indie music can also mutually reinforce an indie 'identity', which can be of particular use in enhancing the indie credentials of both the film on the one hand, and the soundtrack on the other. Both were indie productions that nevertheless contained involvement from larger companies: Paramount, for example, distributed the film, while Virgin distributed the soundtrack (even though it was released on Source Records, a French independent label).

Air's soundtrack to *The Virgin Suicides* should also be considered as an important paratext, part of the film's 'many proliferations' (Gray 2010: 2). Discussing paratexts, Jonathan Gray argues that they are not 'simply add-ons, spinoffs, and also-rans: they create texts, they manage them, and they fill them with many of the meanings that we associate with them' (Gray 2010: 6). So, beyond the marketing functions of the text, we can also think of the soundtrack as enabling certain experiential possibilities in relation to the film. For those who had not seen the film, it may have provided a set of assumptions and expectations about the film itself. Those who sought out the soundtrack *after* they had seen the film might have engaged with it as an extension of the film experience; certainly, for people who engaged positively with the film, it could allow them to sonically re-experience pleasurable cinematic moments. The soundtrack allowed one to explore *The Virgin Suicides* as a sonic, rather than audio-visual, text. It also allowed people to hear fuller versions of the songs recorded for the soundtrack as well as a few selections that were not featured within the film.

Of course, the score by Air only constitutes part of the musical soundtrack. Songs from the era in which the film was set – mostly diegetic – were also released on a separate soundtrack around a month later.

Lost in Translation

Coppola's next feature, *Lost in Translation*, connected to indie music once again, though for this film various artists were assembled to contribute to the soundtrack rather than a single act. Amongst its contributing artists, however, one stood out: Kevin Shields. As the leader of My Bloody Valentine (MBV), Shields had an almost legendary, cult status at the turn of the millennium. MBV were one of the most acclaimed indie bands to have emerged in the UK in the late 1980s; though starting as a somewhat generic jangle-pop band, they shifted gear dramatically in 1988 with the release of their EP *You Made Me Realise* and, later in the same year, their album *Isn't Anything*, both released on Creation Records. These records marked a move into a harder, noisier sound, and the employment of experimental guitar effects by Shields to create strange pitch-shifts and warped textures.

Brian Reitzell – the music supervisor for the film – was key in persuading Shields to contribute new material to the soundtrack, as the two knew each other. Reitzell's past as a musician in indie bands, combined with Coppola's own indie music links, were crucial in recruiting Shields to contribute new tracks for the movie. Such connections are important to note and can often be key in enabling filmmakers to license music. Some music artists take a selective approach to granting permissions for their music to be licensed, in the process avoiding accusations of selling out through allowing their music to be synchronised indiscriminately. The ability to gain permissions from more reluctant artists can, however, sometimes be overcome through personal, often informal, connections and discussions. In this sense, Coppola's social capital would have proven advantageous; her upbringing, combined with her work across different media, have enabled her to meet and befriend many people, including those working within music. Such social connections aid a filmmaker in selecting music which meshes with their broader audio-visual concepts and can help promote the film to key demographics.

In addition to contributing four new music tracks to *Lost in Translation*, Shields also agreed to license a My Bloody Valentine song – 'Sometimes' – to it. The new recordings by Shields enabled the film to gain a lot of attention within the music press; he had not actually released any new material under MBV or his own name since *Loveless*, released in 1991. In a review of the album in *Pitchfork*, five of the seven paragraphs were spent discussing Kevin Shields and his contributions, noting his long absence from releasing any new music, stating that 'though there are eleven other songs here, the Shields material is the drawing card' (Richardson 2003). The remainder of the soundtrack includes contributions from artists such as The Jesus and Mary Chain, Air, Phoenix, Death in Vegas, Squarepusher and Sébastien Tellier. Even though Shields is the dominant presence on the soundtrack, many critics noted how it was quite consistent musically and largely exemplified the sounds of 'dream pop'. Sofia Coppola herself has explained that the soundtrack evolved from 'Tokyo dream-pop mixes' that Reitzell had been making for her based around songs that she liked (Stern 2017). As noted in the previous chapter, dream pop and shoegaze are both often considered introverted, atmospheric and ethereal musical forms, and often overlap, so I will use shoegaze and dream pop synonymously in the following section.

The soundtrack to *Lost in Translation* largely merges the 'shoegaze' sound with ambient textures and snippets. Shields's contributions include songs which exemplify shoegaze music – such as the previously released 'Sometimes' and Shields's 'City Girl' – but other tracks by him are slightly different. They include shorter tracks, such as 'Are You Awake?', a gentle, beat-driven snippet indebted to ambient house; 'Ikebana', an impressionistic, delicate mix of guitar and synthesizer; and 'Goodbye', a subtly shifting set of interlocking drones. The latter tracks mesh with some of the other music on the soundtrack – such as contributions by Air and Tellier – which use gentle, reflective guitar patterns underpinned with atmospheric, slightly lo-fi synthesizer sounds.

Much of the soundtrack functions as a marker of mood and atmosphere, and more specifically – as with *The Virgin Suicides* – contributes to an abstract representation of subjectivity. Journalistic reception of such music often mentioned that it connoted escape, introversion and dreaminess, which link to the film's themes. Crucially, such qualities were sometimes considered the result of alienation from an increasingly privatised society, in which the music provided a kind of bliss-like escape into the 'here and now' (Reynolds 2007: 121). It is notable that many of these tracks are used non-diegetically, in contrast to diegetic music within the film (which includes Chopin on the radio in Bob's hotel room, Peaches' 'Fuck the Pain Away' being played in a strip club, the lounge jazz performed in the hotel bar, as well as the songs that Bob (Bill Murray), Charlotte (Scarlett Johansson) and her Japanese friends perform during their karaoke session). While playing within the fictional world of the represented story, such music often seems disconnected from the main characters: Chopin playing in Bob's room is a good example, as it is matched with still images of Bob sitting on his bed expressionless, and shots of his room presented in a distanced manner that emphasises lack of affect. In contrast to much of the diegetic music – though the karaoke songs are an exception in this regard, as they do mark a moment of human togetherness – non-diegetic music seems less disconnected, more synchronised with Bob and Charlotte's internal states, further underlining how the two characters feel alienated from the objective reality within which they find themselves.

Non-diegetic music is frequently used to accompany either Bob or Charlotte when they are alone, often travelling, and tends to connote the fuzzy, subjective states of minds and bodies drifting through spaces that are unfamiliar to them. These tracks indicate different emotions at different points, including reverie, isolation and escape. When Bob arrives in Tokyo at the beginning of the film – following a brief shot of Charlotte on her bed – he is shown firstly asleep, then waking up in a taxi as it travels through the cityscape on the way to his hotel. These shots of Bob arriving are accompanied by Death in Vegas's 'Girls', a moderately paced, spiralling groove built upon a simple guitar motif and non-lexical, female vocal exhalations, which build in density. The track – particularly its vocalisations and its guitar-led, 'wall-of-sound' qualities – feels influenced by shoegaze rock and sets the musical tone of the film. The non-semantic *aaahs* of the vocalist feel fitting for the scene and the film as a whole: they hint at certain emotions but do not pinpoint them with any certainty. The

Figure 4.2 *Lost in Translation*: Bob awakes jet-lagged in Tokyo

track itself feels slightly dreamy yet also rapturous, which is fitting in that we first see Bob asleep at the back of a taxi, but then he wakes up and starts to look out of the window at Tokyo with a sense of wide-eyed wonder.

The dream-like nature of the soundtrack, in conjunction with the first shot of Bob asleep, draws attention to the importance of 'dreaminess' in the film. We can consider, for example, the lives of Bob and Charlotte as symbolically dream-like in that their 'normal' lives are being held in suspension and they have been plunged into a culture alien to them. In addition to being displaced, the two characters' social isolation also fuels a sense of introversion, another quality associated with dream pop and shoegaze music. Charlotte's introspection is arguably more heightened as she is dealing explicitly with existential questions, though Bob is also quietly introspective, albeit in a slightly world-wearier manner (as though perpetually tolerating unhappiness phlegmatically).

Non-diegetic music is used, for the most part, to accompany the major characters when they are alone and freed from their duties. As Bob is staying in Tokyo for a shorter duration than Charlotte, and as he also spends more time having to fulfil contractual duties, he is associated with such music to a lesser extent. Charlotte, on the other hand, has too much time on her hands; beyond negotiating her unhappy marriage she is left to her own devices whilst her husband is at work. Music accompanies her in her daytime pursuits, whether travelling to a temple or fixing lighting decorations in her hotel room. She is alienated in two senses: from her own marriage and husband, on the one hand, and from the environment that she negotiates daily. As she is living in a hotel room, she is stranded in a kind of non-space which hinders her ability to feel at home with herself, a condition exacerbated by underlying existential uncertainties. Charlotte's dissatisfaction and unease leads to her seeking spiritual meaning at religious sites as well as engaging with self-help books. Her first visit to a temple (Jugan-ji) is accompanied by Brian Reitzell and Roger J. Manning Jr's 'On the Subway': the calming, ambient textures of the track indicate an inner peace that Charlotte searches for, but the persistent, accented beats underpinning the more serene ambient synth lines seem to indicate a restlessness, an underlying anxiety making its presence felt. Her later phone call with her friend Lauren explicitly reveals how she did not 'feel' anything, an admission entirely ignored by her friend and thus further fuelling her alienation.

Amidst her disconnection from other people, Charlotte's relationship with Bob provides emotional solace. Bob is also out of place and alone, but whereas Charlotte is experiencing existential restlessness, Bob seems more numbed: his life in Tokyo vacillates between repetitive commercial work and solitary moments in the hotel, mostly in the bar. It is alone in the bar that he is spotted by Charlotte, who orders him a drink, a gesture which commences a burgeoning friendship between the two. A key scene in the progression of their relationship is when they spend a night out with some of Charlotte's

Japanese friends, where they play around and have fun, including singing karaoke. This scene shows the two characters breaking out of their isolation and coming together; it represents generational differences between the characters, but also bridges cultural differences through song. Eventually, the karaoke session cements connections between Bob and Charlotte, indicated initially by a tender shot in which the bewigged Charlotte rests her head on Bob's shoulder as they take a break from the party. This connection is further emphasised by their journey home in the taxi, which marks the first moment that non-diegetic music accompanies them together. Lying next to a sleeping Bob, a weary Charlotte gazes at the moving landscape through a car window, accompanied by My Bloody Valentine's 'Sometimes'. 'Sometimes' is the only My Bloody Valentine song on the soundtrack, and its use seems to further emphasise the importance of this scene. Kevin Shields and MBV, as noted, act as the fulcrum of the soundtrack with this song (the only previously released music written by Shields included), which is itself important: it stems from an extremely well-respected album (*Loveless*) that is regularly voted as one of the best albums ever made within many alternative/indie music publications. Not only are MBV generally considered pioneers of shoegaze and an example of the sound at its finest, *Loveless* is often considered the pinnacle of the sound. Gentle yet dense, the song features typically blurry musical elements such as shimmering guitars and vocals verging on the threshold of comprehension. Yet the vocals are slightly more comprehensible, at least at selected moments, than some other MBV tracks. Comprehensible lyrics such as 'close my eyes, feel me now' indicate a longing to be lost within physical sensation and mental union, therefore not only emphasising their connection but also hinting at a possible romantic undercurrent to their relationship (a possibility that provides an element of tension to the narrative).

After the friendship between the two characters has blossomed, we can detect small differences in their demeanour, though these are quite subtle; neither character is emotionally demonstrative, so other factors are important in denoting such shifts, one of which is music. An example of this is a comparison of two scenes in which Charlotte visits spiritual sites. As noted, in the first example the track 'On the Subway' functions to foreground an underlying sense of turmoil amidst the serene milieu; later in the film Charlotte travels to Kyoto and the music accompanying her journey this time is Air's 'Lost in Kyoto'. Charlotte visits different locations, including the Heian Shrine, the Nanzenji Temple, and Ryōan-ji, and as such this montage sequence is lengthier than her visit to Jugan-ji. The duration of the sequence, in conjunction with framing, pacing and music, also relates to a slight shift in Charlotte's connection with her surroundings. She seems more serene in this montage: while still distanced from spiritual activities and therefore positioned as a touristic outsider, she nonetheless appears less troubled – indicated by a slight smile – while the gradual motion of her body through space is vaguely matched at one stage with the motion of a newly married couple, hinting that her body is now more in synch with her surroundings than previously. This sense is heightened by the calm music, an ambient synth background overlaid by a gentle guitar and piano melody.

The film concludes with Bob escaping from his airport-destined cab to catch up with Charlotte in a busy street. This tender moment includes Bob whispering into Charlotte's ear, though the audience cannot hear what he says to her. The scene is accompanied by The Jesus and Mary Chain's 'Just Like Honey', which doesn't comfortably belong to the categories 'shoegaze' or 'dream pop' but can certainly be considered an influence on such forms of music. The main point of connection between J&MC and shoegaze is an emphasis on textures that employ distortion, and a more abstract, noisy approach to the pop song. J&MC's *Psychocandy* (1986), which effectively established their reputation, was lauded frequently for its combination of saccharine pop and feedback-enhanced walls of noise; 'Just Like Honey' even lifts the drum intro from The Ronettes' 'Be My Baby'. Though it is one of the less aggressively noise-infused pieces on *Psychocandy*, its sweet, romantic elements are nonetheless offset by slightly spiky, reverberated guitar riffs which build towards a dense, layered conclusion.

In one sense, the inaudibility of Bob's words at the conclusion complements dream pop's tendency towards abstraction, particularly through downplaying the importance of semantic clarity and foregrounding a more amorphous emotional tone, which links to pre-cognitive emotions. However, the song selected to accompany this moment (which closed the film with the track continuing over the end credits) is one of the few non-diegetic tracks on the soundtrack which features fully comprehensible vocals. While the vocal blurriness (or absence of vocals) on the soundtrack meshes with how the scene emphasises emotional flux as more important than semantic detail, the fact that the vocal enunciations on 'Just Like Honey' are clearer than other non-diegetic tracks points to the importance of vocals in this instance, which provide a kind of commentary on the fictional world and a sense of formal closure. The opening phrase 'Listen to the girl, as she takes on half the world', as well as the later line 'Walking back to you, is the hardest thing that I could do', relevantly comment on the characters: the latter echoing Bob's actual actions, the former an indication of Charlotte's newfound resolve following her brief encounter with Bob.

At the time of writing, *Lost in Translation* is Coppola's most commercially successful film. It is also her most critically acclaimed film, and arguably the most beloved amongst audiences. The soundtrack, I would argue, has played an important part in the film's initially positive reception, as well as the continued affection it continues to elicit from audiences. This is not to argue that the soundtrack is the sole factor leading to many people's love for the film, rather to suggest that it is a particularly important contributing element. The film can be considered a cult film in the way it has become embraced by certain niche groups and has remained important for many over time (as well as gaining new devotees), but also through its marked polarisation of opinion. It has the most submitted user reviews out of all Coppola's films on IMDb and enjoys the highest average rating; yet if one looks at the posted reviews, it starkly divides opinion, with a huge percentage of reviews rating the film either 10 or 1. Its embracers often wax lyrically about the film and commonly discuss how it affected them emotionally; its haters often express puzzlement as to why it is so adored and instead highlight its 'boring' qualities. The soundtrack itself, meanwhile, also has an esteemed reputation that has grown over time. On its release it was reviewed favourably in many publications, but it should be noted that it was publicised mostly in alternative/indie-related music publications, both online and offline, including *Pitchfork*, *Consequences of Sound*, *Drowned in Sound*, *Stylus*, *Spin* and *New Musical Express*. In the US it charted in both the independent album charts and the soundtrack album charts, peaking at 13 in both. And its reputation has arguably grown since; in 2019 it was voted as the seventh best soundtrack ever by *Pitchfork*, while in the same year it was re-released on coloured vinyl for Record Store Day. Demand for this limited reissue has been so great that it now sells for around £100 on online record marketplace Discogs, which is indicative of how it has become embraced by a broadly indie/alternative constituency. As I have previously noted (Sexton 2015: 4), the resurgence of vinyl as a medium was particularly marked within independent communities, many of whom were resistant to the mainstream industry's desire to render the format obsolete. The increase in vinyl sales in the mid-2000s, meanwhile, was driven by the independent sector and indie music enthusiasts; Record Store Day itself emerged from the independent sector of the music industry (even though there are now many complaints that it has been corrupted by the increased involvement of the major record companies). Such connections between indie and vinyl have also been made by Ian Garwood, who has argued that 'As adherence to vinyl became a niche option, defined against the mainstream movement to CDs, it followed that this would become available as the sign of an indie sensibility that differentiated itself from mainstream values' (Garwood 2016: 247).

Marie Antoinette

Coppola's next film, *Marie Antoinette*, deploys music in an even more pronounced manner than *Lost in Translation*. This was evident both in how music was used as a core factor to promote the film, and through the sheer amount of music used on the soundtrack. While featuring some modern interpretations of classical compositions, the soundtrack largely consists of a range of post-punk and indie music, which is the most obvious way that it foregrounds its own anachronistic approach to the historical costume drama. The music partly served commercial purposes: as noted by Handyside (2017: 151), the film is targeted primarily at a young, 'hip' audience, and while she notes the importance that fashion plays in this strategy, music is also another crucial factor in this regard. Handyside has further illustrated how *Marie Antoinette* contrasts with 'typical' costume dramas through reference to Coppola's own comments on how she aimed to produce something very different from Masterpiece Theatre costume dramas, or historical dramas typical of the BBC (Ibid.). The film is drawing parallels between the past and present through emphasising key themes: female experience within a patriarchal regime, conspicuous consumption (particularly in relation to fashion and food) and celebrity culture, and by doing so it is also attempting to draw in audiences who might be interested in such themes and be attracted to an unconventional approach to the costume drama. For Handyside (2017: 155), the film's emphasis on fashion – and fashion that combines period detail with modern touches – is the central means by which the modern and the historical are drawn together, and 'a vital tool used by Coppola to overlap her life with the modern Marie Antoinette that she creates in her film'. Music, too, functions to draw connections between the past and present.

The greater presence of licensed music in *Marie Antoinette* can be attributed partly to budget, as this was a much more expensive production than her former features, costing approximately $40 million (her previous films came in at around $6 million and $4 million). Music was then used prominently in marketing the film: the theatrical trailer, for example, features songs used in the film by Aphex Twin ('Ynweythek Ylow'), Gang of Four ('Natural's Not in It'), and New Order ('Ceremony'). The teaser trailer does not feature any dialogue at all; instead, a montage of images from the film is presented with New Order's 'The Age of Consent' playing on the soundtrack. While the title of the track obviously relates to how young Marie was when she became queen, the actual track – unlike the three tracks used in the theatrical trailer – is not even used in the film. The theatrical trailer initially features 'Ynweythek Ylow' as an underscore: its unobtrusive placement on the soundtrack, alongside its sparse, classical sound (made with computer-controlled acoustics), does not initially stand out as unusual; however, the arrival of 'Natural's Not in It' does create an immediate discrepancy between image and sound in terms of prior expectations and this is continued with the use of 'Ceremony'. In addition to the music functioning to appeal to younger viewers, the tracks also announce how this is not an average historical drama. Rather, it is presented as a kind of alternative costume film, indicated by the anachronistic use of music and the music's broader status. The music spans different modes of alternative/independent forms both generically and historically, including post-punk, new wave, electronic music and more modern indie-rock, spanning music from the late 1970s to the early 2000s, which might have also been partly designed to capture different age ranges and tastes beyond the core target market.

Aesthetically, one of the most interesting aspects of the music used in the film is through the intertextual linkages it establishes, which adds further commentary on characters and narrative, as well as Coppola's own relation to the material. The film commences with Gang of Four's 'Natural's Not in It', which plays over the opening title sequence. The use of Gang of Four is important as they were a post-punk band with a Marxist attitude, who often wrote critical songs about alienation and consumerism. 'Natural's Not in It' adds a critical undercurrent to a film which, on the surface, could be read as a straightforward celebration of excessive hedonism. The lyrics to the song, however, pose the idea of consumerism as a problem. Opening with the line 'The problem of pleasure, what to do with leisure', the lyrics declaim the ways in which consumerism is a distraction from understanding how our desires are exploited by capitalist social systems. The credits are simple yet striking: against a black background the font is designed in a style reminiscent of Jamie Reid's cut-out lettering used for the Sex Pistols' 'Never Mind the Bollocks' record. Both music and credit design, then, evoke rebellion and anti-consumerism (Reid himself was an anarchist), but this is counterpoised with a brief, extra-diegetic shot of Marie supine on a chaise longue, surrounded by cake (one of which she takes a lick from) while having a shoe fitted by a maid.

Figure 4.3 *Marie Antoinette*: Marie looks at the camera, accompanied on the soundtrack by Gang of Four

The contrast between the sound/credits and this insert is deliberately created to produce a clash, an apparent contradiction between the opposing currents (and the Reid-style credits typeface also evokes anti-monarchist sentiments, as he also designed the cover for the Sex Pistols' 'God Save the Queen' single.). This clash, along with broader juxtapositions between musical intertexts and images that initially seem incongruous, invite various possible readings. It could, for example, be considered a means to indicate broader context: that is, while we are focused on the life of Marie and royal life, music and credits here evoke the masses whom are largely absent from the diegesis and who, of course, ultimately rebel (we only actually see a glimpse of the rebellion towards the end of the film as an angry mob surrounds Versailles).[2] A second implication is that the credits sequence is an inversion of rebellious tropes: Coppola was probably aware that her decision to focus on the life of Marie Antoinette was going to prove controversial in some quarters, particularly her decision to marginalise the outside world and to only briefly refer to anti-monarchical sentiment (and, if so, she would have been correct). The brief shot of Marie in her epicurean splendour during the credits sequence can be considered a provocation as well as a risk, a subtly subversive manoeuvre which moves away from rebellious clichés. The issue here, as indicated by some reviews of the film, was that this was an insensitive gambit that sided with the oppressors over the oppressed. However, Coppola attempts to move beyond this rather simplistic binary by focusing on Marie's own oppression within a patriarchal regime (and a broader implication is that the hatred towards Marie is a form of scapegoating fuelled by sexism). This brings me to a third implication, which is that the film addresses some of the contradictions that arise from being enmeshed within social systems, even if one is opposed to such systems. It is not merely that the Gang of Four track addresses such contradictions, it can also be related to the fact that they were a Marxist band releasing records via a major company (EMI). Such issues also pertained to the Sex Pistols and to punk more generally, in the ways that its rebellious elements coexisted with commercial considerations: two figures associated with the commercial exploitation of punk are Vivienne Westwood and Malcolm McLaren, both of whom are alluded to within the film.

Punk has long been characterised by tensions between its status as a rebellious, authentic mode of expression and commercial concerns. While it offered a chance for those who often felt excluded from music creation to participate via the flowering and promotion of DIY, and for many to express the rage they felt about society and their position within it, it was also a new style in vogue that presented opportunities for commercial exploitation. As is well-known, the shop SEX, run by Malcolm McLaren and Vivienne Westwood, was centrally linked to punk fashion and music within Britain in the mid-1970s. Tensions and overlaps between commercialism and rebellion can also be detected in the choice of music. While the film alludes to punk through graphics and the inclusion of the post-punk sounds of Gang of Four and Siouxsie and the Banshees on the soundtrack, it also includes other forms of music that grew out of punk and post-punk, including New Romantic music, which was more embracing of the heightened commercial climate of the early 1980s, and is exemplified by music by Adam and the Ants and Bow Wow Wow. Importantly, both acts were managed by McLaren (the latter including members of the former), while Westwood would also be heavily associated with New Romantic fashion. Westwood can also be considered an important influence on the look of the film, for she was inspired by historical fashions but often mixed disparate elements together. Similarly, while *Marie Antoinette* demonstrates attention to historical detail in its costumes, it also takes some liberties; as Handyside (2007: 152) has written, costume designer Milena Canonero 'retains the spirit of historical authenticity while at the same time introducing contemporary touches that offer new perspectives on life at Versailles'.

Allusions to McLaren link to the film's concern with patriarchal control. McLaren was controversial and often considered a Svengali figure due to his skills at manipulation and exploitation. His management of Bow Wow Wow was particularly notorious. Beyond the fact that he'd lured most of Adam and the Ants to form a new, McLaren-designed band, he also recruited a then-unknown thirteen-year-old female, Annabella Lwin, to front the group. He manipulated Lwin into posing nude for the cover of two of their records, which led to a police investigation, and later fired her from the band when she was seventeen. The prominence of Bow Wow Wow on the soundtrack – 'I Want Candy' is used to accompany Marie's consumption spree, while two more songs by the group also feature ('Aphrodisiac' and 'Fools Rush In') – in addition to Adam and the Ants (whose 'Kings of the Wild Frontier' features), foregrounds the figure of McLaren as an historical touchstone. The fact that Marie Antoinette was herself only fourteen when she became Dauphine of France and did not have any choice in the matter is surely no coincidence, and stresses the theme of female manipulation, as well as a more general notion of being thrust into the limelight at such a young age.

Music in *Marie Antoinette* is arguably the most central strategy through which the film conjures intertextual links to create further meanings. Such meanings do not always reinforce what we see but often undercut them. To take an example: the montage sequence of Marie indulging in excessive consumption to the sounds of 'I Want Candy' could be perceived as a pure revelling in that very excess. Yet the spectres of McLaren and Lwin evoked by the track undercut such a straightforward interpretation. Awareness of this reference can encourage an understanding of such behaviour as a response to being enmeshed within a rigid, patriarchal system rather than a straightforward expression of decadent urges. We can consider the intertextual cultural references evoked by some of the music in the film as creating a kind of latent discourse which sits beneath the film's manifest discourse. The numerous critical denunciations of the film that lambasted it for being an empty celebration of consumerism, a defence of oppression and privilege, tended to overlook this element of the film. Many of these intertexts create quite complex meanings, as though elements of the film are in dialogue with each other at times. The use of these texts as cultural referents recalls the concept, introduced by Mikhail Iampolski, of the 'hyperquote', which he argues:

> does not just open a text onto other texts, thereby simply broadening its horizon of meaning. It places a number of texts and significations on top of the other. The hyperquote essentially becomes a kind of semantic funnel, drawing in all competing meanings and texts, even if the latter contradict each other and are not readily reconciled into one unitary and dominant meaning. (Iampolski 1998: 5)

Likewise, Coppola's use of music produces a welter of intertextual meanings which expand the semantic layers informing the film, layers which often produce contradictions as opposed to any smooth, clear meanings.

These musical intertexts, referencing as they do themes of manipulation, consumerism, sexism and contradiction, also relate to Coppola's own life (as previously noted by Handyside). While the issue of female power within a patriarchal system is the most obvious sense in which the film draws parallels between her and Marie's experiences, there are others as well. Another crucial parallel seems to be an issue that has plagued independent and indie music and film for most of its duration: commercial compromise. As mentioned in Chapters 1 and 2, such tensions have long existed, though they have become increasingly marked over the past couple of decades within alternative/indie music *and* film. The fact that much of the 'rebellious' musical intertexts were issued by corporations links to issues of having to make commercial concessions within capitalist social systems. While Coppola's films tend to be considered indie films, and positioned as alternative to mainstream Hollywood, she still must keep commercial, in addition to aesthetic, considerations in mind. *Marie Antoinette*, as mentioned, was the largest budget she had worked with and was 'presented by', and distributed in many territories, by Columbia Pictures, a division of Sony.

The positioning of punk and post-punk intertexts alongside more contemporary indie sounds also forges historical connections between such music: that is, contemporary indie is positioned as a successor to these musical movements. It is now common, following the increased respect for and consequent historicisation (as well as canonisation) of various forms of popular music – including alternative and indie – for connections to be made across history in terms of stylistic developments and influences. Since the growth of the internet, access to historical forms of music has also expanded, which has resulted in a growth in retro-styles of music and a huge expansion of older bands reforming (see Reynolds 2012). *Marie Antoinette* was released when there was quite a notable spike in post-punk retro styles, including bands such as LCD Soundsystem and The Rapture. Therefore, beyond the more complex discursive allusions made through the music, there is also a sense in which it presents a historical lineage of sorts which can potentially appeal to both younger fans of alternative and indie music and older audiences who might not be aware of the newer music but who have strong preferences for punk and post-punk music.

Finally, though this section has focused primarily on the intertextual allusions connoted through music and its interaction with moving images, it should be noted that it also functions more conventionally as a marker of mood and atmosphere at times. So, for example, when Marie first meets Louis, The Radio Dept.'s 'I Don't Like it Like This' plays; its dreamy atmosphere, mostly dominated by melancholy guitar lines over a subtle, metronomic beat, imbues the scene with a contemporary quality and a romantic atmosphere, but the title of course points elsewhere, indicating the forced nature of their coupling and her subjective displeasure. Such displeasure is contrasted with a later scene in which she flirts with Count Fersen at the masked ball and her feelings are heightened by the accompanying sounds of Bow Wow Wow's 'Aphrodisiac', followed by the same band's cover of 'Fools Rush In' accompanying her carriage ride home, reflecting her excitement and desire.

Conclusion

In contrast to Araki's use of music, Coppola's selection of music – both pre-existing music and scores – varies more from film to film, and she has more recently moved away from using indie music to the extent she did at the beginning of her career. For *Lick the Star* she selected many female-fronted indie-rock tracks to match the aggressivity of Chloe; with *The Virgin Suicides* she supplemented the diegetic use of 70s pop music with a retro-flavoured score from Air; for *Lost in Translation* she largely drew on shoegaze and dream pop; in *Marie Antoinette* she licensed a broad range of post-punk tracks spanning several decades. Up until *Marie Antoinette*, music on the soundtracks – beyond its appeal to potential audiences – is mostly responsible for contributing to atmosphere, while also connecting to characters and to broader themes on occasion. *Marie Antoinette*, however, changes tack: in this film, rather than underpinning the emotional tenor of the film complementarily, music often clashes with images and, on an intertextual level, links to meanings that sometimes provide meta-commentary on the diegesis.

Like Araki, Coppola's music choices also link to broader niche cultures and were sometimes used as a means of marketing her films to indie-oriented music lovers. The indie music in Coppola's films was, however, used more consciously in marketing and promoting her films, and this was a process that tended to become more marked by the time *Marie Antoinette* was released. There are two possible reasons for this: firstly, her films had higher budgets – budgets that increased – with studio involvement; secondly, the films were released when the commercial and marketing appeal of indie music was beginning to be noted frequently by industry insiders. Both factors combined to push the music within the promotion of the film and to cross-licence soundtrack albums related to the films.

Since *Marie Antoinette*, Coppola has not engaged with indie music to a great extent. In her fourth feature, *Somewhere* (2010), indie/alternative music features a little, but not to the same extent as her previous films; this is again fitting for a film that often lingers on emptiness and boredom. If *The Bling Ring* returned to a busier soundtrack once again, it was mostly centred around hip-hop, while her next feature, *The Beguiled* (2017), had a more conventional score, albeit by indie band Phoenix. Her most recent film at the time of writing, *On the Rocks* (2020), does feature the occasional indie song – such as inclusions by Porches and Phoenix (who again created the score) – but largely consists of jazz and classical selections.

Notes

1. The tracks included in the film by these bands consist of 'Tipp City' by The Amps and 'Eat Cake' and 'Bowery Boy' by Free Kitten.
2. Otherwise, apart from occasional dialogue that refers to broader unrest, the only scene in which the rebels' feelings are presented is when a portrait of the Queen is overlaid with anti-monarchical inscriptions such as 'Beware of Deficit' and 'Queen of Debt'.

5 DOCUMENTING SCENES AND PERFORMERS 1: PUNK, *SMITHEREENS* AND *SUBURBIA*

In this chapter and the next, I examine how indie musicians and music scenes have been represented within a selection of films. Indie or alternative pop/rock musical artists not only contribute to film soundtracks; many have also appeared within a range of films. In this sense, they follow in a long tradition of music artists appearing in, and contributing music to, films. The 1950s and 1960s witnessed a particularly notable number of films seeking to exploit the appeal of rock'n'roll music. Elvis Presley was one of the most prominent stars to appear in films, though there were of course many others, including The Beatles and The Rolling Stones. Presley, The Beatles and the Stones were huge international stars when they appeared in films, whereas many indie artists are not: in this and the next chapter I largely discuss artists who do not have a major profile.

The appearance of indie/alternative musicians within films can operate in similar ways to more well-known examples, even though the broader status of such musicians and the connotations of specific artists necessitates that one does not treat them synonymously. While prefigured by many examples including those mentioned above, a trend of music stars appearing in films became particularly notable in the 1980s following the increase in 'high concept' film production (Wyatt 1994). 'High concept' reflected the growing conglomeration of film studios through placing heightened emphasis on a film's marketing opportunities; it is, as Wyatt (1994: 13) has written, 'a striking, easily reducible narrative which also offers a high degree of marketability'. Wyatt considered music to be a crucial aspect of high concept as many such films included musical montages and offered cross-licensing opportunities, so that records could promote films in which they featured, while films could draw attention to any associated soundtrack releases and further promote musical artists. While the music artist in many such instances did not actually appear in the film, some both appeared in films and contributed to soundtrack releases. Madonna would be a good example of a major international artist who acted in several films and also contributed soundtrack material to some of these films, such as *Who's That Girl* (Foley, 1987) and *Dick Tracy* (Beatty, 1990).

Many artists covered in this chapter are not stars in the same manner, but can be considered subcultural, 'cult' stars (see Egan and Thomas 2012) and appeal to more niche demographics. Several musicians appear in films which represent local musical scenes, which have been discussed frequently in coverage of indie music. Holly Kruse (2013: 113), for example, has argued that 'Indie pop/rock music, more than most forms of pop music in the United States, was identified by locality (Athens, Seattle, Austin, Minneapolis, Champaign, Olympia, etc.), both by participants and by those outside of particular scenes'. A few examples of scene-based coverage include Barry Shank's 1994 ethnographic study of Austin, Texas; Thomas Howells' 2013 edited collection, *Late Century Dream: Movements in the US Indie Underground* (which covers several regional scenes); Jeffrey London's 2017 analysis of the independent music scene in Portland; and Dewar MacLeod's 2020 book on music in New Jersey.

Music scenes are characterised by clusters of activities which form around musical production and emerge within specific localities. For Woo, Rennie and Poyntz (2015: 288), scenes are:

> a basic part of the social imaginary of urban life. They are typically understood as loosely bounded social worlds oriented to forms of cultural expression. They provide systems of identification and connection, while simultaneously inviting acts of novelty, invention and innovation. Scenes are set within the fabric of everyday life but also function as an imagined alternative to the ordinary, work-a-day world.

This quotation points to several crucial features of musical scenes, as well as the appeal that they can hold for participants: not only do they enable the production and reception of creative works, but in doing so they also provide spaces through which people may form identities and communities, as well as escape less pleasant aspects of their everyday lives. There are many different agents involved within music scenes, including – though not limited to – music artists, producers, engineers, fans, live events staff, promoters, writers, record label staff. Certain music venues and record labels, as well as fanzines (or, more recently, webzines), can become heavily connected with local music scenes: think New York's CBGB venue and its links to the New York punk scene in the late 1970s; or the record label Sub Pop – which of course emerged from the

Sub Pop fanzine – and its associations with the Seattle grunge phenomenon of the late 1980s and early 1990s. When local scenes become documented regularly outside of their locality, especially if they become widely known outside of the US, they foreground how the local is connected to the global, affording opportunities to dissect how more specific socio-cultural phenomena interlink with, and are informed by, broader socio-cultural factors. Dewar MacLeod (2020: 4) has stressed how scenes connect individuals to wider social communities, and how they also link the 'actual' with the 'possible'. Films which represent musical scenes both reflect and construct existing subcultural formations. They are part of broader processes through which various media – such as magazines, newspapers, records and television – disseminate images and ideologies of music scenes beyond specific localities.

In this chapter I focus on two films that document different punk music scenes in detail: *Smithereens* (Seidelman, 1982) and *Suburbia* (Spheeris, 1983). Both these films, and many others covered in the following chapter, include actual musicians in acting roles and/or as musicians performing within the narrative. This tactic often seeks to provide the films with an aura of authenticity, often grounded further in research on and/or immersion within the actual scenes depicted. As many films depicting indie music scenes and musicians are rooted in real life music scenes, they also share some features with music documentaries; though this book is primarily concerned with fiction films, I will make some reference to documentary films in terms of how they share some similarities and influence aspects of fiction films. Music documentaries covering punk music were made frequently, while films about aspects of indie music (usually based around single artists, sometimes based around broader scenes) have continued to be produced regularly, particularly since the 2000s.

Smithereens

Smithereens represents the New York punk scene at a point when the epicentre of punk music was shifting to Los Angeles, a process addressed in the film and which infuses it with an underlying melancholy.[1] It focuses on Wren (Susan Berman), a female punk who moves from New Jersey to New York hoping to make a name for herself within the punk scene, and is often followed by another newcomer to New York, Paul (Brad Rijn). The film's focus on a city in transition includes new styles of music that had connections to punk and would often be classified as post-punk. Some examples of post-punk would come to be termed indie over the years and The Feelies, who provided a significant amount of music for the film, are a band who can be considered, in retrospect, a proto-indie band.[2]

Jimmy Weaver (2013: 180) has argued that *Smithereens* operates 'along the lines of a classic Hollywood cinema of a chronologically revealed story'. Yet, while the film does conform to some Hollywood conventions, it is closer to a verité-style fiction. It exemplifies tendencies within American independent/indie cinema in this regard which, according to Pribram (2001: xi), are 'positioned somewhere in the substantial expanse between, and as a hybrid of, dominant and avant-garde practices'. In some ways *Smithereens*, in its modest difference from Hollywood norms, can be considered a proto-indie picture in similar ways to how The Feelies, who provided music for the film, were at this stage a proto-indie band. The film conforms to the more realistically oriented types of indie films that Newman (2011: 30–1) has outlined, particularly by rooting its characters firmly in social reality, leading to a greater stress on the surrounding social context in which they exist. Newman also claims that while indie films are not often driven by left-wing politics, they tend to be more socially engaged than Hollywood films. As I will go onto argue, this is certainly the case regarding *Smithereens*; while there is no specific ideological agenda fuelling the film, it does connect to socio-political issues. These realist aspects of *Smithereens* support its status as an 'authentic' film, but Weaver (2013: 182; 188) has argued that authenticity within punk cultures existed in tension with a postmodernist stress on bricolage and ideas of identity as masquerade, a tension explored by Seidelman in the film.

Discussing the female-led punk films *Smithereens* and *Ladies and Gentlemen, The Fabulous Stains* (Adler, 1982), Weaver argues there are three main ways that these films create a sense of authenticity: (1) the authenticity of the punk scene depicted within the films; (2) how the female heroines 'demonstrate and display themselves as punk'; (3) the presence of actual punk musicians (2013: 181). In *Smithereens*, punk musician and poet Richard Hell imbues the film with a degree of authenticity, which is bolstered by the verité-style focus on punks in the East Village (including the actual club Peppermint Lounge); while Wren's clothing and lack of respect for anyone clearly mark her as an uncompromising punk character. The authentic aura of actual punk musicians within films would have been heightened by many of them appearing in documentaries; Hell had already appeared in the seminal punk documentary *The Blank Generation* (Král and Poe, 1976), and has also featured as a punk singer in the fiction film *The Blank Generation* (Lommel, 1980), both of which were named after one of the best-known tracks that Hell recorded with the Voidoids. Hell was not originally part of the film; he replaced an unknown actor during an interruption in shooting caused by Susan Berman breaking her leg. Seidelman (2018), in an audio commentary for the film, has explained how this was a fortuitous outcome as it bolstered the film's documentary aesthetics, which were further strengthened by the inclusion of many non-actors in small roles. She further elaborated on how a mixture of actors and 'real people' like Hell was interesting to her as it infused the film with 'a kind of texture and grit that makes it feel authentic' (Ibid.). This verité aesthetic was reinforced by other musicians – such as The Nitecaps – appearing in the film, alongside other people involved in the local punk scene.

Seidelman has stated, for example, that Kitty Somerall – who plays Eric's wife – was someone who hung around the local punk scene and mentioned in the same commentary how she also wanted New York Dolls singer David Johannsen to appear in the film (Ibid.).

Such authenticity markers are not, however, incorporated into *Smithereens* in a straightforward fashion, as the very idea of authenticity itself is questioned throughout the film; in this sense the film exemplifies the tensions between postmodernist masquerade and authentic expression noted by Weaver, and which has also been discussed by Laderman (2010) as a core tension within punk. An example of such tensions within punk can be linked to how many punk performers changed their names. While in one sense this could be considered an 'inauthentic' manoeuvre, in that a 'real' name is rejected in favour of an artificial name, Dave Laing has outlined the complex ways that such names functioned. If names such as Johnny Rotten proclaimed their artificial nature, they also indicated 'real' aspects of a character. Punk performers therefore assumed 'clearly marked artificial names' but these were 'guarantors of a particular punk temperament as individuals' (Laing 2015: 66). Richard Hell's 'real' name, it should be mentioned, is Richard Lester Meyers: in *Smithereens* he plays the role of punk singer, Eric, who is trying to move on following the demise of his band, Smithereens. The film *Smithereens* addresses the difficulties of being authentic within a world driven by capitalism and saturated with images. It is a film that connects to the ideas of Guy Debord, even if links between situationism and punk have tended to focus on UK punk and the Sex Pistols' prankster manager Malcom McLaren and designer Jamie Reid (see Marcus 2001).

Debord's most notable work, *The Society of the Spectacle*, first published in 1967, was a Marxist-influenced analysis of how the mass media had produced the 'spectacle'. For Debord, capitalism and the development of mass media had led to a stage in which images and appearances had replaced 'authentic' existence. Debord claimed that the society of the spectacle was a particular stage within capitalist societies:

> An earlier stage in the economy's domination of social life entailed an obvious downgrading of being into having that left its stamp on all human endeavor. The present stage, in which social life is completely taken over by the accumulated products of the economy, entails a generalized shift from having to appearing: all effective 'having' must now derive both its immediate prestige and its ultimate raison d'etre from appearances. (Debord 1995: 16)

Seidelman's film highlights explicitly the allure of images and how the infatuation with the image erodes authentic existence, and she links this to a prevailing sense of alienation amongst the waning punk scene that Wren so desires to be a

Figure 5.1 *Smithereens*: Wren plasters images of herself on a subway train

part of. The primacy of the image is announced near the beginning of the film: after Wren steals a pair of sunglasses, she then hops onto a subway train and starts posting xeroxed images of herself on the inside of the train, handing one to Paul before she alights (which is their first interaction).

Wren does not pay a great deal of attention to Paul, a newcomer to New York who like herself has no friends and is searching for companionship. She is focused on those people who have status within the punk music scene, as she sees herself as a star who can break into this world. Despite being positioned as a character who is rather desperate to enter the punk music scene, Wren is not a groupie; she rejects sexual advances from Eric's roommate Billy, and later from Eric himself. She wants to be a star, not a sex object, and in this sense even Eric himself functions as a means to an end, rather than an object of romantic desire. One of the implicit ideas underpinning the film is that while punk rejects many of the values and some of the more excessively materialist components of mainstream capitalist society, it is nevertheless enmeshed within such a social system and cannot escape being influenced by it: a compulsive obsession with images and appearances, and associated narcissism, seeped into the structures of both punk and its parent culture.

Hell's appearance as Eric is important because both within the film's diegesis, as well as in its dissemination to audiences, he is the 'star', both within and outside of the film; within the film he is pursued by Wren, whereas outside of the film he would have been known to numerous viewers. He at once is a

Figure 5.2 *Smithereens*: Wren places an image of Eric on a record over a poster of Eric

commodity (someone whose name may attract potential viewers) and a sign of authenticity (an actual punk singer with high cultural status within the New York punk scene). Hell's/Eric's status as an image, or more accurately a series of images, is a core theme in the film. When Wren first visits Eric's apartment, her attraction to him is displaced onto his image; she is more concerned with scanning the images of him – the large poster on the wall, the image of Eric on a Smithereens record – than with his material body. When Wren places the head of Eric's photo from an album cover over that of his head on the poster (two different 'cool' images of Hell wearing sunglasses in the poster, and sans glasses but behatted on the back cover of the album), it emphasises the ascendancy of the spectacle within everyday life, echoing Debord's contention that 'the spectacle proclaims the predominance of appearances and asserts that all human life, which is to say all social life, is mere appearance' (1995: 14).

Smithereens homes in on the alienation and narcissism of the spectacle through frequently drawing attention to images – particularly Wren's obsessive copying and dissemination of her own image – and through framing conversations and relationships in specific ways. The film does not utilise shot-reverse-shots very frequently, a strategy which heightens the chasm separating characters. Seidelman is more prone to frame conversations between characters in two-shots rather than shot-reverse-shots, emphasising lack of direct eye contact: even when Wren first starts talking to Eric in the bar and looks at him regularly, he rarely returns the gaze, instead tending to look off into the distance, absorbed in his own solipsistic world. This aesthetic strategy again connects to another of Debord's axioms, that separation 'is the alpha and omega of the spectacle' (1995: 20). In the filmic universe of *Smithereens*, genuine relations between human beings have been distorted by 'spectacular capitalism'.

Smithereens's musical soundtrack reflects its focus on a punk scene in transition. As noted, at the point of the film's production, L.A. was supplanting New York as the epicentre of punk, and was associated with hardcore punk, a more aggressive, macho mode of punk that was also less focused on image than some of its earlier, New York precursors. The music on the soundtrack would today be considered to consist primarily of post-punk, as opposed to punk, sounds. Hell and the Voidoids are one of the few punk bands on the soundtrack, though even their sounds are far less aggressive than many of the records made by L.A. punk artists around this period. Otherwise, there is a selection of tracks that span genres, including reggae (Singers and Players), minimal funk (ESG) and new wave power pop (The Nitecaps). All these musical genres – at least in some form – had connections to punk subcultures: this was particularly the case regarding post-punk, which refers to music that emerged from punk but often experimented with musical style and expanded punk's musical palette. Many post-punk musicians attempted to approach recognised genres non-conventionally, often producing music with a 'punk' spirit through an amateur-like approach to musicianship, recording music cheaply, and releasing on small, independent labels. Reggae, funk and jazz were all drawn upon by post-punk groups, which not only broadened punk's sonic horizons but also introduced influences from black musical forms. New wave also connected to punk in that it was a more accessible, commercialised form of music that sought to exploit, yet also to some extent tame, punk music.

Most of the music mentioned is used quite sparingly, appearing in brief, diegetically integrated snippets either performed live or on records in clubs and homes. Once again, diegetic music is primarily used to imbue the scenes with a sense of authenticity, communicating as it does a realistic, believable subcultural scene. Music from The Feelies is used more frequently and as a non-diegetic score, therefore functioning slightly differently. Seidelman (2018) has stated how she originally approached John Cale to score the film, on the suggestion of fellow film director Jonathan Demme, but that nothing emerged from their discussions.[3] Demme had also suggested The Feelies as another possible band to score the film, and Seidelman claims that on hearing their music she thought that it was perfectly suited to the character of Wren because of its 'nervous energy' (Ibid.).[4] Rather than providing new music for the score, The Feelies contributed mostly instrumental parts from the following tracks: 'The Boy with the Perpetual Nervousness', 'Loveless Love', 'Moscow Nights' and 'Original Love', all taken from their debut LP *Crazy Rhythms* (1980).

The opening bars of The Feelies' 'The Boy with the Perpetual Nervousness' are the first sounds we hear in *Smithereens*. The film opens unusually, with an extreme close-up of a pair of checkered sunglasses dangling from a woman's hand. Motion has been slowed and the only initial movement is of the glasses moving steadily to and fro. This is accompanied by the opening of 'The Boy with the Perpetual Nervousness', a picked, repetitious guitar line with dampened percussion. As Wren moves into the shot – at this point we only see the top of her fishnet-stockinged legs and the bottom of her checkered miniskirt – a second repetitive guitar line is introduced, prior to Wren's hand snatching the glasses. It is at this point that slow motion ceases, as Wren runs down a flight of subway stairs and is pursued by the victim of her theft. The dynamism of the chase meshes with the music as The Feelies' track kicks into gear, locking into a propulsive yet nervy, rhythmic groove; the song continues through the credits and as Wren plasters pictures of herself on the train, and is then pursued by Paul to the copy shop where she works.

Other music by The Feelies functions in similar ways. The music is a kind of leitmotif for Wren; as noted, Seidelman thought that their nervy, tense, yet dynamic sounds aptly reflected Wren's personality in sonic terms. It also operates on a more dramatic level; while the film does not conform to the dramatic arcs of a conventional Hollywood screenplay, it does contain a few moments where tension and drama become heightened, and such scenes are often accompanied by the instrumental parts from The Feelies' songs. The next scene accompanied by The Feelies' music occurs just under the half-hour mark. The scene again involves a moment of heightened tension: Wren gets locked out of her apartment because she hasn't paid rent and, following her demands to have her clothes returned, is told to wait outside. It is at this point that we can detect, albeit very low down in the mix, the introductory guitar lines from 'Loveless Love', which accompany her down the apartment stairs as a neighbour declaims 'good riddance to bad rubbish'. Wren paces nervously back and forth outside of the apartment block whilst being further irritated by a young boy who is attempting to lure her into gambling, until her clothes are thrown out of the window. Music starts to gradually rise in volume as the tension of the scene becomes heightened: Wren shouts at the woman for flinging her clothes out of the window and onto the sidewalk, briefly runs after the boy, who has stolen one of her bras, then returns as more clothes are flung unceremoniously out of the window. After she yells 'fat bitch' at the landlady, we switch to a high angle shot of her raising her fist and shouting 'you're going to pay for this', before the landlady throws a bucket of water over her. The Feelies' 'Loveless Love' has, at this point, locked into an insistent, multi-layered rhythm, its nervous energy once again contributing to dramatic tension, while also indicating Wren's agitated mental state. As Wren angrily exits the scene, the camera follows her legs as she walks through the streets, a recurrent motif within the film. For Wren, an uncompromising and tetchy character, walking is important: defiant and living hand-to-mouth, she must regularly take flight and seek new spaces to exist in.

There are two further scenes in which The Feelies' music is used prominently, and they both soundtrack further tense, dramatic moments. The track 'Moscow Nights' is used to accompany Wren and Paul breaking into the apartment where she previously lived, so that she can steal back her possessions. At first, as they quietly break into the apartment, the music is mixed low on the soundtrack, but it rises to the fore when they are discovered by the landlady. When Wren and Paul run out of the apartment – leading to Wren falling over before they escape in Paul's van – dramatic tension is again heightened by The Feelies' music, with two prominent, echoed riffs concluding the scene. The final, prominent employment of The Feelies' music comes towards the end of the film, as Wren finally comes up against multiple barriers to her movements. After she is cajoled by Eric into stealing from a stranger, she expects to then elope with Eric to L.A., but when she visits his apartment, finds that he has already gone. She then tries, but fails, to stay with her friend Cecile, whose flatmate will not even allow Wren to enter the apartment. Following these scenes, as Wren walks down a sidewalk – camera once again following her and focused on her legs moving through space – The Feelies' 'Loveless Love' accompanies her perambulations around the city, shifting between the foreground and background of the soundtrack, coming to prominence at fraught moments: for example, it comes to the fore when she breaks into the Peppermint Lounge and tries, unsuccessfully, to latch onto The Nitecaps' singer, before being violently ejected (and once again having to haul herself off from the sidewalk). In contrast to previous uses of The Feelies' music, this placement also includes vocals, which connect loosely to the film's content: 'Loveless Love' obliquely recounts the frustrated feelings of a singer who is on the receiving end of 'loveless love', a condition which befits Wren's – and Eric's – largely functional approach to romance and relationships. Wren's hopeless attempts to find a place to stay are partially a consequence of her somewhat parasitic lifestyle: after being kicked out of Peppermint Lounge, she further attempts to phone her sister – hanging up when her brother-in-law answers the phone – and then visits Paul, only to discover that he has sold his van and left. Alone at the end of the film, and walking out of Manhattan across the George Washington Bridge, she is courted by men in cars trying to pick her up; the camera then freezes, in a seeming nod to *The 400 Blows* (Truffaut, 1959), as Wren turns to look at one of the drivers offering her a ride.[5] The ending of *Smithereens* is deliberately open-ended, though somewhat downbeat. In one sense, it is circular; András Bálint Kovács (2008: 79) has argued that circular narratives are common in modernist art films, which *Smithereens* is indebted to, and that they commonly involve a story going 'back to its starting point without a solution only to end there'.

Whereas much of Wren's walking has been driven by a desire to latch onto a person and find a place to stay, these options have dried up by the end of the film. There is a rather distasteful indication that she might be subject to sexual harassment following this pick-up, even though she has been presented as a fighter and someone who can repeatedly pick herself up from the floor and get on with things. Another possibility – and one that Wren herself would despise – is that she returns to New Jersey, possibly to live with her parents. Her escape from, and possible return to, New Jersey further lends relevance to The Feelies' music: the band are themselves from New Jersey, so the frequent bursts of their music on the soundtrack partly function as a reminder of what Wren is escaping from (in case we are in any doubts about her feelings for the place, she states to her sister Terri at one point, 'I'm not setting foot in New Jersey again, ever').[6]

The mixture of non-professionals from the music scene with trained actors appositely reflects the content of *Smithereens*, which concerns the difficulties of being authentic within a culture informed by narcissism and image-worship. The film's focus on a recalcitrant female punk emphasises the possibilities that punk cultures afforded some of their participants, but also foregrounds the limits of such freedoms. There is, further, an emphasis on the transience of scenes and the opportunities they afford. This concerns both the specific character of Wren, who fails to 'make it' and runs out of options by the film's conclusion, and broader punk cultures. As mentioned, New York had by 1982 been supplanted by L.A. as the epicentre of punk within much media coverage. While the New York scene was already splintering into more sonically diverse directions, L.A. was host to a more aggressive, less 'arty' punk explosion.

SUBURBIA AND HARDCORE PUNK

Hardcore punk emerged across different cities in California in the late 1970s, with L.A. its most notable centre. Hardcore punk divested itself of the more postmodern tendencies evident in the earlier New York and London punk scenes. It pushed the music in even faster and more aggressive directions, and further emphasised a DIY ethos, but was often beset by regressive social stigmatisation. Ryan Moore writes:

> Hardcore music was louder, faster, and angrier than its punk predecessors, and hardcore shows were frequently more violent and male dominated. Yet for all its stylistic homogeneity, hardcore represented even more divergent political possibilities than punk: in some circles it could be not simply nihilistic but shamelessly homophobic, misogynist, and racist, while others used the do-it-yourself ethic to mobilize resources into one of the very few social movements to challenge the Reagan agenda from a radical, multi-issue perspective. (Moore 2010: 52-3)

Moore argues that the shift towards more authoritarian and corporate politics in America – heralded by Reagan's presidency – influenced much hardcore punk. While several northern Californian bands adopted a direct, politically activist ethos, Moore contends that the L.A. scene was more politically conservative overall and 'exhibited nihilism and violence as even more dominant tendencies than they were in Britain or other parts of North America' (Moore 2010: 51). Jon Lewis also touches on the anti-social characteristics of L.A. hardcore:

> For the duration of its brief hold on the disenfranchised youth of urban L.A., punk unapologetically paraded a variety of misanthropic and misogynistic tendencies: Nazism, fascism, racism, and self-hate. No youth movement before or since has hinged so tenuously on bizarre and frightening ceremonies of attraction and repulsion and public displays of anti-social behaviour. (Lewis 1998: 87)

It was the more sensational elements of this subculture which were largely focused upon in media coverage, partly because of the threats that they posed to social order, but also because of additional factors such as morbid fascination. In the remainder of this section, I will focus on two films by Penelope Spheeris which further foreground the violence of the L.A. punk scene, but not from a position of moral outrage. I will largely focus on the fiction film *Suburbia* (1983) but will also discuss Spheeris's earlier documentary *The Decline of Western Civilisation* (1981), which informs the former film in several ways, much like how earlier New York punk documentaries such as *The Blank Generation* fed into subsequent fiction films which incorporated documentary aspects.

The Decline of Western Civilisation has become a cult film since its release, chiefly due to its enduring appeal amongst punk music fans; as the film has aged, early 1980s L.A. hardcore has increasingly gained historical importance. While it is true that the film only features a few bands connected to the scene and is therefore highly selective in its focus, it nevertheless captures footage of hardcore bands playing in 1980 and includes many interviews with several key hardcore bands, fans, as well as fanzine producers. In some ways, it can be considered a seminal text in the same ways that *The Blank Generation* was in relation to late 1970s New York punk. If that former film fed into some later fictional productions, including *Smithereens*, then *The Decline of Western Civilisation* acts as a kind of urtext for *Suburbia* in a more direct manner because the two films were directed by the same person.

The Decline of Western Civilisation has undoubtedly gained a reputation as an 'authentic' document of the L.A. hardcore scene in the early 1980s. While it did receive some negative reactions, most responses have been positive, attesting to the film's importance as an historical document. Spheeris's film further benefits from synch sound, unlike *The Blank Generation*, as well as being shot in colour (though some interviews with fans are in black-and-white). While there has been occasional griping from viewers about the bands covered, Spheeris did manage to film some of the most lauded bands from the era, including Black Flag, Circle Jerks, The Germs and X. And while the film does focus largely on the performers – including extensive concert footage and interviews with band members – it also includes footage of fans and fanzine producers, therefore emphasising punk as a broad scene in ways that *The Blank Generation* did not.

Even more so than *Decline*, *Suburbia* focuses on a broader subcultural scene rather than punk performers; while it features more performance footage overall than *Smithereens*, the performers themselves are arguably less important to the main protagonists in this film than they are in *Smithereens*. In *Smithereens*, Wren is drawn to band leaders because of their prominent status and cultural cachet. She is interested in them because she wants to become a star image herself rather than being a fan of their music per se. This star worship is largely absent from *Suburbia*; the music in the film is something that binds the individuals and enhances group identity. Despite the film's greater attention to subcultural characters associated with punk music, these teenagers do not actually seem to be engaged in any mode of cultural production: we do not get a sense that any of the characters themselves are in bands, neither are they involved in fanzine production. In contrast to Wren's desire to break into the music industry and become a star, the gang in *Suburbia* do not seem to have any expectations about breaking out of their current situation, which lends the film a quite depressing, nihilistic tone.

Suburbia is an ensemble film that centres on the T.R. gang ('The Rejected') and depicts many of the more sensationalist elements of the punk scene, such as violence and robbery. As noted, it has often been considered an authentic representation of punks of this era, which is bolstered by the inclusion of staged concert performances from actual punk bands D.I., T.S.O.L. (True Sound of Liberty) and The Violators, and because many of the actors and other personnel came from the punk scene: for example, Jack is played by Chris Pederson, who had never previously acted but had been in several punk bands (The Dumps, SIN 34 and The Patriots); Joe is played by Wayne Walston, who became a bassist for the band U.S. Bombs; Razzle is played by Flea, who of course became bassist for the Red Hot Chili Peppers. The soundtrack for the film, meanwhile, was produced by Alex Gibson, who had formerly been in punk bands Little Cripples and BPeople, and who would go on to form another band, Passionel.[7] As with *Smithereens*, the inclusion of non-professional actors aligned with the scene depicted creates a degree of verité authenticity, which was aided by Spheeris's previous immersion within the culture and by her extensive research on media reports of punks. She stated to Patrick Goldstein (1984: 18): 'Almost everything in the film came from watching the news. I've

Figure 5.3 *Suburbia*: D.I. perform 'Richard Hung Himself' in concert

spent lots of my time with kids who live like squatters in these abandoned crash pads near Western Avenue, places like Hotel Hell, Skinhead Manor and the Oxford House.' Her extensive engagement with media reports of the subculture, combined with an ethnographic immersion within that culture, lends the film a dual tone which veers between earnest documentation and media sensationalism; the latter factor was, according to Spheeris, influenced mainly by Roger Corman's involvement in the film's production.

Suburbia was co-produced and co-financed by Roger Corman, and distributed by his company New World Pictures. A successful exploitation film producer, Corman was often very strict about including sensationalist content within his films, and this is evident in *Suburbia* through the focus on violence and the inclusion of nudity. Spheeris herself has discussed this tension, which indicates how the film combined verité and exploitation registers:

> Roger Corman had co-financed it and he kept trying to make it into an exploitation movie because that genre was his specialty. I kept trying to make it into a meaningful coming-of-age movie about social outcasts. There are some scenes I would have not included, but I had to in order to get the movie made. Roger's orders were that there *had* to be either some sex or violence every ten minutes. Hard to deal with that when I was trying to make a movie with some substance. (MacInnis 2018)

As such, the more documentary-style aesthetics of the film sometimes clash with these exploitative elements. Spheeris does, however, incorporate exploitation aesthetics in a way that links to actual occurrences within punk subcultures, particularly violence. She manages to avoid merely depicting the punks as senseless, anti-social menaces through two main strategies: firstly, via occasional self-reflexive scenes that draw attention to how mass media reportage of punk subcultures are themselves aesthetic exaggerations and, secondly, through an often-sympathetic depiction of the gang.

Two scenes in particular reference other movies, a strategy which foregrounds the film as a construction, and which pulls away from the predominant verité style. The first is when the gang walks down the street in slow motion, following scenes where they have been stealing food from homes. The slow motion, long-lensed frontal shot is reminiscent of a scene from *A Clockwork Orange* (Kubrick, 1971) when Alex suppresses a planned coup by his gang, the droogs. One gang member is even wearing a bowler hat and has a cane slung over his shoulder, in a nod to Alex, who often walks around with a sword cane. This intertextual reference to *A Clockwork Orange* functions in several ways. Firstly, it links to another film about gang violence, which resonated with many punks in the late 1970s and early 1980s (Wigley 2019; Barber 2006: 69); T.S.O.L.'s 1982 album *Beneath the Shadows*, for example, featured the band's full name (The True Sound of Liberty) prominently placed across the top of the cover in orange lettering reminiscent of Philip Castle's lettering for *A Clockwork Orange*'s promotional posters. The film was also incredibly controversial; in Britain numerous media articles cited the film as a causal factor in actual violent attacks by youths; in the US there were also many concerns about the film's possible impact stressed in reviews, many of which claimed it was nihilistic, even fascistic, and linked it to growing tendencies in American society more broadly (Kramer 2011: 100–7). The allusion to *A Clockwork Orange* further draws attention to a film which combined graphic violence with a serious exploration of morality, signalling in the process its own similar intentions. Through this reference to *A Clockwork Orange*, *Suburbia* acknowledges its status as a fictional text, drawing attention to how these menacing images of punks are exaggerated tropes that have been fuelled by media reports. Of course, the film itself is also presenting the subculture in a partially exploitative manner, though according to Spheeris these are elements that she was urged to include: through self-reflexive scenes like this, she incorporates a meta-level commentary pertaining to media representations of subcultures so that the film – like *A Clockwork Orange* – fuses sensationalism with a more serious examination of this subcultural phenomenon.

Another prominent self-reflexive scene within the film occurs when violence breaks out at a funeral for gang member Sheila, who has committed suicide. After Sheila's father tells the gang that they are not welcome at the funeral, an altercation breaks out as Joe declaims the father's abuse of Sheila. When the father starts grappling physically with Joe, Skinner punches him, which leads

PUNK, SMITHEREENS AND SUBURBIA

Figure 5.4 Frontal shot of the gang in *Suburbia* which references *A Clockwork Orange*

Figure 5.5 Frontal shot of the gang in *A Clockwork Orange*

to further scuffles and punches being thrown. Once the violence commences, the style becomes more exaggerated: there is a very dramatic, low-level close-up of the father on the floor with a pained expression, glasses knocked askance across his face and blood dripping prominently down his forehead. As a brawl between the gang and other churchgoers breaks out, frenetic punk music – The Vandals' 'The Legend of Pat Brown' – accompanies the chaotic action before we cut to the outside of the church and the T.R. gang burst out of the doors in another frontal shot.

The scene recalls the funeral scene from *The Wild Angels* (Corman, 1966), an older exploitation film which focused on a subcultural group with a reputation for danger within the mainstream media of the time, particularly as both scenes result in the main patriarchal authority figure lying helpless on the ground (in *The Wild Angels* it is a priest who is beaten to the floor). Spheeris here references previous modes of subcultural exploitation that the film belongs to (and a film that was produced and directed by Corman), but she also differentiates her film from such predecessors. Thus, while the film does incorporate these sensational elements, they are incorporated reluctantly; through referencing *The Wild Angels* Spheeris even indicates – via the Corman connection – who is chiefly responsible for their inclusion. Yet by referring to other films, Spheeris draws attention to such sensationalist spectacle as a *media construct*: this does not mean that punks did not engage in violence and other forms of criminality (crowd violence features in *The Decline of Western Civilisation*), but it does emphasise that much media coverage of punks tended to exaggerate and overly focus on this aspect of the subculture. Spheeris moves beyond pure sensationalism by counterbalancing the more exploitative aspects of the film with a humanist depiction of the T.R gang. *The Wild Angels* did this to an extent, in that while it largely revelled in the anti-social antics depicted, it did imply these were symptomatic of broader social issues, such as unemployment and a growing disaffection amongst working-class youth (Barton-Fumo 2013). The social causes of such behaviour are only glimpsed, however, and are outweighed by the more sensationalist focus on their immorality, which peaks in the extended funeral scene. Spheeris presents the T.R. punks in a more sympathetic light: it is interesting, for example, that while the biker gang members in *The Wild Angels* are associated with Nazi imagery, Spheeris deliberately does not associate *Suburbia*'s punks with Nazi symbols, even though some punks at the time did occasionally parade swastikas in a deliberately provocative fashion. While the funeral scene in *Suburbia* ends in violence, it is more justified and briefer than the corresponding scene from *The Wild Angels*. In *Suburbia*, the punks have gone to the funeral of one of their friends but are told to leave, ostensibly because of their appearance. The initial response to this is polite, with one of the girls stating to Sheila's father that 'we didn't have any nice clothes, we're sorry'. But such politeness does not get them very far, and the hypocrisy of the father is exposed when his physical and sexual abuse of Sheila is called out. Spheeris also depicts some of the social factors which rationalise the criminal acts of the gang, most notably parental neglect and abuse. The funeral scene in *The Wild Angels*, meanwhile, is drawn out and is much darker, descending as it does not only into chaotic violence, but also sexual abuse of the female gang members.

The foregrounding of social issues including parental abuse, as well as unemployment and lack of opportunities, presents a very different picture of suburban living than was being heralded by Ronald Reagan. John Taylor (2017: 14) has argued that both *The Decline of Western Civilisation* and *Suburbia* 'serve as powerful counter-narratives that resist the dominant conception of suburban existence in the early 1980s'. Reagan was heralding family values and home ownership, particularly within the suburbs, which were promoted as idyllic spaces of opportunity; *Suburbia* depicts, contrastingly, the prevalence of crime, unemployment, poverty and alcoholism in the suburbs, while the families – the fulcrum of Reagan's vision of a prosperous society – tend to be dysfunctional. Taylor notes that while the pains of suburban living had been addressed in the 1950s and 60s – most notably in *Rebel Without a Cause* (Ray, 1955) – by the onset of the 1980s 'the suburban landscape was restored in the popular imagination as a place of renewal and reparation' (17).[8] While I agree with Taylor's argument, it should be mentioned that there were some cinematic predecessors to Spheeris's focus on suburban alienation in the 1970s. One of the most notable of these was *Over the Edge* (Kaplan, 1979), which focuses on extreme teenage alienation in the suburbs. The film is, like *Suburbia*, a low-budget production which employed unknown actors and emphasised its connection to real events in its opening titles, highlighting problems of suburban planning. The film was inspired by a rash of newspaper articles on teen violence in the suburbs from the early 1970s; writers Tim Hunter and Charles Haas also conducted extensive interviews with families, the police and schools (Goldstone 1978: 22). While *Suburbia* presents an even more depressing situation than that film, it nevertheless echoes some of its thematic concerns and aesthetic strategies.

A prominent means by which *Suburbia* humanises the T.R. gang is through its rather negative depiction of parents. This is evident in the first two scenes of the film, which both occur prior to the credits. Firstly, we see Sheila, who has left home, hitchhiking. While this scene focuses more on the driver's baby daughter being attacked viciously by a stray dog, we are already introduced to a future T.R. member escaping her family. In the next scene, following a shot of a child (Ethan) circling outside a house on his tricycle, we cut inside to his house and see his brother, Evan, watching television. His mother then arrives home, drunk and abusive; after accusing him of drinking from her bottle of vodka, she rants at him for not taking the litter out, eventually throwing a bottle at his head (which misses and smashes on the wall) and then slapping him. This leads to Evan leaving home; after aimlessly walking the streets at night, he follows a group of punks to see D.I. play live. Initially, the scene focuses on some rather distasteful occurrences: Evan has his drink spiked unawares (by gang member Keef); the club manager shouts out towards a fracas that threatens to spill into violence; someone has their pocket picked; most egregiously, a woman is harassed and then has her clothes ripped off (by the T.R. gang's most violent member, Skinner), while audience members circle around and taunt her. But if Spheeris here presents an almost-cliched exaggeration of anti-social and misogynistic tendencies that had been reported frequently, she balances such coverage with a more humanistic focus. Firstly, Casey Royale, the singer of D.I., eventually stops the performance and pleads for the goading audience members to leave the harassed girl alone and return her clothes; this eventually leads to the manager coming on stage and cancelling the show (which becomes a running joke throughout the film; the first three of four live performances in the film are abruptly cancelled due to the unruliness of the audience). More importantly, after being found slumped on the club floor adjacent to a pool of vomit, Evan is carried out of the club by security and dumped outside. He is spotted by Jack, the nominal leader of the T.R. gang, who helps him up and offers to give him a lift home.

After Evan tells Jack that he doesn't have a home, he joins the T.R. himself, and the gang provide him with greater support than his own family, a point driven home later in the film when Evan collects his young brother Ethan following his mother's arrest for drink driving. Spheeris presents some unpleasant elements apparent within the punk scene but moves beyond them and, consequently, expands on their purely negative coverage in mainstream media. The scene with Evan and Ethan's single mother highlights how even more toxic violence and abuse can be found in families. Domestic violence is not, importantly, located only in broken homes: Sheila, introduced in the opening scene, has been raised by married parents but the abuse from her father is even more shocking, the evidence of which is etched across her back with huge scars. While the T.R. gang engage in criminal and sometimes dubious behaviour, such antics are partly explained by their upbringings, as well as their poverty: they rob, for example, to survive. They look out for each other consistently and therefore provide emotional comfort and support absent from their family upbringings. The gang are also contrasted with members from a group called 'Citizens Against Crime', two of whom – Jim Tripplett and Bob Skokes – they come into frequent conflict with. Despite their ostensive opposition to crime, Jim and Bob come across as aggressive and violent; we first see them shooting at stray dogs, and their manner throughout the film suggests that their allegiance with the law stems partly from a desire to enact violence without recompense, and once again draws attention to divisions between sanctioned and unsanctioned, demonised violence. At the end of the film, after a series of skirmishes, Jim and Bob eventually attack the T.R. house, ultimately running over and killing Ethan. This tragic incident ends the film with the gang all in shock, reminiscent of a grieving extended family. This ending also echoes the beginning of the film through the death of a young child; if the baby's death at the beginning of the film encouraged Jim and Bob to enact a kind of vengeance against stray dogs, the ending emphasises their violent tendencies – and hypocrisy – as they themselves become child killers.

The self-reflexive moments within *Suburbia* facilitate meta-commentary on the depicted events: through intertextual exaggeration and pastiche, the predominant verité aesthetic is interrupted occasionally. While such moments are the most overt examples of a verité approach being undercut by self-conscious artifice, the film itself sometimes blends fictional and documentary registers uneasily. The presence of actual performers, as well as non-professional actors who were part of the punk scene, is another facet of the film which blends documentary and fiction. Spheeris's experience of having shot extensive footage of live punk bands for *The Decline of Western Civilisation* would have informed her approach here. In that film, multiple cameras were used to construct dynamic concert footage which shifted perspective between band members and the audience. The live performances in *Suburbia* mirror such scenes to an extent – the bands perform live music in a real space to a punk audience – but there is more emphasis on the audience here. The four live sets featured within the film foreground the band's performances prominently, but they also cut away from the musicians frequently, sometimes for extended periods. In this sense, the film extends *Decline*'s focus on the punk audience and broader subculture; its fictional framework allows Spheeris to probe the subjectivity and existential travails of some members of this subculture. *Suburbia* inverts the focus of *Decline*: the latter largely focuses on the bands (both on stage and through interviews), with some coverage of the fans and broader subculture; in *Suburbia*, the subculture takes centre stage, with the bands and their music providing a backdrop to the T.R. gang's existence.

The live music in *Suburbia* is foregrounded as an attraction in one sense, yet the live music sequences only focus on the live performers intermittently, as focus shifts to members of the T.R. gang and other groups and individuals within the venue. Outside the live performances, diegetic punk music on the soundtrack is shifted even further into the background; much of the music – such as The Vandals' 'Urban Struggle' – is heard as background music, played within the T.R. squat but not foregrounded. One of the few times diegetic music (that isn't being performed) is prominent on the soundtrack is when

Jack and Evan visit Joe, and he is playing The Germs' 'No God'. As they enter Joe's bedroom, the music loudly blasts from a record player; a close-up of the seven-inch record playing is briefly glimpsed before Jack turns the record off to talk to Joe. Once again, even when diegetic music is prominent on the soundtrack, it quickly shifts to the background. Within the film, diegetic music contributes to an aura of actuality, contributing to a 'realistic' audio-visual environment within which the fictional events – themselves based on real events – unfold. Beyond its status within the film itself, the music also contributed – and continues to feed into – the film's appeal amongst punk fans. As a low-budget feature, the film would not have expected to reap large commercial rewards; it was instead more of a niche film, catering primarily to audiences who themselves felt alienated from mainstream culture. The music in the film therefore functioned as a marketing lure, and this commercial component of the music led to a soundtrack album being released, which consisted partly of Alex Gibson's score and of live performances by the bands featured within the film. The inclusion of live performances also contributes to a sense of authenticity on the one hand, and potential commercialism on the other. In commercial terms, songs which had been released in studio form were now available in less polished, more direct forms which had not been released previously. (If the tracks had been presented in studio form, the soundtrack might have been less appealing to potential buyers if they already had those recordings.)

Conclusion: Authenticity and Representation

The combination of authenticity and commercialism may initially appear paradoxical, but this isn't necessarily the case. I consider authenticity to be a relative, rather than essential, concept, and historically it has been located (by critics, audiences, etc.) across cultural forms that have been released as commercial products. According to Philip Auslander, authenticity plays a crucial role in the reception of rock music, but he argues that though fans and critics may discuss authenticity as an essence, it is in fact 'an ideological concept and [. . .] a discursive effect . . . a matter of culturally determined convention, not an expression of essence. It is also a result of industrial practice: the music industry specifically sets out to endow its products with the necessary signs of authenticity' (Auslander 2001: 82).

In films that portray punk subcultures, the notion of authenticity becomes heightened as many fans and practitioners of punk considered it to be a more authentic mode of expression than many other forms of music. Auslander has argued how the concept of authenticity in rock music often depends on differentiation from other contemporary forms, which are deemed inauthentic, and in this respect rock authenticity is conservative, as 'authenticity is often located in current music's relationship to an earlier, "purer" moment in a mythic history of the music' (83). Such manoeuvres were common in punk during its emergence in the late 1970s, when it was often presented as a more authentic alternative to the bloated complexities of progressive rock, which for many punks had become divorced from the 'real'.[9] *The Decline of Western Civilization* commences with a brief snippet from an interview with a punk called Eugene, who discusses his attraction to punk by emphasising how it is both new but also harks back to rock'n'roll: 'It's something new and it's just reviving old rock'n'roll'. He then goes on to claim that punk 'is real . . . it's not bullshit, there's no rock stars'. His claims about punk being just rock'n'roll but also 'new' foregrounds how punk harked back to an earlier, 'purer' era of rock music: simpler, less dependent on studio trickery, earlier rock'n'roll was considered a form of music that was more directly connected to authentic expression. Punk took this as a model and transformed it through cranking up speed, volume and attitude.

While there were no large-scale Hollywood depictions of punks to contrast films like *Smithereens* and *Suburbia* with, other films were considered less authentic. Two examples are *Times Square* (Moyle, 1980) and *Ladies and Gentlemen, The Fabulous Stains* (Adler 1982), which were mentioned in Chapter 1. *Times Square* was generally dismissed as an overly contrived and diluted representation of punks, as was *Ladies and Gentlemen, The Fabulous Stains* initially, despite featuring actual punk musicians Steve Jones and Paul Cook of the Sex Pistols, and Paul Simonon of The Clash. The film's reasonably large budget, the involvement of a Hollywood studio in its production, and its comparatively glossy look were factors that might have affected its initially disappointing reception. The film was also considered compromised by many because of tussles over the script written by Nancy Dowd and based on research by music journalist Caroline Coon. Dowd eventually quit the film and it was not released until 1982, after director Lou Adler had tacked on an MTV-style music video at its conclusion. Despite some of these factors leading to negative judgements of the film, its reputation has slowly grown over the years, embraced by a newer generation of viewers including many involved in the riot grrrl movement. This highlights how judgements of authenticity are far from fixed and can alter over time as films and music move across different contexts.

The employment of punk musicians, whether in an acting capacity or through inclusion of punk music on a film's soundtrack, is a strategy capable of bridging commercial concerns and authentic values (though this is not guaranteed). As low-budget films, *Smithereens* and *Suburbia* were attempting to depict punk subcultures in broadly realistic ways, but the musicians featured could also act to promote the films. It is not only within these two films that commercial and authentic values overlap in this manner; *Ladies and Gentlemen, The Fabulous Stains* also attempted to do so through its inclusion of members of the Sex Pistols and The Clash. Allison Anders' debut feature, *Border Radio* (1987), co-directed with Kurt Voss, also featured several artists prominent within the L.A. punk and alternative music scene, and Anders has stated how the music within the film was an important component in enabling her and Voss to attain completion funds (Anders et al. 1995: 134).

There is no agreed upon 'reality' of punk culture(s), or the various factions that constitute punk culture(s); consequently, there is no straightforward assessment of whether a film has authentically represented such cultures. Rather, punk films – including documentaries – are important elements that contribute to the media construction of subcultures. I here draw on Sarah Thornton's arguments about how media are central to the development of subcultures. Even though she is discussing early 1990s rave culture in the UK, her arguments have broader application. She contests the idea that subcultures develop organically, only to be distorted by the mass media, arguing that 'media sights, sounds and words are more than just representations; they are mediations, integral participants in music culture' (Thornton 1995: 112). She further notes how earlier subcultural theorists such as Stanley Cohen only paid attention to mass media, whereas she focuses on a range of other media including niche media (such as specialist consumer magazines) and what she calls micro-media (such as fanzines and promotional flyers). In punk music, and punk films, there was at first – as is the case with numerous subcultures in their early stages – a perceived gap between how punks were addressed by mass media and specialist niche media. If mass media reports – particularly within newspapers and television coverage – tended to frame punks negatively, as a social menace, then micro-media such as fanzines presented a very different, more positive angle on punk. Both *Smithereens* and *Suburbia* should be considered niche media due to their low budgets and limited screenings, as well as through the ways that they present less judgemental, alternative representations of punk artists and fans. Within various forms of punk subculture, many would have placed more trust in niche media as they are more likely to be perceived as emerging from the culture that they represent, whereas some of the more negative reports in mass media would have been considered as the views of outside figures with little understanding of the lived experiences of punks.

Punk has continued to materialise in new forms since its original emergence in the late 1970s and early 1980s. The next chapter looks at the filmic representation of cultures related to broad, punk-influenced movements with links to alternative music and indie cultures: grunge and riot grrrl. Notions of authenticity continued to be a pressing issue in the reception of these films, while questions focusing on independence within a commercial landscape became even more heightened when grunge – which emerged from indie cultures – entered the mainstream.

Notes

1. This sense of a waning scene was even more prominent when the film was released, as it was delayed because of Berman breaking her leg. Whilst it commenced production in 1980, it was not released until 1982.
2. The Feelies would become more commonly referred to as an indie band over time, as the label became employed more frequently. They would not release their second album *The Good Earth* – after undergoing some personnel changes – until 1986, six years after their debut album *Crazy Rhythms*. Co-produced by R.E.M.'s Peter Buck, the music still features repetitious use of jangly guitars but employs more acoustic instrumentation than their debut.
3. Seidelman (2018) indicates that Cale had drug issues at the time and was a little 'unreliable'.
4. Demme was obviously a fan of The Feelies, as they appeared in *Something Wild* (Demme, 1986) – under the guise of 'The Willies' – where they played a number of songs at a high school reunion, including 'Loveless Love', 'Crazy Rhythms' and covers of David Bowie's 'Fame' and The Monkees' 'Daydream Believer'.
5. European art cinema is an obvious influence on the film, as Seidelman has noted in her director commentary. Not long before the frozen ending, the French New Wave is explicitly referenced by an unnamed character in Paul's ex-van as she reads a newspaper report about a 34-year-old woman (unnamed, though presumedly referring to Candice Bergen) finding what she has been looking for: French director Louis Malle (the story also links to Wren's own star-seeking trajectory). The film is also loosely inspired by *Nights of Cabiria* (Fellini, 1957), in which a woman unsuccessfully seeks romance with a film star.
6. The Feelies also developed a reputation for not travelling outside of New Jersey very often to play live. While they did play Manhattan, and developed a reputation there, they would increasingly shun New York. As Jesse Jarnow (2012: 72) has written, 'after a few years in the New York trenches they started to decide playing in Manhattan didn't suit them'.
7. Little Cripples did not release any recordings, but of historical interest is that the band featured Michael Gira, who would go on to form influential no wave band Swans after he moved to New York. Gibson himself would eventually become a film music editor.
8. He contrasts Spheeris's depiction of the suburbs in *The Decline of Western Civilisation* and *Suburbia* with the films of John Hughes. While Hughes's films did often portray teenage angst in the suburbs, Taylor argues these were focused much more on middle and upper-class characters. Even though working-class characters did appear, the films tended to 'elide class difference' and present teenage life as a 'rite of passage through which the teens must pass in order to join a normative adult order' (Taylor 2017: 19).
9. A prominent, much remarked upon example is Johnny Rotten's 'I Hate Pink Floyd' T-shirt, in which Rotten had just scrawled 'I Hate' over the top of a Pink Floyd T-shirt, thus negating his former illegitimate tastes and proclaiming his status as a real punk.

6 DOCUMENTING SCENES AND PERFORMERS 2: GRUNGE AND RIOT GRRRL

This chapter focuses on grunge and riot grrrl, two modes of punk-inspired indie and alternative rock that emerged in the late 1980s and early 1990s. These movements demonstrate the continuing influence of punk, both in terms of sounds and attitudes, and both connect to issues that have been frequently addressed within indie cultures. In the case of grunge following its commercial breakthrough, questions about retaining anti-mainstream values in a market that was seeking to 'co-opt' alternative culture were regularly voiced. Riot grrrl, meanwhile, was a movement that stressed gender issues and sexism within indie music scenes. While it was much more opposed to engagement with mainstream media than many grunge acts were, and therefore at the time of its emergence in the early 1990s was far less popular than grunge, its influence has continued to grow over the years and has inspired a number of films, some of which are discussed in this chapter.

Grunge and Mass Media

While punk continued to influence various areas of music culture throughout the 1980s, the early 1990s witnessed a resurgence of a new form of punk music, grunge, which was commonly perceived as a merging of punk sounds with influences from metal. In this section, I want to focus on how grunge, which would eventually break into the mainstream, led to vociferous discussions around well-worn debates in indie music circles, such as 'selling out' and mass media's detrimental effects upon the integrity of previously niche subcultures.

I will commence this discussion through analysis of the independent documentary on grunge, *Hype!* (Pray, 1996), for even though this book largely focuses on fiction films, this documentary on grunge highlights such issues extremely prominently, albeit in ways that I will argue are problematic.

Hype! focuses on the Seattle music scene, particularly the grunge phenomenon, but it critiques the mass media reporting of the scene and purports to offer a more accurate overview of Seattle's music culture in the 1990s. As mentioned in Chapter 2, the huge success of Nirvana's 'Smells Like Teen Spirit' single and *Nevermind* album in 1991 elevated music that had emerged from punk/indie scenes to unprecedented levels, both in terms of sales and media coverage. Though the album was released by DCG (a subsidiary of Geffen Records), Nirvana were a core part of indie music in Seattle in the late 1980s, recording previously for the independent label Sub Pop. This moment created, however, a sense of crisis for many people affiliated with indie cultures; while on the one hand it exposed such music to a greater audience, on the other it threatened the exclusiveness of such music that many people prized (and, as mentioned in the Introduction, this crisis led to an increased use of 'indie' over 'alternative rock' within the United States).[1] Grunge music – and Seattle itself – was suddenly being covered by a variety of mass media outlets, and a raft of grunge bands were signed to major labels. For many participants within indie cultures, this resulted in oversaturation, common misunderstandings of the culture by mass media organs, as well as an overall dilution of the culture.

Hype! largely concerns itself with the mass media's reporting of grunge, though it is also partially a history of the Seattle indie music scene during the 1990s. The film presents the Seattle music scene as under threat from oversaturation and media hype. This threat is not from the media per se, however, but from corporate media. *Hype!* positions itself as an informed media product, created by people with an intimate knowledge and understanding of Seattle's music culture, and in doing so differentiates itself from the mass media, which is contrastingly represented as clueless and exploitative. The first point introduced in the film is that mass media have tended to *distort* the Seattle music scene, through focusing on grunge at the expense of other forms of independent music being performed and produced within the city.

The film's critiques of mass media coverage of grunge are not problematic per se, but the arguments aired tend to exaggerate demarcations between specialist media and mass media. As such, specialist media coverage is barely scrutinised in a critical manner, whereas mass media is considered purely critically. It is worth returning to Thornton's arguments about subculture here, particularly her contention that the media's role in *constructing* subcultures is often overlooked. While not explicitly stated in the film, *Hype!* implies that the independent music scene within Seattle is an organic, authentic culture that has been misrepresented by mass media; specialist media, in contrast, are important because of their more accurate reports of this culture. For the most part, the specialist media's role in contributing to the broader media images of Seattle's music scene in the early 1990s is largely overlooked, even though such processes are engaged with occasionally, most notably when Sub Pop's invitation to British music journalist Everett True is documented. True, a writer for alternative music weekly *Melody Maker*, was courted so that he could promote the emerging grunge sound to a British audience, and therefore potentially expand the market of such music (a process that was largely successful). Yet Sub Pop's core role in constructing an image of grunge that was then continued in the mass media following Nirvana's commercial breakthrough – albeit in sometimes ill-informed ways – is not examined sufficiently. Michael Azerrad, for example, has outlined how Sub Pop commonly hyped itself to the specialist music press and established 'a mythos about the label based on exaggeration' (Azerrad 2001: 440); while Ryan Moore has argued that Sub Pop 'constructed many of what would eventually become the early 1990s clichés about grunge and, by extension, Generation X, alternative music, "slackers," and so forth' (Moore 2010: 124–5).

Sub Pop began as a record label in 1988, though it was previously a fanzine started in 1979 by Bruce Pavitt from Olympia, Washington. Pavitt relocated to Seattle in 1983, where he continued the fanzine, wrote record reviews for music paper *The Rocket*, and presented a music show on the University of Washington radio station KCMU (Azerrad 2001: 412–14). In 1988 Pavitt created the Sub Pop record label with Jonathan Poneman, who had also hosted shows on KCMU. In *Hype!*, the label's contribution to mass media hyperbole is largely papered over and mostly displaced onto mass media.[2] Sub Pop was, however, extremely significant 'in the marketing and dissemination of the Seattle "sound", the Seattle "scene", and in the process, key narratives regarding the city of Seattle' (Lyons 2004: 124) and has been described by Michael Azerrad as 'more calculated than any previous American underground indie' (Azerrad 2001: 412). *Hype!* downplays the tactical and commercial aspects of local niche media to sustain its broad distinctions between niche and mass media. In doing so, it cannot confront how niche media 'like the music press construct subcultures as much as they document them', or how mass media coverage 'develop youth movements as much as they distort them' (Thornton 1995: 117). Consequently, the film adopts a somewhat elitist stance, most overtly expressed via clips of local independent music fans complaining about the music becoming too big and that the wrong kinds of people are now listening to it. At such points, issues around exclusivity and its loss come to the fore; but these are again not probed in detail, and such egregiously elitist attitudes are attributed to individual fans as opposed to the filmmakers.

Hype! also overlooks important questions related to the raced and gendered nature of the Seattle music scene. Grunge was largely performed, with a few exceptions, by white males, and many others involved in the scene – most prominently music writers – tended to be male. The film does include some interviews with females, but most interviewees are male. Despite the film's focus on the independent music scene in Seattle, it still privileges a largely white, indie-rock/alternative rock sound, conveniently overlooking other modes of independent music produced in the city. In this it once again reproduces some of the homogenising tendencies of the mass media that it purports to critique (and these homogenising tendencies were also evident in niche media's coverage of the Seattle music scene). While Seattle did not in the early 1990s have a huge non-white population, African Americans nevertheless accounted for approximately 10 per cent of its demographic, while Asian Americans accounted for 11.5 per cent (Lyons 2004: 65–6). In foregrounding whiteness, both mass and niche media further perpetuated implicit associations between indie music and whiteness, a topic which will be explored in more detail in Chapters 7 and 8.

Grunge music had already featured heavily in *Singles* (Crowe, 1991), a feature film that also depicted grunge musicians in Seattle. The film was widely debated and often dismissed as inauthentic by many grunge fans; in some ways it kickstarted debates around the co-option of a previously 'indie' scene and was the type of product that *Hype!* was railing against. While the film is a studio release (produced and distributed by Warner Bros.), it is worthy of discussion here as in the contemporary climate it might be considered an indie production due to its status as low-budget and specialist (though at the time its studio provenance was a factor in its dismissal); Warner Bros. did not at this stage have a specialist subsidiary.

The general tenor of arguments voiced by participants in *Hype!* – of the exploitation and dilution of the grunge movement and Seattle scene – were also applied frequently to *Singles*. Such perceptions would have been encouraged by the fact that the cultural currency of Seattle and grunge were key factors leading to the film finally being greenlit. The script of the film had been written long before the grunge phenomenon, but Crowe had trouble gaining studio interest. In a 1992 *New York Times* article, Michael Walker wrote how Crowe's 'penchant for making deliberately eccentric movies about real people in low-key situations baffles studio marketing departments accustomed to high-concept, plot-driven films' (Walker 1992: 7). Eventually, it was the commercial potential of grunge that led to the film being picked up by Warner Bros. The film's background in conjunction with the increase in media coverage of the Seattle scene, and a raft of rock-based indie bands being signed to major labels, were factors influencing the film's general dismissal within specialist and niche media. Kurt Cobain apparently hated the film, while Kaya Oakes (2009: 134) has written that the film was an example of the co-option of indie in the early 1990s and 'was enough to make an indie musician puke'.

The film received a warmer response, though, in more mainstream critical circles, a situation that arguably fuelled further negative reactions from those who felt that they understood the scene more intimately.

Many aspects of *Singles* can be considered slightly alternative through diverging from more common conventions of larger-budgeted Hollywood films. While it was far from radical, it did feature a moderately fragmentary narrative, an ensemble cast, and extensive spoken-to-camera diary moments, in which characters broke the fourth wall. Such aspects, alongside the lack of any obviously marketable components which could be used in promotion – such as special effects, or top-ranking stars – meant that the film was considered a hard sell initially. The soundtrack, however, enabled the film to be exploited in more conventional ways. The *Singles* soundtrack represents a mode of generic packaging, which Jeff Smith has noted became prominent in the 1990s (though it had started in the 1970s). He links this to Justin Wyatt's notion of 'high concept', where simple, marketable elements of the film could be easily pitched to industry executives on the one hand, and audiences on the other (Wyatt 1994: 8). Smith quotes Dick Wingate, senior Vice President of marketing at Arista Records: 'The most successful soundtrack albums have a focus, and to be fully focused you must have a genre of music that's the center of the album' (Smith 2001: 137). The soundtrack to *Singles* certainly reflected this, organised as it was largely around grunge and featuring tracks by acts including Pearl Jam, Soundgarden and Alice in Chains. There were a few tracks that were not classed as grunge on the soundtrack, but these were tracks that were nevertheless related to alternative/indie music, such as Paul Westerberg's two solo tracks and a track by the Smashing Pumpkins. Released prior to the film, its aim of appealing to grunge fans worked; it had sold 700,000 copies only ten weeks after its release on Epic Soundtrax and went on to achieve double platinum status. Not only did the sales of the soundtrack help to advertise the film, but other songs not included on the soundtrack album also played heavily on radio as a means of promotion. In the early 1990s, grunge and other forms of indie-rock were commonly connected to Generation X, leading to an increase in films – both independent and studio-produced – that focused on youthful disaffection and incorporated indie-rock prominently on their soundtracks. This led to tensions between the alternative/indie ethos that many fans of such music espoused and the increasing commercialisation of such sounds, tensions evident within *Hype!* and in numerous responses to *Singles*. The co-option of indie cultures was far from new – indie bands had long been signed by major labels and sometimes been accused of selling out – but the explosion of grunge and frequent articles on Generation X marked a particularly heightened relationship between indie and mainstream commercial cultures. The early 1990s was, according to Naomi Klein, a period when 'commercial co-optation was proceeding at a speed that would have been unimaginable to previous generations' (2001: 65). *Business Week* devoted a cover story to Generation X in December 1992, which indicated their importance as consumers: 'Grunge, anger, cultural dislocation, a secret yearning to belong: they add up to a daunting cultural anthropology that marketers have to confront if they want to reach twenty-somethings. But it's worth it. Busters do buy stuff' (quoted in Duncombe 2008: 137).[3] Alisa Perren (2012: 89) has noted how the indie film market also started to cater towards the Gen X constituency around the mid-90s as they became recognised as 'a prominent consumer force and cultural entity in their own right'. Within such a context, there could be extreme sensitivity to co-option: the dismissals of *Singles* by many who felt connected to indie scenes was indicative of such sensitivities. However, as mentioned in Chapter 2, a film such as *Clerks* used grunge music as part of a commercial strategy but was not dismissed in the same manner. Commercialism is not the only factor in judging a film's authenticity; other factors – including the provenance of the film – were also important in their reception: *Singles* stemmed from a Hollywood studio and was perceived as a calculated attempt to cash-in on a phenomenon, while *Clerks* was perceived more as an outsider film linked to a specific authorial vision.

SLAVES TO THE UNDERGROUND: POST-GRUNGE DILEMMAS AND GENDER ISSUES

Debates about selling out and authenticity were explicitly embedded within the script of *Slaves to the Underground* (Peterson, 1997). The film is set in Seattle and focuses on the independent music scene during a period when the Seattle/grunge phenomenon had begun to fade from mainstream consciousness, despite the continuation of many bands performing punk-inspired indie-rock. Directed by a woman – Kristine Peterson – and focusing on a female rock band, *Slaves to the Underground* moves beyond the themes addressed in *Hype!* to probe the masculinity and sexism of indie-rock scenes. The band, No Exits, are noted in promotional materials for the film as a 'grunge' band, and the film seeks to redress the often-overlooked female dimension of grunge: though a number of bands with significant female representation were connected to grunge – including 7 Year Bitch, Dickless, Hole and Babes in Toyland – such bands were more commonly overlooked than male bands.[4] The film also draws on the riot grrrl movement to an extent, which is not surprising considering its emphasis on female participation and because there were some overlaps between grunge and riot grrrl, such as the emergence of these movements in the Northwest of the US and the influence of punk on both (both musically and through a commitment to DIY).

Slaves to the Underground's main themes are the tensions between commercialism and independence, sexism within indie-rock scenes and generational specificity. As Ryan Moore has argued, the impact of Nirvana led to

Figure 6.1 *Slaves to the Underground*: Shelly and Suzie performing onstage with their band No Exits

the transformation of many indie communities 'as those in the corporate music industry came to believe that alternative music could be commercially lucrative after all, and so major-label representatives began to comb the local nightclubs in various cities in search of the next big thing' (Moore 2010: 114–15). *Slaves to the Underground* is set in the aftermath of grunge's commercial popularity. The impact of such commercialism, however, is evident throughout the film, notably in discussions and monologues that express antipathy towards corporate values; but such anti-commercial sentiments are also portrayed as difficult to sustain within a commercially driven society. For example, the character Jimmy (Jason Bortz) – who runs a fanzine – constantly expresses an anti-corporate ethos in earlier parts of the film. When his friend Dale (Peter Szumlas) turns up after being away for a year and mentions he has an interview at Microsoft, Jimmy accuses him of being a sell-out 'like everybody else in this town', accuses Bill Gates of being Satan, and claims that he 'wouldn't be caught dead working for Microsoft'.[5] Directly following this scene is a direct-to-camera, jump-cut montage of Jimmy standing in front of a stack of fanzines, discussing how they represent the future and dismissing mainstream media for being simplistic and superficial. He further argues that zines tell the truth as opposed to the lies peddled by mainstream media. Jimmy's logic exaggerates differences between independent and mainstream media and overstates the possibilities of mainstream media dying out. As such, while the film sympathises with his stance, it also implies such opinions are difficult to sustain when facing some of the harsh realities of everyday life. The main reality obstructing such ideals in the film is the need to survive, with such needs increasing as one gets older and takes on more responsibilities. When Jimmy renews a relationship with his former partner Shelly (Molly Gross), singer and guitarist in the band No Exits, he adopts a more responsible approach to life to support her. The irony is that he gets a job at Microsoft, therefore betraying his earlier-expressed ideals. Even after the two break up, Jimmy is saying that 'it is a really cool place to work'. Despite such harsh realities intruding on Jimmy's idealism, the film concludes with a commitment to independence and idealism: Jimmy still produces zines whilst working for Microsoft, and eventually is handed the reins of running the music venue by Big Phil (Bob Neurwith), who is stepping down.

Shelly, meanwhile, is making music as a solo artist. While No Exits are offered a record contract, their lead singer Suzy (Marissa Ryan) decides to leave the band to pursue political activism. Shelly concludes the film with a straight-to-camera sequence (mixed with her playing a solo gig at Jimmy's club) in which she extols independence, naming Ani DiFranco as a particular inspiration because she has released her music on her own label. Ultimately, then, the film does side with a commitment to independence and a desire to avoid selling out, pointing towards the possibilities of doing so through Shelly's reference to DiFranco; but it also demonstrates how difficult it is to sustain such independence and seems to warn against overly exaggerated distinctions between independence and commercialism.

While the film celebrates independent music culture, it doesn't present it in an entirely positive light. The most negative aspects of the indie scene presented are undoubtedly male-dominance and sexism. While writers such as Bannister (2006a; 2006b) and Houston (2012) have stressed how many men in indie-rock scenes have challenged 'hegemonic masculine norms' (Houston 2012: 160), they have also stressed the continuation of some forms of masculinity and sexism. Houston, for example, claims that 'the indie rock scene is predominantly a male space. Thus, even though it reportedly provides a place to construct alternative masculinities, it still has characteristics that limit women's presence and participation in the scene' (Ibid.: 172). Maria Raha (2005: xi) has argued that while punk and indie music communities tend to reject 'societal and cultural norms . . . that same community falls prey to those same traditional and confining notions of behavior in regards to gender and sexual identity'.

Riot grrrl culture, which emerged in the early 1990s, was focused on confronting sexism within indie/punk cultures, as well as within society more generally. While females had previously been involved in punk culture, and had often challenged sexism, punk cultures tended to remain a difficult space for women to exist in. This was particularly the case regarding hardcore punk, which, in the words of Gottlieb and Wald (1994: 257), 'negated gains women made in the punk movement'. Julia Downes has argued that even prior to the emergence of hardcore, female punks often had to repress their femininity:

> Women were able to carve out a powerful role within punk, albeit on the condition that women collude with the symbolic repression of the feminine deemed necessary for the constitution of punk subcultures. However, these identifications carried high costs: the rejection of conventional femininity effectively alienated women from each other and perpetuated a patriarchal devaluation of the feminine. (Downes 2012: 208)

Downes claims that riot grrrl culture constituted a far more explicitly feminist attack on punk's masculinist values (Ibid.: 208–9). The beginnings of riot grrrl are usually traced to Washington State and Washington DC, spearheaded by a number of core bands such as Bikini Kill, Bratmobile and Heavens to Betsy (Spiers 2015: 2), but the movement quickly broadened its influence beyond these places; Marion Leonard (1997: 233) has stated that as 'information about riot grrrl spread, networks of girls and women grew up across America and in Britain, communicating in letters, at meetings and through zines'.[6] Through their music and their writing – disseminated largely via zines – riot grrrls drew on feminism to express themselves, and would frequently address issues such as 'rape, assault, and the physical and psychological abuse of women' (Ibid.). While writings about these issues were sometimes painfully raw, they enabled riot grrrls to externalise their inner pain, gain confidence and make social contacts with other women to bring such issues to wider attention and effect change.

In *Slaves to the Underground*, it transpires that Shelly was raped by Dale when she was dating Jimmy. It is significant that sexual assault is perpetrated by someone within Shelly's group of friends, and that she does not even tell Jimmy about it (it is only later, following their separation, that he discovers this). This relates not only to the prevalence of sexual abuse being perpetrated by people known to the victim, but also demonstrates how such abuse could occur in supposedly progressive music scenes, issues that many riot grrrls had also confronted when they addressed the rife sexism within indie-rock. As Sara Marcus has written, 'In a subculture that congratulated itself for presenting an alternative, in a realm that should have been a refuge, they found more of the same crap' (Marcus 2010: 140). Many riot grrrl bands actively campaigned for women at gigs to move to the front, so that their concerts offered a safer, more comfortable space for women. While *Slaves to the Underground* does not represent such activity, the aggressive confrontation of sexism is evident, particularly via the character of Suzy, No Exits' lead singer. When Jimmy turns up at a gig to see No Exits with his friends Dale and Brian, Shelly spots Dale as she is about to perform (ironically, he is standing next to a 'Womyn's Resource Alert Phone Network').[7] Informing Shelly about the presence of her abuser,

Suzy – who is at this point Shelly's partner – proceeds to confront and then violently assault Dale, causing him such damage that he leaves the venue. Later in the film, when No Exits play a gig attended by record label reps, Brian and Jimmy are asked to leave the venue. The band's refusal to play unless the two leave is greeted with hostility, particularly from males, and leads to a mass brawl; Shelly then attempts to perform, but the other band members don't: Suzy, as the most aggressive band member, instead gets involved in the fighting.

As well as addressing sexism, the film also explores sexuality and sexual orientation, particularly through Shelly. At the beginning of the film Shelly is in a relationship with Suzy, but it is soon made clear that she has previously had a relationship with Jimmy. The three main characters therefore represent different sexual orientations. The film does not gloss over Shelly and Suzy's relationship and features scenes where they are intimate with each other. It seems, however, at around the mid-way point in the film, that Shelly's homosexual inclinations are going to be negated. It transpires that she broke up with Jimmy because of the trauma of her rape, so when she does split with Suzy and gets back together with Jimmy, her lesbianism appears to have been only a phase. The film does ultimately avoid such an unsatisfying conclusion: Shelly's renewed relationship with Jimmy does not satisfy her, and she once again leaves him, while Suzy leaves the band and Seattle. Shelly's address to the camera at the conclusion of the film indicates that she still desires other women (noting that she would like to 'fuck Ani DiFranco'), as well as stressing her newfound strength and independence (deciding to play music as a solo musician and not signing to a major label with No Exits).

The focus on lesbianism within *Slaves to the Underground* also connects to riot grrrl culture, as many riot grrrl artists 'identified as queer or lesbian' (Keenan 2020: 18). Both Keenan (Ibid.) and Kearney (1997: 217–22) have argued that the queerness of riot grrrl was often played down within media reports of the phenomenon, despite the overlaps between riot grrrl and 'queercore'. Queercore referred to queer punk musicians; many artists associated with queercore would also, like riot grrrls, produce fanzines and create networks to support other queer punk and indie artists. *Slaves to the Underground*, while not mentioning explicitly the term 'queercore' – or, for that matter 'riot grrrl' – nevertheless draws on both these movements in a manner that stresses their overlaps and linkages, rather than playing down such connections.

Slaves to the Underground also comments on generational issues, most notably the concept of Generation X. The term itself – along with another oft-used word applied to this generation, the 'slacker' – is mentioned by Jimmy in his rant about mainstream media discussed earlier. Within his monologue, he indicates that terms such as Generation X and 'slacker' are mass-mediated constructs that are frequently drawn upon in attempts to describe a generation, but are merely superficial generalisations: 'Look at what I'm wearing, look at my haircut. Am I a slacker? Do I belong to Generation X? The mainstream media wouldn't focus on me and they would label me in a second.' Jimmy indicates that mainstream media accounts of indie culture are framed by people from outside of the culture, who have limited knowledge of the people and scenes they report upon, tending to frame them as others in ways that overstress style and appearance at the expense of substance. Of course, generational attitudes and ideologies were also reported, though Jimmy's reference to slackers indicates that these were also liable to simplification and exaggeration, at least as far as cultural insiders were concerned. Jimmy might not be financially secure, existing as he does tangentially to mainstream culture, but he is far from work-shy or cynical; rather he is constantly busy and very positive about the potential of indie media production. Shelly and the other members of No Exits are also far from apathetic or cynical, either. The direct-to-camera monologues in the film function partly to distance it from being a standard mediated product that incorporates stereotypical 'Generation X' tropes as a means of catering to that very generation (or at least notable portions of it). There had, as mentioned in Chapter 2, been a spate of studio-backed films that licensed numerous indie-rock tracks and harnessed them to rebellious and cynical young people railing against their elders, and/or which valorised independence over corporate culture, including *S.F.W.* (Levy, 1994), *Reality Bites* (Stiller, 1994) and *Empire Records* (Moyle, 1995).[8] While *Slaves to the Underground* is certainly less cynical than some of these films, it is still an attempt to represent – and in the process make money from – indie music cultures related to Generation X. Further, while Jimmy's monologue questions

Figure 6.2 *Slaves to the Underground*: Jimmy discusses independent media in a direct-to-camera monologue

the generalised simplifications of Generation X, Shelly's direct-to-camera monologues often reflect on the demarcation between Gen Xers and Baby Boomers.

The first of Shelly's monologues is positioned early in the film, which opens with a focus on her rehearsing with No Exits. The song immediately sets the tone of anger in response to sexual assault, as she sings lines such as 'I'd like to fuck you up, I'd like to see you scared, I want to see you drop', and this theme is reinforced through a brief intercut scene of her scrawling the name of 'Dale Edmonds' (her abuser) in a toilet cubicle amongst other graffiti including 'no more rape' and 'womyn take back the night'. The next scene shows Shelly briefly watching television, and then discussing *The Graduate* (Nichols, 1967) in a direct-to-camera monologue. Shelly uses the film to frame a discussion on the differences, as well as some continuities, between her and her parents' generation. Noting that the film is her mum's favourite movie, she proceeds to emphasise the creepy sexual politics of the film, asserting that Benjamin is really a stalker and a 'selfish, irresponsible, proto-slacker'. That the film was largely received as romantic fuels her disgust of the Baby Boomers who embraced it. While Shelly does here draw on broad generational schisms, she nevertheless indicates overlaps when stressing the proto-slacker credentials of Benjamin in *The Graduate*. She therefore complicates some of the broad distinctions commonly noted between Baby Boomers and Gen Xers (while at the same time drawing on those distinctions). The slacker was the 'most pervasive stereotype' (Hanson 2002: 40) adopted to describe Gen Xers and tended to refer to aimless, cynical, disenchanted youths. Through drawing a connecting thread between Benjamin and the modern slacker figure, Shelly also emphasises gender divisions within generations and stresses issues of sexual abuse across both generations, particularly the sexual immaturity of many male slackers (and proto-slackers).

Slaves to the Underground attempts, like the documentary *Hype!*, to move beyond the stereotypes associated with Generation X and indie-rock cultures (particularly, but not limited to, grunge) and proffer a grittier, more authentic vision of this culture. It is a more complex reflection than *Hype!*, however, mainly because it moves beyond the unreflective male focus of that film and adopts a slightly more nuanced engagement with independence/mass media debates. While some of the sentiments expressed in the film denote firm distinctions between indie and mass media, with the film positing the former as more ethical and authentic, indie cultures are not presented as unproblematic: in addition to highlighting gender issues, the film also stresses the difficulties of living outside of the oft-denigrated mainstream. Even though the two main characters – Shelly and Jimmy – continue to pursue their passions at the conclusion, Jimmy has already worked for Microsoft (and softened his hatred of the corporation), while Shelly has been caught up in attempting to get her band No Exits signed to a label, before deciding to pursue a more independent path.

Slaves to the Underground, like many of the punk and post-punk films discussed in this chapter, values authenticity but also highlights the difficulties of being authentic within a mass-mediated landscape. The film exemplifies some traits associated with Generation X in its rather ambivalent, often cynical, relationship to mass media despite a heavy immersion in such media, particularly television, cinema, music and video games. Peter Hanson (2002: 51) has argued that Gen Xers were exposed 'to nonstop junk culture' and 'given countless opportunities to peer behind the curtain of said junk culture'. He further stated:

> These opportunities helped produce unprecedented media-related savviness, which often manifests as cynicism (a been-there, done-that attitude toward entertainment) and/or fascination (an endless appetite for behind-the-scenes information). In fact, an ambivalent mixture of cynicism and fascination probably is the most prevalent attitude toward pop culture reflected in Gen-X cinema. (51)

This media savviness also led some members of this generation to become suspicious of overt advertising and other ways of being 'sold' something. It was fuelled also by the huge increase in advertising across different areas of life: Naomi Klein (2000: 83) has argued that by the early 1990s, youths were being bombarded by marketing messages to an unprecedented degree. While she stresses that advertisers targeting youth was not new, she argues that the growing youth market now became one of the most important demographics within marketing following a drying up of Baby Boomer spending and the early 1990s economic recession. To successfully target youths, however, marketing tactics would need to change; Klein (2000: 86) outlines how branding was key here:

> It was not going to be sufficient for companies simply to market their same products to a younger demographic; they needed to fashion brand identities that would resonate with this new culture. If they were going to turn their lacklustre products into transcendent meaning machines – as the dictates of branding demanded – they would need to remake themselves in the image of nineties cool: its music, styles and politics.

Brands were increasingly linked to ideal lifestyles that one either felt part of or wanted to belong to. However, because the Gen X demographic was considered media savvy, advertisers created more self-conscious and ironic messages in efforts to avoid perceptions amongst young consumers that they were being sold to in a direct, obvious fashion. Jim McGuigan (2009: 109) has elaborated on the intricate tactics of 'cool advertising':

Consistent with the assumed scepticism of such groups, the advertising industry denies its own effectiveness, thereby seeking to undercut critical claims concerning its own overwhelming influence. A game of reflexive knowingness is played out in the interaction between cool advertising and its most favoured subject groups: the hard-sell is frowned upon and everything is done in a tongue-in-cheek manner, not to be taken seriously.

Naomi Klein has stressed how presenting oneself as 'indie' was also a way to appear cool, and therefore attractive to the youth demographic. This was, after all, a period in which 'alternative' and/or 'indie' rock was appealing to large swathes of youths with disposable income, and the appeal of indie cinema was also growing. As mentioned in the opening chapter, takeovers of both indie music labels and indie film companies were occurring regularly during this period, along with the establishment of specialty indie-style divisions. Klein (2000: 86) has noted how youths became increasingly aware of such tactics, which led to an increase in more ironic forms of mass cultural consumption. But this argument overlooks how ideas of authenticity within indie cultures were still important to many (it is probably more accurate to consider ironic forms of consumption as co-existing with authentic engagement). The emergence of cool capitalism, ironic consumption and lifestyle segmentation informed a very complicated network of socio-cultural relations which were beset with many contradictions. By the mid-1990s it was incredibly difficult to live outside the orbit of commercial/consumer culture; one could certainly distance oneself from it, but only often by degrees.

Slaves to the Underground was a low-budget film without studio involvement. Even though director Kristine Peterson had mainly worked in low-budget, often straight-to-video genre films, this film was slightly different in being grounded in knowledge of indie-rock music scenes. It was written by Bill Cody, who had previously produced a documentary film about the mid-1980s independent music scene in Athens, *Athens, Ga. – Inside Out* (Gayton, 1987), but the most important symbol of authenticity was – like other films discussed in this chapter – conveyed via music and performance. The soundtrack contains numerous indie tracks, mostly punk-related, sourced from independent labels.[9] Many artists featured were not high-profile, and – chiming with the focus on female musicians – the soundtrack was dominated by female artists: music licensed was either by solo female artists, all-female groups or bands that had significant female representation, except for Mike Martt, who provides the score. Martt, a solo artist who has also been a member of many bands including T.S.O.L. and The Gun Club, further contributed to some of the music performed by fictional band No Exits. The majority of No Exits' songs, however, were written by Beth Carmellini and Jenni McElrath from L.A. punk band Red Five. Two artists featured had a bigger profile than most:

Abby Travis, singer of L7, sang a cover of 'Give Me Just a Little More Time' with the band Mommy; while Joan Jett also features on two tracks as part of the band Evil Stig. Jett had by this point become an icon amongst female indie-rockers as a female rock artist who had set up her own record label (Blackheart Records), and she produced and performed on Bikini Kill's 1993 'New Radio' EP. Evil Stig consisted of Jett and members of the band The Gits, and formed to perform a series of live benefit concerts to fund an investigation into the murder of former Gits singer Mia Zapata, who was raped and murdered in 1993. Her appearance thus links to two major themes of the film: females performing rock music and the assault of women.[10]

Some other films also demonstrated a riot grrrl influence in the late 1990s and 2000s. In the remainder of the chapter, I focus on one film that centres on an all-female indie-rock band – *Down and Out with the Dolls* (Voss, 2001) – and on one film that is inspired more by the political activities of riot grrrls than their music (though music is nevertheless an important presence): *The Itty Bitty Titty Committee* (Babbit, 2007). Music associated with riot grrrl had already appeared on the soundtrack of some independent features. A notable case is the lesbian drama *All Over Me* (Sichel, 1997), which includes music by Sleater-Kinney and other female artists such as Ani DiFranco, Babes in Toyland and Patti Smith. While the film does not centre on a music scene per se, it does focus on two protagonists who occasionally attempt to play music together, albeit lacking much commitment, and features a band playing in one scene that includes Leisha Hailey from The Murmurs and Uh Huh Her. Hailey has a minor role in the film as Lucy, who becomes romantically involved with central character Claude (Alison Folland). Riot grrrl culture does not inform the content of the film as directly in this film as it does *Down and Out with the Dolls* and *The Itty Bitty Titty Committee*, hence my decision to focus on these films in more detail.

Down and Out with the Dolls

Some of the themes explored within *Slaves to the Underground* also inform *Down and Out with the Dolls*, though *Dolls* is a more comedic, satirical – and occasionally campy – take on the issue of women in indie music scenes. The film is directed by Kurt Voss, who as noted in Chapter 2 has co-directed a trilogy of films based around musicians with Allison Anders. With this film, he teamed up with Nalina 'Deedee' Cheriel, who co-wrote the film. Both Voss and Cheriel had backgrounds in music and were members of the band The Hindi Gods. The film is loosely based on Cheriel's background: she was involved in the Northwest indie music scenes in the 1990s and was a member of all-female bands such as Teen Angels, Juned and Adickdid (which also featured Kaia Wilson of Team Dresch).

Down and Out with the Dolls is set in Portland, Oregon, and centres on fictional band The Paper Dolls. As with many other films depicting indie music cultures, numerous scenes unfold in recurrent spaces such as the independent record store and the local nightclub. The film is populated by fanzine writers, music label owners, producers and other people who work in the independent music scene, and includes varied musical performances such as rehearsals, live performances and studio recording. As with many films discussed in this chapter, the musical performances are authenticated by the input of actual musicians, despite the film's comedic tone. It features appearances by actual musicians, three of whom are responsible for creating the music performed by The Paper Dolls. These are Zoë Poledouris, Coyote Shivers and Jerome Dillon. None of these musicians can straightforwardly be deemed indie, and they were also based in L.A. rather than in the Northwest. This might be linked to how the film is not a straightforward, 'serious' representation of an all-female music band, but also reflects the schisms within the fictional band The Paper Dolls, who are split between independent, integrity-focused values and more commercially ambitious desires. The film also features independent Canadian music artist Kinnie Starr, who plays Reggie, and a rather bizarre cameo from Motörhead's Lemmy, who lives in Fauna's closet.

Poledouris's character, Fauna, overtly represents naked ambition in the film. Near the beginning, she has an argument in a bar with her bandmate and partner, Paulo, leading to the demise of their band, The Snogs. Snogs fan Kali (Nicole Barrett), who is serving at the bar and is also in an all-girl band, spots an opportunity to play music with Fauna, but her earnest request to play is met with a non-verbal, icy dismissal. Fauna is immediately presented as rather aloof and selfish, traits which become even more pronounced as the narrative progresses. She does soon join Kali's band, The Paper Dolls, in an opportunistic manoeuvre, but her attitude is immediately contrasted to theirs. The scene in a bar where Kali attempts to connect with Fauna also introduces the theme of gender and rock. Reggie, who serves at the bar and is also in Kali's band, has a partner Mulder (Brendan O'Hara), who complains to her and Kali about not being allowed in the band. This leads to the following exchange:

Kali: 'Mulder, this is a girl band, get it?'
Mulder: 'You know, there was a time when men ruled rock. They fucking ruled.'
Reggie: 'Yeah, well that time is over.'

Kali and Reggie subsequently fist bump in solidarity, emphasising their strength. Mulder himself is a rather pathetic figure: he is constantly ordered around by Reggie and adopts a role that would more traditionally be considered 'feminine': he hangs around the house that the band move into like a groupie, desperate to be involved in their band. The partner of fellow Paper Dolls band member Lavender (Melody Moore), Discourage Records owner Clark (Shawn Robinson), also displays a jealous attitude towards her involvement in the band, which becomes more pronounced as they start to attract increased interest from record labels.

The second time Fauna encounters Kali is in a bar when the latter is talking to musician Levi, whom she knew when she was younger and has reintroduced herself following his performance at the Discourage record store. Fauna, seeing Kali talking to Levi, now asks her about possibly joining her band. When Kali tells Fauna that they are an all-girl band, Fauna lowers her eyes in contempt and reluctantly states 'I guess that's okay'. Fauna has only really joined the band because she is both desperate and sees this as an opportunity to get closer to Levi, who has status within the indie music world (though he has performed solo, he is a member of a New York-based band, The Suicide Bombers). Her unenthusiastic reaction to joining an all-girl band demonstrates how she has internalised some of the male perspectives on female rock musicians. Her views will increasingly place her at odds with the other band members: she lacks any solidarity with them, often belittles their skills and wants to move them in a more commercially viable direction. Her cravings for fame and money also lead her to sexually seduce men in positions of power, such as Levi and the record label owner, Bill Black.

While Kali is mostly presented as a positive indie female rocker in contrast to Fauna, there are occasional moments which undermine this dichotomy. Fauna may be opportunistic and mostly unpleasant, but she is also a commanding performer who acts as an inspiration for Kali and helps to improve the band. Their first informal performance, in a private garden to a small audience, is dynamic: Fauna is a compelling, confident performer who grabs attention. Performing the punchy, punk-pop 'Dig Butt', she strides around the small, impromptu stage in commanding fashion. The dynamism of the performance is heightened by the way it is filmed: rapidly edited, it shifts shot scales and angles frequently, capturing different members of the band (but most prominently Fauna) and the small crowd gathered to watch, including a disgruntled Paulo, who is tending the barbecue. Compared to many of the live musical performances discussed in this chapter, *Down and Out with the Dolls* has a more kinetic feel, facilitated by digital cameras, which gels with the film's hyperreal aesthetic. At one point during a rehearsal, Fauna attacks one of Kali's songs in a nasty, patronising manner, which initially comes across as a straightforward schism between the honesty and raw authenticity of Kali and the ambitious commercialism of Fauna (she responds to Kali's defence of her lyrics as expressing her feelings with 'your feelings aren't commercial'). However, later in the film, following a successful gig in front of a packed audience, Kali's voice-over narration states: 'chalk it up to the benefits of creative

Figure 6.3 *Down and Out with the Dolls*: Fauna performs for the first time with The Paper Dolls in a private garden

conflict, but with that show The Paper Dolls sounded better than we ever had before'. So, while authenticity and honesty are celebrated in the film, there is – via Fauna's challenges and her contribution to the band's improvement – an implicit critique of an insular, overly amateurish approach to music-making informing the film. While she proves almost impossible to work with because of her incredible selfishness, Fauna acts as a catalyst: by the end of the film, following the demise of The Paper Dolls, Kali has become wiser about the music business and adopts a more 'professional' commitment to her art, but without compromising her need to express herself. A voice-over by Lavender informs us that Kali eventually joined up with the surviving members of The Suicide Bombers following Levi's overdose and concludes with Lavender and Clark playing one of Kali's records at Discourage. Fauna, meanwhile, is symbolically punished for her transgressions: she is in a band with her former partner Paulo and his new partner, reduced to playing second fiddle as a backing singer/tambourine player (and looking very miserable).

The film not only features many musical artists as actors and/or musical contributors, but the character of Fauna seems loosely based on Courtney Love, who herself was involved in the Portland rock scene when she was younger (she would later, following a period in England, return to L.A., where she formed Hole). Love was a controversial figure and, though many media reports of her were undoubtedly exaggerated, she was nevertheless ambitious and highly motivated, which put her at odds with the riot grrrl movement at times. She would criticise the movement for its inwardness and homogeneity, and for labelling her a 'wrong' kind of feminist. She even wrote a withering song for Hole about riot grrrls ('Rock Star', from Hole's 1994 breakthrough album *Live Through This*), and reportedly punched Kathleen Hannah at the 1994 Lollapalooza festival. While Fauna is not directly modelled on Love, her ambition, calculatedness and tendency to offend do allude to her (or at least media portrayals of her). In films based on actual music scenes – however loosely or seriously – it is inevitable that some connection to real-life figures will occur, even if characters are not directly modelled on actual people. Such films play rather complex games: they often feature actual musicians to bolster their credibility as 'authentic' depictions of musical scenes and figures, and allude to other figures and actual scenes, but incorporate these elements into fictions that adhere to conventions that sometimes pull away from credibility. This is even the case with a film like *Down and Out with the Dolls*, which is highly exaggerated but also still rooted in a 'real' scene (in this case, feminist-inspired musicians within the Portland indie-rock scene).

The Itty Bitty Titty Committee

The Itty Bitty Titty Committee is a film about a radical feminist group directed by Jamie Babbit – who had previously directed the conversion camp satire *But I'm a Cheerleader* (1999) – and produced by POWER UP, an organisation devoted to promoting the visibility of gay women in the media.[11] While the film is not focused directly on a music scene, it was inspired by the riot grrrl movement and features extensive use of female-fronted indie-rock music, including some scenes at a music venue. Babbit (2007: 3) herself noted the importance of riot grrrl music in the film's press release, claiming that it 'changed my ideas about feminism and politics', and that she 'wanted to create a film that was the cinematic equivalent of this music'. The film's focus on a group of direct-action political feminists, rather than on a music scene, foregrounds how riot grrrl culture was involved in political activity and organisation beyond the music scene, particularly in attempting to update feminism for a new generation and actively challenging patriarchal dominance.

The film's narrative follows Anna (Melonie Diaz), a middle-class Latina lesbian who works at a cosmetic surgery clinic and who has recently been dumped by a girlfriend. Despite her lesbianism, she is otherwise presented as a rather straight, naïve character. We initially see her trying on dresses for her sister's impending wedding, working at the reception of the clinic and brooding over her former girlfriend. Her world is turned upside down when she spots someone spraying feminist graffiti – 'A woman is more than her parts' – over the front of the clinic where she works. Hiding behind a bush, Anna initially attempts to alert the police but is caught by the graffitist, who turns out to be Sadie (Nicole Vicius), a member of radical feminist group C(i)A (Clits in

Action). Sadie informs Anna of the group and invites her to a meeting they are having in the evening. When Anna does appear at the meeting, she is viewed suspiciously by some of the members, particularly Shulamith, who criticises her for working in a cosmetic surgery clinic. While Anna has only gone to the meeting because of an attraction to Sadie, she becomes much more committed throughout the narrative after being 'schooled' by Sadie and participates in many of the public stunts that the group undertakes.

The idea of schooling not only informs the narrative of *The Itty Bitty Titty Committee*; as B. Ruby Rich (2013: 206) has argued, the film is also a 'history lesson', so has the potential to school audiences.[12] The film itself is partially an attempt to highlight – and spur further interest in – other feminist movements, people and cultural expressions, which are not restricted to riot grrrls. One other central text that the film is inspired by, and alludes to, is Lizzie Borden's *Born in Flames* (1983), a low-budget, feminist docu-drama set in an alternate near-future, ten years after a socialist revolution. It follows different feminist groups highlighting the continuing subjection of women in everyday life, who are actively organising for change and increasingly subject to police surveillance. The film has gained a reputation for its radicalism and for its intersectional approach to feminism. It does not present feminism as a unified movement but instead focuses on different groups, both white and black; although differences between these groups are foregrounded, they do eventually come together despite their disagreements to fight for a common cause (sparked by the suspicious death of black political activist Adelaide Norris in police custody). Borden's focus on lesbian activists, and on media – both official media and alternative media, most saliently represented by pirate radio broadcasts – are also crucial influences on *The Itty Bitty Titty Committee*. Babbit also mirrored Borden's production methods: both films were made by a largely female crew and shot on 16mm (though *The Itty Bitty Titty Committee* does also include some scenes shot in Super 8mm).

Beyond these core influences, the film alludes to numerous other important cultural and political referents. B. Ruby Rich has noted how it assembles a raft of intertextual links:

> Babbit invokes an entire roster of names with this film, a blast from the past, as though she'd synthesized a mixtape of lesbian and feminist Greatest Hits into the shapes, politics, and subtexts of her screenplay in a bid to make once-powerful ideas live and breathe again. (Rich 2013: 203)

The antics of the group are also inspired, as Babbit (2007: 3) has noted, by the Guerrilla Girls, a feminist art collective established in 1985, who donned gorilla masks and created performance actions and other art to protest the male-dominated art world. In the same press pack, Babbit also states that PETA were an influence on the film's activist performances, and further claims that the group run by Courtney – the more conventional feminist NGO Women for Change – was based on the National Organization for Women. She further describes the film's visual aesthetic as influenced by punk zines, 'punk photos from the CBGB's days', and Jill Reiter's short *Frenzy* (1993), a queer film about rock groupies that starred Kathleen Hannah. The film also features a scene in which an Angela Davis effigy is dumped outside city hall, while the character Shulamith is named after Shulamith Firestone, the radical feminist who wrote *The Dialectic of Sex: The Case for Feminist Revolution* (1970). Many cast members and other crew had links to feminist and/or lesbian culture which encourages, in Rich's words (Rich 2013: 205), 'her publics to recognize their lineages on the screen and invest accordingly'. Guinevere Turner, who plays the news reporter Marcy, was in Rose Troche's seminal NQC film *Go Fish* (1994) and Cheryl Dunye's *The Watermelon Woman* (1996); Daniel Sea, who plays Calvin, had played a trans character in the ensemble television series *The L Word* (Showtime, 2004–9), a show centred on lesbian and bisexual characters; Jenny Shimizu, who plays Laurel, is a lesbian model who shot to fame when she was hired to model for Calvin Klein in the 1990s; while Melanie Mayron, who plays the older Courtney, had starred in Claudia Weill's acclaimed feminist feature *Girlfriends* (1978). Many of the crew had also been involved in gay and lesbian film productions and the film's composer – Radio Sloan – has a background in indie music, having played in queercore band The Need and many other bands; Sloan also contributed to Le Tigre's 2005 album *This Island* and has toured with electro-punk artist Peaches.

As riot grrrl is a key influence on the film, it is unsurprising that the film is saturated with music cues and other references to feminist-oriented, female-led music. The soundtrack features much riot grrrl music, mainly songs from Bikini Kill and Heavens to Betsy. The singers of these respective bands – Kathleen Hannah and Corin Tucker – are also heavily represented through the groups they subsequently formed, Le Tigre and Sleater-Kinney. Other artists featured on the soundtrack include The Need, Peaches, Slant 6, Slumber Party and Team Dresch. The music is largely punk-influenced: even Le Tigre and Peaches, who use more electronic sounds than other artists on the soundtrack, are often considered electro-punk through their incorporation of digital music into punk-inspired sounds and attitudes. Music is not merely a frequent sonic presence in the film, it also informs the mise-en-scène: Anna's transformation into a politicised feminist is visually highlighted by the way that she transforms her bedroom after she scrawls feminist graffiti over her walls and adorns them with posters and flyers, including a Le Tigre poster. We also see her participate in her first series of activist disruptions with the C(i)A in a Super 8mm montage sequence, culminating in Sadie introducing Anna to numerous books and music CDs (as part of her education), including releases by The Gossip,

P. J. Harvey, Sleater-Kinney, Tiger Trap and a Kill Rock Stars compilation.[13] This montage sequence highlights the importance of music and politics, linking certain artists with other important inspirations, including writing on DIY culture and feminism.

The music venue is also an important space within the film: many C(i)A members go to see live music being played and it functions as a backdrop to some of the interpersonal dynamics being played out between Sadie and Anna. Sadie takes Anna to the venue when they are getting to know one another, and the band are playing Bikini Kill's 'Rebel Girl', one of the most well-known riot grrrl songs. Later, Anna becomes intimate with Aggie – mainly to spite Sadie following her inability to fully commit to a relationship – and the band are playing Heaven to Betsy's 'White Girl'. As with many films that document performers and music scenes, the band – The Cheerleaders – consists of real musicians, most notably Patty Schemel on drums (probably best known for being a member of Hole) and Camila Grey on guitar (member of numerous indie-rock bands, including Uh Huh Her). This inclusion of real musicians is, as noted, a strategy that imbues the film with a sense of authenticity on the one hand, though in this film it also links to the plethora of linkages established via casting and other intertextual references.

The character Courtney represents a different type of feminist to the C(i)A members and it is through this contrast that generational differences are also limned. Courtney is associated with more formal, legitimate attempts to effect political change, in contrast to the C(i)A's more transgressive, subterranean strategies. Courtney's group, Women for Change, participates in mainstream political commentary and holds board meetings that make use of official statistics to outline gender inequalities. Her relationship with Sadie leads to differences between the groups being openly debated on occasions, during which critiques of their respective positions are aired: while Women for Change are perceived by C(i)A as rather dry, boring and compromised, Courtney considers the C(i)A as puerile and ineffective. As the film focuses mainly on the actions of C(i)A members, their position is presented to the audience as exciting and appealing, but Courtney's criticisms of the group do point to some limitations of their activist approach. Firstly, Courtney indicates that by merely undertaking symbolic performances outside of official legislation, their ability to concretely improve the lives of women is limited. Her authority within discussions is heightened by the fact that she provides for Sadie and is in a relationship weighted in her favour; Sadie's role, by contrast, is somewhat parasitic. Through operating more formally, Courtney can not only effect political change – even if this is sometimes compromised – but also attain a secure livelihood. The more extreme and radical acts of the C(i)A place them outside of more mainstream institutions, which leads to problems of survival. So, while they do not have to compromise by engaging with mainstream institutions, including mainstream

Figure 6.4 *The Itty Bitty Titty Committee*: Sadie graffities a wall as part of a Super 8 montage

media, and can therefore politicise in more direct, radical ways, they do have to compromise in terms of forging alliances with women who can finance their lifestyles. Courtney is the most notable of such figures, but Laurel is another character who provides for them. She tells Anna at one point that she 'has a real job' and pays 'real rent, so you so-called political feminists can camp out on the floor for free'. Such criticisms point to the difficulties in sustaining underground movements, whether culturally and/or politically, and mirror the previously discussed issues of attaining independence within a commercialised environment. Their sustainability may also be imperilled by interpersonal tensions, as is the case with the C(i)A, who eventually split because of them (before reassembling towards the conclusion to pull off their biggest stunt). Yet even though the revolutionary ideals of the C(i)A are difficult to sustain, in contrast to the more realistic, grounded attempts to make incremental changes within the system represented by Women for Action, they are presented as appealing. The excitement and dynamism of their direct actions, bolstered by the energetic riot grrrl and associated music, is fully communicated by the briskly edited immediacy of the montages.

B. Ruby Rich has argued that the C(i)A can be considered carnivalesque, in the sense that they perform symbolic actions that can feed the imagination and point towards better worlds:

> Culture does not follow the linear track of political action: it works on perception, subterranean and subtle, and lodges in dreams. To act, in

life as in film, we must first imagine acting . . . A carnivalesque action frees the imagination to envision a different world, a sort of voluntary amnesia in which obstacles and disciplines can be 'forgotten' long enough to be flouted, with the fond hope that they won't necessarily be 'remembered'. (Rich 2013: 210)

The importance of the imaginary in inspiring political action and consciousness is evident in the main influence on the film itself, riot grrrl culture. Riot grrrls were sometimes criticised for their naivety and dependence on revolutionary slogans, but there is no doubt that they have had a huge cultural impact over the years and have introduced many to feminist politics. *The Itty Bitty Titty Committee* aims to have the same impact through focusing on the excitement of participating in direct action and attaining a more liberated, feminist consciousness. The aesthetic of the film seems to reinforce its meshing of concrete action and imaginary fancy: while it is rooted in authentic nods to punk on the one hand through its hand-held Super 8mm and 16mm footage, music and depiction of underground cultural production, it also contains fairytale elements. Babbit herself has stated how she has always admired, and drawn on, fairytales, and described the film as 'a punk feminist fairytale for everyone wishing the world was a more enlightened place' (Babbit 2007: 3). In light of such comments, and following the point made by Rich, it is less important whether the actions depicted in the film are realistic so much as that they spur the imaginations of audiences.

Conclusion: Race and its (Relative) Absence

Despite being inspired by *Born in Flames*, Babbit's *The Itty Bitty Titty Committee* is relatively coy in its approach to racial issues. While Borden's film acknowledged the importance of racial differences in framing feminist politics, Babbit's film does not do so to the same extent, despite centring around a Latina character (and including, albeit in a much more minor role, an Asian American in Laurel, played by Jenny Shimizu). While Anna is positioned as an outsider to the C(i)A group, these outsider characteristics are largely attributed to her conventional lifestyle and naivety: her racial difference is not overtly addressed within the film. Likewise, *Down and Out with the Dolls* focuses on a band led by an Asian American character, Kali, but her race is once again largely absent from discussion. There is one scene where it is addressed, and dismissed, by Fauna, which does allude to racial tensions within riot grrrl cultures, albeit very briefly. When Fauna attacks the song Kali has just written, she also includes the line 'How am I supposed to sing it, I mean I'm not half Thai'. The film mainly glosses over Kali's ethnicity, however, and focuses much more on questions of commercial compromise and female participation within indie-rock. *Slaves to the Underground*, meanwhile, only features white major characters: while we can occasionally spot a person of colour in the background of live performances, there is again an absence of discussion of such matters.

This is slightly surprising considering that the whiteness of riot grrrl cultures and indie music more generally has been discussed. Kearney writes:

> While we might want to applaud the gains many riot grrrl bands have made in male-dominated punk scenes, we do well to investigate how the privileging of riot grrrls as the revolutionary musical offspring of punk reaffirms, rather than deconstructs, the popular understanding of rock's heterosexual whiteness. (Kearney 1997: 217)

There were some women of colour involved in riot grrrl culture, but according to Mimi Thi Nguyen they often felt excluded and frustrated at the tokenistic roles they were assigned. Many complained that when they did raise objections, their voices were quickly drowned out. White riot grrrls often assumed commonalities between all female members, regardless of other differences, and this was particularly pronounced in terms of overlooking the very different historical experiences of black people. As Nguyen argues:

> The raising of consciousness did not aim to end structural determinations, and instead ossified its categories of class or gender as an absolute reality to predict social expression . . . But how then could experience yield revolutionary knowledge about race, where the dominant experience was whiteness? (Nguyen 2015: 179)

Slaves to the Underground perpetuates the dominant whiteness of female indie-rock, while the inclusion of women of colour in central roles in both *Down and Out with the Dolls* and *The Itty Bitty Titty Committee* does not really move beyond a tokenistic incorporation of racial diversity. While Anna in *The Itty Bitty Titty Committee* may undergo a schooling in feminist politics that moves her away from a previously naïve political position, this is an education provided by a predominantly white feminist group, so she is also moving away from her ethnic background, which becomes largely invisible when she becomes fully ensconced in the C(i)A.

White dominance, privilege and racist assumptions are not merely limited to riot grrrl cultures, however, but are firmly linked to many areas of indie music, particularly indie-rock, its most dominant mode. In the next chapter I will explore some of these issues in more detail, paying attention to films made by African American filmmakers.

Notes

1. The commercial breakthrough of Nirvana, and other grunge acts, brought to the surface tensions that have often existed within various indie music scenes: between an avoidance of the mainstream and commercial compromise on the one hand, and a desire to seek wider audiences and earn more money on the other. People involved in such scenes were more likely to embrace the former in an ethical sense, but some proclaimed antipathy towards the small-scale insularity of indie scenes, while even those who embraced the small-scale ethos might be led towards expansion – such as making deals with major record labels – due to financial necessities. Kurt Cobain himself seemed more conflicted than many over these tensions and found it difficult to deal with the move to a major label and the attendant publicity it generated.
2. The film does not completely ignore Sub Pop's strategies, and there is even an interview with Chris Eckman featured in the film which critiques the label for promoting itself above its artists. This interview clip, alongside the material detailing how the label commissioned Everett True to write an article about the Seattle scene, are the closest the film gets to analysing how the Seattle music scene was a construction prior to the mass media being alerted to it. But it never arrives at this conclusion.
3. The original article is Laura Zinn et al., 'Move Over Boomers: The Busters are Here – And They're Angry', *Business Week*, December 14 1992, cover story, p. 78.
4. Generally, female bands were less commonly referred to as grunge bands. Definitions of grunge are quite hazy and many aggressive, punk rock-influenced bands were classified as grunge at the time, but it was more likely that male-led/dominated bands would be referred to as grunge.
5. Microsoft's headquarters are based in Redmond, Washington, part of the Seattle metropolitan area and fifteen miles from the city of Seattle.
6. The spread of riot grrrl-affiliated (and inspired) writers and musicians would increase over time, though connections were made between artists in different regions quite early. For example, Bikini Kill released a split album with British band Huggy Bear – *Yeah Yeah Yeah/Our Troubled Youth* – in 1992, and the two bands toured together in 1993.
7. 'Womyn' is a long-standing feminist term but has become increasingly controversial due to its associations with anti-trans views. For example, one of the first organisations to use the term was the Michigan Womyn's Music Festival, which commenced in 1976, and which only admitted 'womyn-born-womyn'. The growing campaigns against this policy eventually led to the discontinuation of the festival in 2015. Despite the controversies around the festival – which go back at least to the early 1990s – Kathleen Hannah's band Le Tigre played at the festival twice (in 2001 and 2005), which led to demands for her to apologise (see Rusty 2004).
8. This is in line with Alisa Perren's assertion that the more commercialised indie sector in the 1990s took a particular interest in various 'niche' and 'taste' cultures, and cultivated Gen Xers, particularly male teenagers and young adults. She writes that '1990s-era indie companies regularly promoted their films through locally oriented alternative weekly newspapers along with a rapidly growing range of cable channels suited to a specific film's demographic profile' (Perren 2012: 99).

9. Reflecting the complexities of 'independent', the film culls tracks released on both fully independent labels and semi-independent labels, such as Sub Pop (which in 1995 became partly owned by the Warner Music Group, which purchased a 49 per cent stake in the company) and Interscope Records (originally formed in 1989 as an independent, it formed a partnership with Atlantic Records – which was owned by the Warner Music Group – in 1990, then briefly became an independent company after Warners' sold back its stake in the company in 1995 before being sold to UMG in 1996).
10. Since the film was released there have been claims by former Runaways members that Kim Fowley, their manager, was abusive. Michaela Steele has claimed that she was forced to leave the band after refusing Fowley's sexual advances, while Jackie Fuchs (then named Jackie Fox) claimed in 2015 that she was raped by Fowley when she was in the band (Cherkis 2015). Fuchs also stated that fellow Runaways Joan Jett and Cherie Currie were present when the rape occurred; both Jett and Currie have denied this (Roberts 2015).
11. POWER UP stands for 'Professional Organization of Women in Entertainment Reaching Up'. It was founded as a non-profit organisation in 2000 and has helped to fund and assist several films, mostly shorts. *The Itty Bitty Titty Committee* was the first feature it produced; its first film was a short film directed by Babbit, *Stuck* (2001).
12. Audiences of the film will vary in their knowledge, of course, but the film can potentially act as a gateway to interest in other feminist movements and people for some audiences.
13. Kill Rock Stars is an independent record label based in both Portland, Oregon and Olympia, Washington, which released many records by riot grrrl bands. While founded by men, in 2006 it became notable for having all-female staff (though in 2019 co-founder Slim Moon returned to manage the label). The majority of the music licensed in *The Itty Bitty Titty Committee* is from this label.

7 INDIE MUSIC, FILM AND RACE 1: *MEDICINE FOR MELANCHOLY* AND *PARIAH*

In this and the next chapter, I explore more marginal conceptions of indie music, particularly those related to modes of music typically encoded as black. Such conceptions challenge the dominant whiteness of indie music. While there are a range of ethnicities in the US, this chapter will focus specifically on African American filmmaking and music due to the extensive range of music and filmmaking produced by African Americans. As noted in the introduction, indie was originally just a shorthand for 'independent' and gradually began to accrue further, often generic, connotations (a process which has also occurred within film). In practice, however – and this applies to both music and film – indie is often used in different ways, and it is still used in some cases merely as an abbreviation of independent. I would stress, then, that it is imperative scholars remain cognizant of the different ways that indie is employed discursively. This does not mean that we must necessarily *agree* with the ways it is being used; but even if one has a strict working definition, it is important not to lose sight of alternative ways that the term functions in everyday practice. (It is also the case that even if we create a strict working definition then this definition is subject to historical change, indicating a need for at least some openness and flexibility in our understanding of the term.) In short, while dominant ideas of indie refer broadly to alternative modes of guitar rock-pop, there are more marginal conceptions of indie that tend to use 'indie' more as an adjectival modifier than as a genre-like noun.

Across a range of American independent films directed by black filmmakers, indie music in its more familiar generic guise does not tend to feature prominently. But if we think about indie more as an economic marker, as well as an adjectival modifier, then 'indie' music is a more noticeable presence. Extending the limits of indie in this manner might be considered unhelpful by those who demand a more precise conceptualisation of the term. Furthermore, the term 'indie' is not used extensively by those working outside of the indie rock-pop continuum, so some might object to this manoeuvre on the grounds that it does not conform to dominant generic conceptions of indie *or* to prevalent discursive uses of the term. I would counter, in considering the latter point, that while indie might not be used prevalently in such a manner, it *is* nevertheless used occasionally and there are signs that it is becoming more frequently employed in this sense. It has been more common for hip-hop that is released on smaller, independent labels and/or which demonstrates a non-mainstream sensibility to be called 'underground hip-hop'. Yet indie hip-hop is also used to refer to such releases: Spotify hosts a number of 'indie hip-hop' playlists, *Fact Magazine* published a '100 best indie hip-hop records of all time' list in 2015, and the term can be used in record titles – an example being the 2005 album *Wu-Tang Clan Meets the Indie Culture*. As with other forms of indie music, indie hip-hop is also often connected to a broader DIY, anti-corporate aesthetic. Indie hip-hop has also been the subject of academic scrutiny: Christopher Vito (2019: 3) has distinguished between indie and underground hip-hop, classifying underground hip-hop as 'unsigned and emergent' artists, and indie hip-hop as music released on independent labels without any ties to the three major music corporations (UMG, Sony, Warner Bros.). Yet he also acknowledges that such terms can be used in different ways and are not entirely fixed: he notes, for example, that many artists who have been classified as underground hip-hop do not fit his criteria as they have released records on major labels (Ibid.). Motti Regev, meanwhile, includes in his discussion of 'indie pop-rock' the category of 'alternative rap' (Regev 2013: 143). Hip-hop isn't the only mode of black music that has its indie variations: we could also consider indie variants of other types of music heavily associated with blackness: indie R&B, for example, has been used as a designator occasionally. Though not adopted as frequently as indie hip-hop, it tends to connote either R&B artists who record on smaller, independent labels and/or are considered as 'alternative' to mainstream R&B in terms of their sound. The former tends to be the primary way that 'indie R&B' is used, as it is, for example, in the 'indie' section of online magazine *This RNB*. Meanwhile, certain modes of R&B – such as neo-soul – are often positioned as 'alternative' or eccentric examples even when not being discussed as indie.

In addition to these indie modes of more notable 'black' genres, many black artists and music fans are involved in more traditional modes of music associated with 'indie pop-rock'. Even though they are far outnumbered by white producers and fans of such music, they nevertheless are important to consider. There has, in fact, been some work discussing black people involved in predominantly white music scenes, including James Spooner's 2003 *Afro-Punk* documentary, Maureen Mahon's academic study of the Black Rock Coalition (2004), Leila Taylor's reflections on being a black fan of goth music (2019) and Stephanie Phillips's work addressing racism within indie and punk rock scenes (2021). These texts engage with the convoluted identity politics black people must negotiate when attaching themselves to musical cultures regarded as white. Taylor writes:

> I used to feel a cheat for my inability to latch on to R&B, my dislike of saccharine love songs, my general indifference to hip-hop and rap, and my utter disdain for gospel music somehow made me less black. I thought perhaps I was missing some genetic predisposition to melisma and that not liking 'Black' music was somehow a sign of self-loathing and betrayal of my race. (2019: 132)

Taylor contends that black people who have 'white' interests and who belong to predominantly white subcultures are 'twice marginalised' (Ibid.: 25), both from the dominant white culture on the one hand and from black communities who view such musical tastes as suspicious. Phillips, meanwhile, who is a member of the black British female indie-punk band Big Joanie, and involved in the establishment of the Decolonise Fest – a punk festival for people of colour which commenced in 2017 – has written of her own experiences in white-dominated indie music scenes:

> The indie rock and punk scenes I experienced in the 2000s were predominantly white, in terms of people who took up space and were celebrated in the scene. It does not mean that there were no people of color there, but I highlight the fact that many people of color were often pushed to the sidelines and very rarely on stage. (Phillips 2021: 76)

Such experiences were common, also, amongst the many black punks interviewed in Spooner's *Afro-Punk* documentary, some of whom claimed that they were often the only black person at punk gigs, and that they also faced hostility from black people for being unusual and not conforming to more stereotypical notions of what black Americans should listen to and look like. While they often fraternised with white people, many black punks nevertheless stated that they could not discuss racial issues comfortably within such milieus.

In this and the next chapter I explore how indie music has figured within three African American films released since the millennium: *Medicine for Melancholy* (Jenkins, 2008), *Pariah* (Rees, 2011) and *Sorry to Bother You* (Riley, 2018). These three case studies allow me to look in detail at how the inclusion of indie music within black filmmaking often leads to questions around identities, and in particular the exploration of non-normative notions of African American identity. Such films, as I will go on to argue, tend to not only question the identity of people but also the broader identity of indie: these include engaging with the often implicitly raced issues that feed into indie music cultures (*Medicine for Melancholy*) but also an attempt to present a broader, more inclusive, less white range of indie music (*Pariah* and *Sorry to Bother You*).

Indie and Whiteness

There have not been many films made by, and featuring, African Americans which use indie music as it is more commonly understood in an extensive fashion (that is, as a broad mode of alternative rock-pop music). This is evident within the very coverage of this book, which largely explores indie music produced by white people being used in films made by white directors and/or predominantly centred on white protagonists. The major factor influencing this situation is undoubtedly the fact that indie music, and indie-rock music in particular, is often considered a white mode of music: it is largely produced and consumed by white people, and many commentators have positioned it as a mode of music that has largely divested itself of the influences of 'black music'. In recent years, discussion of indie's whiteness has become more prominent. In a 2007 article for *The New Yorker*, Sasha Frere-Jones argued that indie music had divested itself of too many 'black' musical influences, namely a lack of blues, soul, reggae and funk, and this has had a detrimental impact on indie-rock. He claimed white musicians were at one time heavily influenced by black modes of expression, noting how rock music emerged from the blues, but contends that since the 1990s there has been an increased ghettoisation of both black and white musical forms. While there are certainly criticisms one can make against Frere-Jones's arguments – such as selectively cherry-picking artists to support his argument, his at times essentialist language (despite his own awareness of this issue) – the main point about how modes of music are often raced is important and continues to be a heavily debated issue.

In 2015, Sarah Sahim wrote a provocative article for *Pitchfork* entitled 'The Unbearable Whiteness of Indie'. In contrast to Frere-Jones, Sahim is herself a person of colour, a position which leads to an impassioned denunciation of indie music's colour blindness. She writes:

> In indie rock, white is the norm. While indie rock and the DIY underground, historically, have been proud to disassociate themselves from popular culture, there is no divorcing a predominantly white scene from systemic ideals ingrained in white Western culture. That status quo creates a barrier in terms of both the sanctioned participation of artists of

color and the amount of respect afforded them, all of which sets people of color up to forever be seen as interlopers and outsiders.

She differs from Frere-Jones in her attacks on how white artists often appropriate and 'attenuate' black musical styles and reap rewards for being innovative: 'White musicians seemingly can have it all: their almost impenetrable music scenes as well as their bastardization of most any other cultures. The root work by artists of color effectively disappears.' While Frere-Jones's position was largely from a musical perspective (the problem with indie music is that it does not draw on enough black influences), Sahim is more focused on the structures of indie music cultures, and how such cultures often marginalise black performers.

While Sahim's focus on racist elements within indie music is important (and will inform some of the analysis later in this section), some aspects of her article can be questioned. For example, she seems to slide between her uses of 'indie' in support of different argumentative threads. She begins by using the term 'indie', then discusses 'indie rock', only to begin using the phrase 'independent' in the latter stages of the article. Sahim, however, seems to slightly shift her perspective when altering her terminology, in line with the specific point she is making. Thus, she decries the whiteness of indie-rock, but then claims that she 'can count on one hand the number of prominent performers in the independent scene that look like me'. This shift from indie-rock to independent scene allows her to include in her list of non-white independent artists figures such as M.I.A. and Heems, neither of whom tend to be considered 'indie-rock' (even if M.I.A. certainly does draw on elements of indie-rock and was often lauded within indie scenes). In one sense, we could consider such a manoeuvre as highlighting indie's whiteness problem, in that Sahim has had to broaden her category to even list a handful of non-white independent artists. This is certainly true to an extent, but if we are considering independent artists of colour then she is overlooking a huge swathe of artists (and in this sense is guilty of further propagating the whiteness of the independent scene through her own processes of marginalisation).

Noah Berlatsky has argued that indie music became more hybrid from around 2000 onwards and that artists who worked with electronic beats and created sounds considered innovative and alternative were increasingly considered 'indie'. He argues, however, that white artists are far more likely to be positioned as indie artists than black artists working in similar musical territory:

> Genres like rock and indie are for many people defined by whiteness – that is, white skin becomes the genre marker, rather than the music itself. There are few artists of color in the indie scene because artists of color who make what could be called 'indie music' get classified as something

> else. . . . Performers like SZA, FKA Twigs, or Dawn Richard all work with spacious, off-kilter beats and psychedelic electronica flourishes – they sound like peers of Björk, not Beyoncé. But Björk is considered central to indie, and SZA, FKA Twigs, and Richard are all R&B with an asterisk. (Berlatsky, 2015)

Indie's dominant associations with rock music has undoubtedly been a core factor influencing its whiteness. Despite being rooted in black cultural forms – emerging as it did from R&B, with black artists such as Little Richard, Chuck Berry and Bo Diddley considered key musicians in the development of rock'n'roll – rock music has since become largely perceived as a white mode of music. Maureen Mahon (2004, p. 6) has argued that, following the death of Jimi Hendrix, black people were increasingly marginalised from rock music. Black participants do exist, however, as marginal participants in indie-rock performance and consumption. Indie-rock is often considered as having emerged from punk, which itself was dominated by white participants. There have, of course, been some black performers within punk music: the American hardcore band Bad Brains, for example, or Poly Styrene, the lead singer of the British punk band X-Ray Spex. The annual American festival Afropunk, founded by *Afro-Punk* director James Spooner and commencing in 2005, also points to the participation of black artists within punk – as does the previously mentioned Decolonise Fest – even though it has been criticised for moving away from its roots into a more commercial and generically more diverse direction. More recently, non-white participants in indie-rock have included Benjamin Brooker, Big Joanie, Santigold's former band Stiffed and TV on the Radio. While this is just a small sample of non-white indie-rock artists, black indie-rock remains marginal, which is neatly captured in The Cocker Spaniels' track 'The Only Black Guy at the Indie-Rock Show' (2010), whose lyrics include the line 'I look like just a thug amongst the dressed-down Pavement fans'. Singer Sean Padilla's repeated pleas that 'it shouldn't really matter' point to how being a participant in the indie-rock and pop scenes continues to be an issue. The marginality of black indie music, and of its black audience, is addressed in Barry Jenkins's debut feature *Medicine for Melancholy*.

Medicine for Melancholy

An intimate, low-budget film, *Medicine for Melancholy* follows Micah (Wyatt Cenac) and Jo (Tracey Heggins) exploring San Francisco the day after they have had a one-night stand. The film opens with Micah washing his face in the mirror, while the next cut shifts to Jo in bed as she realises – following a brief, canted POV shot of Micah – the awkwardness of her situation: not only has she had a one-night stand, it later transpires that she has a partner.

This partly explains why Jo seems so initially hostile to Micah when, after leaving the house where a party had occurred the previous night, he attempts to engage her in conversation. After a quick coffee, over which Micah tries to grill Jo with questions about herself, the two get a taxi but Micah's desire to converse with Jo is frustrated when she abruptly leaves the taxi to walk home. In her haste to flee Micah, she accidentally leaves her purse in the cab, so Micah subsequently tracks down her address with the help of MySpace. What proceeds is an occasionally awkward, sometimes intimate, often challenging, meeting of minds and bodies between the two, with race the central fulcrum of conversation.

Medicine for Melancholy blends everyday realism with a broader, symbolic dimension: it is both a low-key, observational drama spanning twenty-four hours and an interrogation of race and identity. The film's unusual colour palette – markedly desaturated in the majority of scenes – alludes to the decreasing black population in San Francisco. While the two characters conceive of their identities differently in relation to race, they are both marginal 'black hipsters' living in San Francisco. Micah is a San Franciscan native who, while friends with many white people, is highly conscious of racial and class-related issues; Jo has moved to the city more recently and is committed to seeing the world beyond race. Discussions around race begin as soon as Micah enters Jo's apartment upon returning her purse. While she is initially hostile to his presence, he eventually eases some of the palpable tension when he picks up an acoustic guitar and performs Fred Rogers's 'Won't You Be My Neighbour', which causes Jo to laugh. Underlying friction is still evident, though, when Micah questions her about her apartment. He assumes correctly that her partner is white (he is an art dealer) and they begin to discuss racial issues. Micah's concerns about race are reasonable, though his interrogation of Jo's blackness is also slightly aggressive and is undoubtedly affected by his desirous feelings towards her and his accompanying jealousy of her absent white partner. He is also corrected by Jo on his erroneous assumptions about why Black History Month is in February, while his questioning of her living with a white boyfriend is somewhat hypocritical considering we later discover – via Jo's later glimpse of his MySpace page – that he was formerly in a relationship with a white woman. His questioning of her colour blindness, however, is important in generating a discussion of black experience and identity in a contemporary city that has increasingly gentrified, resulting in a significant dwindling of its black population. At the time of the film's release the African American population in the city was less than half its size in 1970 (Lim 2009). Micah's greater knowledge of San Francisco's history enables him to introduce issues of class in relation to race, while his and Jo's walk around various areas of San Francisco reveal 'a place impacted by redlining, urban redevelopment, gentrification, displacement, and a dwindling African American population' (Gillespie 2016:

122). This complicates any straightforward expression, and embodiment, of black identity. For example, during their walk around the city, Jo and Micah visit the Museum of the African Diaspora (MoAD). While on the one hand the museum represents an acknowledgement of black experience within the city, it was developed out of a San Francisco redevelopment programme and is hence intertwined with the city's gentrification; while it constitutes a symbolic honouring of African American subjects, many poorer, black citizens of San Francisco have been increasingly erased from the city.

As someone married to a white art dealer, and who herself makes T-shirts honouring female filmmakers, Jo is positioned as the more middle-class of the two. In contrast to Jo's husband's spacious if somewhat bare apartment, Micah's space is cramped: he lives in a tiny studio apartment and his vocation – aquarium installer – is more manual. He is, nevertheless, more intellectually questioning than Jo. She thinks his constant discussion of race limits who he is and how he can live; for him, he believes it is crucial to remain keenly aware of race and how it structures life. The use of indie music on the soundtrack – and at one moment in the film as a point of explicit discussion between the two characters – connects to issues of race (as a predominantly white musical mode) and class (while indie is enjoyed across classes, it is often considered to appeal mostly to middle-class fans [Fonarow 2006: 12]). The film largely features guitar-based rock-pop and lo-fi synth pop by artists with minor profiles. The presence of music is quite subtle, largely used as a low-key background

Figure 7.1 *Medicine for Melancholy*: Micah and Jo dance intimately in the nightclub

soundtrack. It bursts to the fore, however, in a key scene where Jo and Micah visit a nightclub, accompanied by loud snippets from indie bands including White Denim, Canoe, Bloodcat Love, The Octopus Project and The Answering Machine. They both appear to have a good time at the club, indicated by laughter and dancing, while the more frenetic pace of this scene – bolstered by the foregrounding of the music – diverges from the predominantly languid, quiet tone of the film. If the scene appears to signal the coming together of Micah and Jo, their subsequent walk home together belies such harmony.

It is obvious from how the nightclub scene is presented that Jo and Micah are minority black presences. While both characters enjoy themselves regardless, their post-club discussion signals how Micah is acutely aware of the issue, even if his outburst can partly be explained by his jealousy of Jo being in a relationship with a white man. The talk between the two characters at first is friendly, but Micah starts to become more aggressive after Jo speaks to her boyfriend on the phone. Commencing with a comment about black people dating outside of their race, Micah shifts discussion onto the indie scene and race: 'Everything, everything about being indie is all tied to not being black.' Jo states that she does not want to talk about it, but he continues, noting at one point: 'Friends who are indie? White. Bands who are indie? Like, okay, you got TV on the Radio. But the rest of them are white.' This leads him back into issues of interracial dating, but Jo wards off his increasingly aggressive attack by exclaiming 'You think because I'm black and you're black that we should be together. You're so fucking crazy.'

As mentioned, gentrification is posited as a major factor that has hastened San Francisco's dwindling black population, a point emphasised when we see Jo and Micah observe a Housing Rights Committee meeting, where the displacement of poorer residents is discussed. In the context of the film's themes – racial identity, class, gentrification – indie music's function is partly symbolic. Not only is it a mode of music that has been connected to whiteness, but it is also sometimes connected to the idea of *hipsterism* (see Newman 2017). In recent times hipsterism has also been associated with whiteness (despite its rootedness in black experience), with gentrification (Maly and Varis 2016: 648–9) and with indie cultures (Greif 2010: 23). Indie music is, therefore, an appropriate mode through which to explore intersections of race, class and gentrification. Despite its major contours, hipsterism can nevertheless cross class and racial borders, and in the 2000s there was an increased discussion of the 'black hipster' or 'blipster' (see Olopade 2009). The largely negative ways that the modern hipster has been framed, however, can lead to problematic prejudices. Jace Clayton (aka DJ /rupture) has argued that the hipster is often scapegoated for many ills, which tends to block a complex analysis of issues. Clayton writes that 'criticizing the hipster is often a way of discussing gentrification and change – while exempting oneself from the process' (Clayton 2010: 55). He argues that the arrival of hipsters in specific locations is often a sign that a locality has already become gentrified; that is, hipsters might be a symptom of gentrification, but they are rarely its main engineers.

Medicine for Melancholy engages with hipsterism partly through its more common stereotypical features, but it also delves beyond such stereotypes. As Michael Gillespie (2016: 150) has argued, 'the brand of hipsterism that Micah and Jo seemingly subscribe to negates the assumption that all hipsters are white poseurs or aesthetes, and they are certainly greater than the pithy overtones of "blipster." Cool and hip, their style praxis might wrestle with enduring veracity critiques, but it remains an indisputable source of nonprescriptive pleasure.' Elements of Micah's identity and social relations position him as a black hipster: it is implied he has a lot of white friends (the party is at a white friend's house, his ex-girlfriend is white), and other moments align him with hipsterism, such as telling Jo that he will fix the breaks on her bike and then trying to persuade her that she should switch to a fixed-gear bike (the fixed-gear bicycle has become associated with hipsters, and Micah himself uses one). Jo is also associated with hipsterism through her love of indie music as well as her interest in art. If Jo and Micah are positioned as non-typical hipsters, they are also not typical exemplars of blackness, at least as it is more stereotypically codified in relation to taste and style.

The club scene that features a lot of indie music was, originally, not even an indie club night, but a Northern Soul club night (Gillespie 2016: 147). Northern Soul generally refers to cultures in the North of England (hence the name) that emerged from the Mod scene in the 1960s, which was devoted to tracking down rare American soul records. It has, however, continued to be popular in some areas, with San Francisco a specific city in which Northern Soul has more recently enjoyed avid interest. Jenkins would have likely chosen a Northern Soul club night because of its links to racial, national and classed exchanges: originating from largely white working-class British hipsters who congregated around a mode of music primarily performed by black Americans, it then became transplanted to America primarily amongst the white middle-class. Within this mix of cultural exchanges, Jo and Micah's blackness adds to the complexity of their situation, in which identity negotiation is often fraught due to the sometimes prescriptive, occasionally proscriptive, notions around taste, race and class. According to Gillespie, the scene eventually employed indie music for reasons of cost. In some ways, though, indie music is a more appropriate mode in the sense that it has been discussed quite frequently in relation to race and is predominantly white. If we had witnessed the two characters dancing to soul music, it would not have had the same jarring effect: black people dancing to soul music on film is not uncommon; black people dancing to indie-rock is. (Though the shift to indie does not indicate processes of appropriation in the manner that the original soul music would have.)

As a mode of music with links to hipsterism and whiteness, indie music offers pleasures that are nonetheless jarring to Micah, whose political concerns clash with his personal enjoyment. The club scene is key in condensing these elements into a charged moment: while Jo and Micah are visibly enjoying themselves in the club, their subsequent argument is indicative of the issues underpinning how such pleasures are more broadly informed by political forces beyond one's immediate control, a situation which feeds Micah's rage: though he is politically aware of racial issues and more specifically the historical gentrification of San Francisco, he also feels a sense of powerlessness. He does have a framed poster of a 1962 San Francisco redevelopment programme announcement with 'LIES' superimposed over it pinned to his apartment wall, but whether he is actually involved in wider political actions to oppose gentrification is open to question (the fact that he and Jo stand outside of the Housing Rights committee meeting is telling – he is interested but does not enter the space and remains an observer).

The indie club scene and its aftermath seem to encapsulate many tensions and contradictions that run through the film, without offering simple answers. Jo's concerns with racial issues are more distanced than Micah's (hence, she uses a formal manner when informing him of the reasoning behind Black History Month being in February, as though she is repeating a firmly memorised piece of information); his relationship to race is more embodied and impassioned. Jo wants to transcend the confines of race in contrast to Micah's insistence on making connections between race and broader social issues. Her ideals might in some respects represent a more comfortable and sensible negotiation of experience considering Micah's tendency to rage, but such idealistic aspirations can run the danger of overlooking very real injustices and inequalities. In one scene at Micah's apartment, after they have shared a joint, he discusses how being black is the foundational category which he identifies with over all others (more so than being a man). Jo refuses to explain herself in one word in the same manner, stating that 'people aren't that simple', and later tells him: 'You feel you have to define everybody. You limit them to the point that they're just a definition and not people.' She is correct to remind him of the complexities of any individual's identity, but when she discusses how he is much more than his blackness, he responds with 'That's not how society sees it'. Despite her response of 'Fuck what society thinks', his point is valid: individuality is not a transcendent outcome of self-creation but is shaped in many ways by socio-historical factors, and a person cannot just wish systemic racism away.

The actual music used on the soundtrack of *Medicine for Melancholy* represents a diverse range of indie-rock and pop, with a couple of exceptions such as Yesterday's New Quintet and Tom Waits. Even these tracks, however, are related to indie and 'alternative' music: Waits himself now records for an independent label and is also considered non-mainstream (and liked by many indie fans); Yesterday's New Quintet is an alias of Madlib, one of the most acclaimed indie hip-hop artists to have emerged in the late 1990s, who creates jazz-infused hip-hop under the Yesterday's New Quintet name. Many of the artists who feature on the soundtrack are relatively obscure, such as Gypsophile, The Changes, Bloodcat Love and the local San Francisco act Casiotone for the Painfully Alone, whose music plays over the opening and end credits. Much of this music shares lo-fi production qualities, a prominent trait in much indie-rock and pop music. This quality, along with the nature of many of the tracks and how they are used – with the exception of the club scene music – contributes to the film's reflective tone.

Casiotone for the Painfully Alone's songs – 'New Year's Kiss' and 'Tonight Was a Disaster' – are intimate and melancholy. These slightly morose, introspective songs would be more typically used to soundtrack white, angst-ridden teens and young adults. Jenkins's use of such music, however, is an important component of his wish to probe black identities in a predominantly white locale. In addition to contributing to the film's focus on race and identity, and its somewhat muted tonality, a lot of the music has been chosen for apposite lyrical content. The two Casiotone for the Painfully Alone tracks, for example, vaguely match with the narrative situations and emotional tone of the scenes they follow. After the brief pre-credits scene in which the one-night stand has been established, the lyrics to the first verse of 'New Year's Kiss' are: 'Woke up with fingers crossed/In a boy's bed with your pants off/After polite declines of coffee and toast/Walked home itching in last night's clothes'. These lyrics of course reflect the awkwardness of the one-night stand and relate in particular to the shame and guilt that Jo experiences. 'Tonight Was a Disaster' follows the final scene of the film, when Jo refuses to stay the night and is observed by Micah from his apartment window as she cycles off. 'Tonight Was a Disaster' as a title, and the final line of the song, reflects to some extent Jo's feelings once again. The opening lines of this equally downbeat track are: 'You went out with your best sweater on/ With every intention of dancing till dawn/But when the DJ played that song, it all went wrong'. Of course, this doesn't completely synchronise with the narrative of the film – the night goes downhill *after* the two have left the club – but it does capture her feelings of pleasure and excitement both leading up to and including dancing at the club, and the later souring of her mood following Micah's emotional outburst. It is notable that the lyrical content of the two tracks relates to Jo more than Micah, as he is generally the more assertive and argumentative of the two. Jo is certainly not afraid to stand up for herself and argue with Micah – as she does occasionally – but she is the less vocal character. In this sense, some of the musical tracks function to provide insights into her thoughts and feelings, therefore highlighting her perspective.

Anahid Kassabian (2000) has argued that compiled music is more likely to generate what she terms 'affiliating identifications', in contrast to the composed score which attempts to draw audiences into the film via 'assimilating identifications'. She uses the term 'identification' not just to refer to audiences identifying with a specific character, but as a broader characteristic which draws audiences into a filmic world. The concept of identification in her work refers partly to the ways that specific musical elements – most typically leitmotifs – can link to specific characters, settings, themes, etc.; but she uses it more commonly to denote 'the encounters between film texts and filmgoers' psyches' (2000: 1). This notion of identification stresses how viewers may be drawn into a film and identify with not only characters, but also narrative elements and ideologies. In some ways, this idea of identification overlaps to an extent with the concept of immersion, especially her concept of 'assimilating identifications', which 'are structured to draw perceivers into socially and historically unfamiliar positions' (2000: 3). Affiliating identifications are less likely to absorb spectators into a unitary filmic universe; Kassabian argues that compiled scores 'bring the immediate threat of history' because if the spectator knows the song, 'perceivers bring external associations with the songs into their engagements with the film' (Ibid.). We could add that compiled songs used on film soundtracks might also 'bring external associations' even if viewers do not know the specific track, as it might resemble other tracks and be aligned with other, similar types of music (and accompanying connotations) from related genres.[1] *Medicine for Melancholy* deliberately uses indie music for its external associations, particularly in relation to race. If assimilating identifications absorb spectators in a self-contained filmic world, the use of music in *Medicine for Melancholy* deliberately connects its concerns to the world outside of the film. Yet indie music does not merely function in this manner; it is also used for other purposes, such as indicating mood and, as with the use of Casiotone for the Painfully Alone tracks, pointing towards how a character might be feeling beneath the surface of exterior articulation.

Despite its multiple functions, the music used in *Medicine for Melancholy* primarily relates to issues of race and identity. In this sense, the film – including its title – can be linked to Paul Gilroy's notion of 'postcolonial melancholia' (Gilroy 2005). This concept relates to the ways in which colonial and imperialist legacies have not been properly worked through, resulting in hostility towards multiculturalism and ethnic minorities. Gilroy uses the term melancholia in a Freudian sense, as a pathological, unacknowledged response to loss, though Jenkins's film seems to draw on both the more psychoanalytical idea of melancholy and its more common meaning. Gilroy warns against going back to essentialist conceptions of race, however, and contends that being resigned to 'natural' racial characteristics 'supports enabling analogies and provides legitimation in a host of historical situations where natural difference and social division are politically, economically, and militarily mediated' (Gilroy 2005: 8). This does not, however, entail the disavowal of racial difference; instead, Gilroy argues for an openness to other identities as well as historical and geographical understandings of how racial discourse 'generates a field of ethics, knowledge, and power that contributes its unique order of truths to the processes that produce and regulate individual subjects, conditioning the intimate consciousness through which they come to know and understand and indeed constitute themselves as racial beings' (Gilroy 2005: 12). *Medicine for Melancholy* grapples with similar issues: the need to acknowledge difference whilst not being bound by natural, essential ideas of race, yet also highlighting how racial discourse and historical factors have produced systemic inequalities. Ultimately, Micah's interest in indie music and his hipster status, combined with his colour, leads to an overinvestment in Jo. As he clearly has many white friends, his one-night stand with a black woman with similar tastes leads him to think there is a deep connection between them. The ending of the film, however, refuses such a neat and tidy conclusion, highlighting the complexities of identity.

Pariah

Dee Rees's *Pariah* also explores racial identity in relation to music often coded as white, but it also concerns sexual identity. It follows the character Alike (Adepero Oduye), a black lesbian adolescent negotiating her identity whilst concealing her sexual orientation from her parents, particularly her strict, religious mother. In line with her conflicted identity ties, music on the soundtrack is split between more beat-driven hip-hop and R&B on the one hand, and modes of indie-rock and spiritual soul on the other. All the music used, though, can be considered to be broadly indie in the sense of being independent; as with *Medicine for Melancholy* the film's low budget results in lesser-known acts being licensed for the film. Whereas *Medicine for Melancholy* employs music from mostly white artists, *Pariah*'s compiled music is from black female artists. This is important because *MfM* was focused partly on the question of black erasure, which is not an issue that *Pariah* negotiates (the film is set in Brooklyn and features mostly black protagonists).

In *Pariah*, Alike is distanced from 'normative' black identities in two major ways: firstly, and most significantly, through her attraction to other women and, secondly, through her interest in alternative styles of music. While her musical tastes are not divulged immediately, her sexuality is. The film opens on close-ups of anonymous bodies outside of a nightclub, with sounds of people speaking and distant musical beats from the interior of the club. After we are shown tickets being stamped, we are introduced to the inside of the club, and music now dominates the soundtrack. The track is Khia's 'My Neck, My Back (Lick It)', a salacious, bass-heavy rap song underpinned by insistent snares and kick drums, and probably the most widely recognised song on the soundtrack at the time of the film's release (the track charted in many countries, though it was released on then-independent label Artemis Records). Slow motion movements of a go-go dancer are then shown and intercut with the first shot of Alike. As the music moves from the foreground to the background of the soundtrack, the film starts to show people in the club, who are mostly black women. Neon colours, salacious dancers and 'dirty rap' music are usually associated with male and heterosexual cultures on screen, yet the track features a female rapper voicing her desires in an explicit fashion. It is true that some women have been associated with sexually explicit rap – such as Lil' Kim and Nicki Minaj – but it remains male-dominated. The theme of queerness has been indicated through the film, opening with a quote from black lesbian writer and activist Audre Lorde – 'Wherever the bird with no feet flew, she found trees with no limbs' – though the spiritual nature of this quote does not fit closely with the club scene in any obvious manner. The film explores, instead, a more spiritual notion of the erotic, which aligns with Lorde's belief that it is a 'resource within each of us that lies in a deeply female and spiritual plane, firmly rooted in the power of our unexpressed or unrecognized feeling' (Lorde quoted in Kang 2016: 275).

While this opening scene establishes the milieu of a black lesbian club, it is clear that Alike does not seem as comfortable in this environment as many others, most notably her friend Laura (Pernell Walker). The first shot of Alike is telling, in that we cut to her framed at a canted angle of about ninety degrees, before rotating in slow motion back to a parallel position (intercut with shots of a go-go dancer). Slow motion footage and the absence of ambient sounds in the club last for around thirty seconds before a sound edit introduces voices of clubgoers and 'My Neck, My Back (Lick It)' shifts to the background of the mix. This brief slow-motion sequence not only introduces the main character of the film but also indicates her separateness from the scene within which she is embedded; her subjective space is marked, via camera angle and motion, as out of kilter with her surroundings. As the scene proceeds, Alike's double outsider status is further cemented. Firstly, she tries to impede her friend Laura throwing too many bills at the dancer (who replies, 'What you doing man, what did you come here for?'). She then leaves to sit down on her own, next to a couple, and looks unhappy: it is at this point that the film title briefly appears on the screen, as if to underline her 'pariah' status. The scene proceeds with Alike eventually persuading a reluctant Laura that they must leave, as she needs to get home on time. Outside the club they talk for a while before going home, which establishes Alike's outsider status even further: it transpires that, in contrast to the sexually active Laura, she is a virgin, and that she has difficulties getting other girls' phone numbers (she initially pretends to Laura that she has picked up some girls' numbers at the club, but Laura realises that the people Alike cites are mainly her classmates).

Alike looks up to Laura. It transpires that not many people know about Alike's sexuality, so Laura is someone she can talk to about her desires without fear of censure. As such, she goes to clubs with Laura to meet a potential partner, and she also dresses similarly to Laura, in a rather masculine outfit consisting of baseball caps and casual, loose-fitting shirts and trousers (we later see Laura advising her on clothing, suggesting that some of the clothes may be Laura's). But she is not like her and on their way home on the bus she seems irritated that Laura wants to wait to get off at Alike's stop. After Laura does reluctantly alight the bus at her own stop, Alike is left alone on the bus. A gently strummed guitar then begins on the soundtrack as Alike moves her position on the bus and takes off her cap, do-rag, and polo shirt – revealing a more 'girly' piece of attire, a pink T-shirt with the word 'Angel' prominently displayed – then puts on earrings. Initially it seems she might be divesting herself of a uniform that she is not completely happy with, but we will learn that the primary reason for her change of uniform is because her strictly religious mother (Kim Wayans) is not fully aware of her sexuality and is constantly trying to get her to dress in a more stereotypically 'feminine' manner (and her irritation with Laura – who is 'out' – is because she wants to conceal this somewhat shameful process). When Alike goes to school, she immediately visits the restroom and changes her costume again, this time shedding more feminine elements of clothing and adopting a more butch appearance.

Alike's struggles with her identity are not only emphasised by the ways her image is reflected prominently in the bus window, but also through the

Figure 7.2 *Pariah*: Alike feels conflicted as she rides home on the bus, prior to changing her clothes

non-diegetic song on the soundtrack. The track is Sparlha Swa's 'Doing My Thing' and the lyrics directly relate to Alike's subjective turmoil, expressing the need to keep going through troubled times, particularly the repeated line of 'Got to keep on doing my thing', whose insistent repetitions are sometimes undermined by doubts such as 'Sometimes I feel like I just won't make it'. Other lines are also related to Alike's experiences, such as 'Chasing after the wrong crowd' and 'You don't know who I am'. 'Doing My Thing', like other non-diegetic music used within *Pariah*, links to Alike's subjectivity. This subjective musical dimension is important in indicating Alike's feelings as she often conceals them to friends and family, even Laura. The song itself contrasts greatly with the bass-heavy hip-hop heard in the club; a sparse solo acoustic guitar is the sole accompaniment to Swa's soulful, emotive vocals. This song expresses spiritual urges that contrast with the more physical, sexualised music in the club, indicating how Alike is more concerned with a romantic connection than casual sex. This is established further when she asks Laura to hook her up with a girl at her school, Mika, whom Laura vaguely knows through a friend. Laura is sceptical of Alike's insistence that Mika likes her and says to her: 'All I know is I been trying to get you to holla at girls in the club for the longest', to which Alike replies, 'I don't want to holler at girls at the club'.

While Laura is a friend who she can be candid with and who can provide advice regarding lesbianism, Alike's explicit rejection of Laura's advice marks the beginnings of an active pursuit of her own desires, as opposed to those desires which are thrust upon her by others (whether her mother's fierce attempts to mould her into a feminine, heterosexual subject, or Laura's guidance on where to go, how to dress, who to date). Although Laura has helped Alike come to terms with her sexuality, the two are very different: Alike is intellectually gifted, does well at school, has a flair for writing poetry and is growing up in a middle-class family; Laura, on the other hand, has dropped out of school early after becoming estranged from her mother, works at a restaurant whilst studying for a GED in her spare time and is struggling financially. Such differences are further emphasised through music. Laura is associated with hip-hop and electronic R&B sounds, often with assertive, raunchy lyrics, which match her confident personality. Alike is associated with the more soulful, spiritual songs of Sparlha Swa, and – as the film progresses – harder rock sounds. Their shared commonalities – sexual orientation and difficult relationships with their mothers – have nevertheless helped them to forge a connective bond.

Later in the film, Alike is reluctantly paired with Bina, a daughter of her mother's friend. Alike's mother introduces her to Bina (Aasha Davis) because she wants to steer her away from Laura. Despite her initial reluctance towards befriending Bina, the two eventually become closer and bond through music. When they first meet, Alike refuses to even engage with Bina; they eventually agree to be more cordial with each other for the sake of convenience, but musical connections bring them much closer together. Bina starts discussing music with a visibly disinterested Alike, asking if she likes certain commercial R&B and hip-hop, such as 'Destiny's Kids' (supposedly Destiny's Child), 'Jay-Z' and 'Fifty' (Cent). Irritated, Alike replies 'No, I don't really like any of that commercial bullshit'. Pressed further by Bina on what music she *does* like, she is again somewhat disengaged from the conversation as she is still looking at texts on her phone rather than making eye contact with Bina. She replies that she likes 'More underground stuff, none of that crap they play on radio'. Pushed to name specific artists by Bina, she is again dismissive of her, saying 'People you probably never heard of. Conscious stuff.' When pressed again, she does finally list some artists that she likes. Here she mentions acts which sound like 'Trees' and 'Black Circle', though it is unclear who she is referring to here considering there are a number of musical artists with these names.[2] What is established is that, whilst she does like hip-hop, she does not like the same types of music that Laura listens to. When Bina actually starts discussing enthusiasm for some of this cited music, and herself notes if Alike knows of Bahamadia[3] – a 'conscious' hip-hop artist – Alike starts to become engaged in the conversation for the first time, and her initial assumptions about Bina are challenged. After a pause, during which Alike finally stops looking at her phone, Bina asks if Alike likes rock. 'It's cool', replies Alike, before getting up to leave, but Bina stops her to listen to some music that she plays. The aggressive punk rock of Tamar-kali's 'Boot' is played briefly, with a solitary expression of 'Wow' from Alike, before a cut to the next scene.

Music functions to forge connections, as well as erect barriers, between characters in *Pariah*. Rees has herself stated how she wanted different genres of music 'to heighten the character's voices' arguing that 'Alike's voice is kind of acoustic soul. And then the punk is kind of Bina's voice; this kind of alternative music [represents] an alternative way to be. And then hip-hop is Laura's voice' (Harris 2011). These musical signifiers aren't entirely fixed, though. Alike may be associated primarily with the acoustic soul of Sparlha Swa – which non-diegetically accompanies moments of her journey – but she also discusses her passion for alternative hip-hop and develops an interest in rock. The diversity of her musical interests in contrast to, say, Laura, reflects her position as the central, most complex character within the film.

If the non-diegetic music indicates elements of Alike's hidden personality beyond her external presentation to others, some of the diegetic music – particularly the music played in the presence of Bina – functions as a means of extending and exploring her identity. After she and Bina have made a connection through music, we briefly witness a scene in which Laura arrives at Alike's house and is harshly told by her mother that she is not in. The next brief scene cuts to Bina's bedroom, with Bina and Alike listening to more rock – Honeychild

Figure 7.3 *Pariah*: Bina puts on a Honeychild Coleman record for Alike

Coleman's 'Echelon' – and now visibly closer (in terms of physical distance and, unlike previously, making notable eye contact). Alike is now nodding her head to the music, proclaiming 'This shit is hot', and proceeds to ignore a call from Laura, claiming that she wants to stay the night with Bina instead of meeting up with Laura as she had planned.

The music of Tamar-kali reappears to cement their growing closeness when Bina asks Alike if she wants to go to a party. The party, which features a live performance by Kali – who is performing 'Pearl' – mirrors the opening scene at the lesbian club with its prominent dark neon colours and Alike reacting to a stage performer. However, rather than being confronted with a go-go dancer, she is watching a black female singer emoting in an energetic, though non-sexualised, performance; and in contrast to the earlier scene where she looks uncomfortable, in this scene she is dancing and smiling in an uninhibited fashion. The increased closeness between Bina and Alike, sparked by joint listening to Tamar-kali, has now risen in intensity and eventually they sleep together in the evening.

Simon Frith has argued that 'identity is mobile, a process not a thing, a becoming not a being' and that 'our experience of music – of music making and music listening – is best understood as an experience of this self-in-process' (2016: 294). He also claims it is not so much that music *reflects* existing identities so much as *constructs* them; that is, 'social groups agree on values which are then expressed in their cultural activities (the assumption of the homology models) but that they only get to know themselves as groups (as a particular organization of individual and social interests, of sameness and difference) through cultural activity, through aesthetic judgement' (2016: 295–6). Such a perspective insists that music is an important means through which identities can be constructed, but that this process is far from fixed. While different types of music can be associated with different groups, they are not confined to such groups. In *Pariah*, music is used as a crucial shorthand to express identities but can also – as in Alike's embrace of rock – be used to extend identities and forge new connections. Unfortunately for Alike, she invests perhaps too much into her musical connections with Bina. While music is therefore posited as a crucial element through which identity can be constructed/negotiated, it co-exists with many other factors. It is merely one symbolic identity strand amongst many, and in this instance has created a false alignment between Alike and Bina.

Alike's thwarted desires next explode in outbursts of anger and frustration: she slams the door shut on Bina, leaves her apartment, and then kicks bins outside as the aggressive guitars of Audio Dyslexia's 'Parallel' soundtrack her anger. The introduction of aggressive sound at high volume – accompanied by jerky hand-held shots and jump cuts – underpins the explosive internal impact this rejection has had on Alike. As there has been an absence of music on the soundtrack building up to this explosion – the intimate coming together between Alike and Bina takes place without musical accompaniment – the visceral nature of the scene is heightened. Alike's turmoil continues when she returns home, as she goes to her room and starts trashing it. She is now accompanied by woozy, backward loops (from Chewing Pics' 'Migromelodi'), which hint at the mental churn and turmoil she is now experiencing. While these scenes focus on the anger, rage and pain of Alike, they nevertheless mark a crucial point within her life and open the way for a more independent identity. She subsequently tells her parents that she is a lesbian, and though this again leads to an explosion of anger – this time from her mother, who beats Alike when she states that she is a lesbian repeatedly and throws her out of the house – the film ends on a positive note.

A montage in which Alike seeks solace from Laura, accompanied by Sparlha Swa's 'Song of the Morning', encapsulates Alike's spiritual growth following her painful rejection by Bina. The song injects the montage with hope through its lyrics, which emphasise inner strength and the need to develop 'essential' elements of the self and attain independence:

> Now inside myself I go diving. Knowing nothing else can satisfy. The deeper needs within me. The most essential in me. I close my eyes to find the space of revelation in me. 'Cause only I can be the creator of my high.

Thus, despite the downbeat visual elements of the montage, non-diegetic music is used to position this as a process of healing, a difficult yet necessary stage in attaining independence and sexual identity.

At the end of the film Alike travels to Berkeley, having attained an early scholarship. While still on talking terms with her father, her attempts to speak to her mother are rebuffed. However, she has now embraced herself and is no longer quite so dependent on the advice of others. While she is staying temporarily with Laura, she no longer feels the need to ape Laura's style and is now more assertive: she refuses her father's offer to come home, but expresses to him that this is her choice, that she is not running, she is *choosing*. These sentiments are repeated when Alike reads a poem in class – which is edited into a montage of her saying goodbye as she leaves for Berkeley – which includes the lines: 'I am not running, I am choosing. Breaking is freeing, broken is freedom. I am not broken, I am free.'

The final shot of the film mirrors the scene on the bus near the beginning. In that shot, set at night, Alike's conflicted identity is indicated by her surreptitious clothing changes and her reflection in the window. We now see Alike on a bus but now in the daytime; rather than returning home to a place in which she conceals her true self, she is on her way to a new life where she can hopefully express herself more independently. We do not see a visible reflection of her in the window as she is no longer concealing a fundamental aspect of her identity, while music is now absent because she has at this moment attained peace of mind.

In addition to music's function in *Pariah* as a symbolic indication of character, other intertexts are used for thematic and character-related purposes. The most important of these is the work of poet and essayist Audre Lorde, who as previously mentioned has a fragment of her writing quoted at the beginning. This is from her memoir (or as she calls it a 'biomythography') *Zami: A New Spelling of My Name* (1982), which Rees has claimed was an important resource when she was coming to terms with her own sexuality (Anon: 2011). Nancy Kang (2016: 296) has argued that *Pariah* 'envisions *Zami* as an intertextual model, resulting in a kind of cinematic palimpsest, a visual text signifying upon a written precedent'. Both Rees's personal experiences and Lorde's *Zami* (as well as other writing by Lorde) inform *Pariah*. Perhaps the most notable overlap is the need to acknowledge one's true sexuality amid forces denigrating and denying such an identity; issues such as parental disapproval, specifically problematic maternal relationships, are also themes of both texts. Lorde stressed the necessity of acknowledging inner feelings and transforming these into thought and action, despite the dangers of doing so, for this was preferable to the pain of remaining silent (Lorde 2007: 88). Alike's journey throughout the film mirrors Lorde's beliefs in being true to one's inner feelings and transcending others' shaping of the self. The pain Alike has had to experience also reflects Lorde's emphasis on this being a difficult process: Alike has attained peace of mind at the end of the film, though she is on a journey – both literally and metaphorically – and will undoubtedly have to encounter more difficulties along the way.

As *Pariah* centres on an African American who does not adhere to broad stereotypes of blackness, music functions partly to expose what Mahon describes as 'dominant, flattening stereotypes of blackness' prominent in media representations (Mahon 2004: 8), which have rarely included black lesbian characters; DeClue (2018: 226) has noted that when *Pariah* was released it was only the 'second feature film made by an out black lesbian director to have a national theatrical release in the United States.' DeClue (2018: 232) also argues that the film 'works to destabilize the imposed political divisions and essentializing conceptions of blackness that obfuscate black queerness'. Alike herself can be considered a 'post-soul eccentric' (Royster 2012) through her queerness, musical tastes and nerdish qualities; her more bookish inclinations align her with the figure of the 'black nerd' or 'Afro nerd'. Francesca T. Royster has noted how novels featuring black nerd characters – such as Zadie Smith's *White Teeth*, Paul Beatty's *The Whiteboy Shuffle* and Danzy Senna's *Caucasia* – tend to:

> explore coming of age in a global Post-Soul landscape of shifting racial, gender, and sexual identity. In each of these novels, recently integrated schools and blurring neighborhood color and class lines, as well as the ghostly return of histories of racial violence, become the backdrop for the production of nerdy, eccentric, or 'strange' selves, forged between the cracks of family and community. (Royster 2012: 5)

Pariah is also important for featuring a black female nerd figure, a figure which, as Jonathan Charles Flowers (2018: 185) has argued, is rarer in popular culture than white female nerds. Finally, Alike, Jo and Micah can be considered black bohemians. Reniqua Allen (2013: 509–513) argues that there is a long tradition of black bohemianism, but that such figures were largely overlooked not just by Hollywood but also within much independent production until the release of *Medicine for Melancholy*.[4] Black bohemians, hipsters, nerds and eccentrics can all be linked to a broader idea of alternative black culture and the 'alt-black lifestyle', which is becoming more notable within various media representations, including film and music.

Conclusion

Medicine for Melancholy and *Pariah* both, in different ways, employ a range of 'indie' music to explore black selfhood. Further, these representations can also – to refer back to Frith's argument – help to *construct* identities through disseminating representations of 'eccentric' black identities which refute more conventional depictions of blackness in favour of 'understanding blackness as multiaccentual and multidisciplinary' (Gillespie 2016: 6). *Medicine for*

Melancholy features a range of music that would more commonly adhere to dominant perceptions of indie music – lo-fi, mostly guitar-driven, often confessional music by white artists – to interrogate issues such as racism and hipsterism in a city with a dwindling black population. The whiteness of indie music is foregrounded in Micah's rant, and it serves to both construct, and probe, 'non-normative' black identities and question culturally engrained stereotypes around black selfhood. Micah and Jo evade stereotypical black identities, but Jenkins seems to ask at what cost such liberation comes, particularly via the character of Micah. While Jo seems relatively comfortable with her own being, Micah is more conflicted and worries about his predominantly 'white' tastes and white friends, conscious of how his cultural habits and networks are shaped by intersecting forces in a city undergoing black erasure. In this sense, his experiences have similarities to some of the noted issues raised at the beginning of the chapter, in which black people who embrace rock music – particularly indie-rock – sometimes feel as though they are marginalised both from the white communities that they participate in and also from other black people.

Within *Medicine for Melancholy*, indie music functions as a broad genre, a subset of rock music. Indie, however, is also as an abbreviation of independent and can function as an adverbial modifier of other genres rather than a self-contained genre. Categorising indie through an adverbial, rather than generic, lens more frequently could help to address the overwhelming whiteness of indie music. *Pariah* is interesting in this respect as it incorporates a range of black indie music which spans different genres. Its main character is drawn to certain forms of black indie music (though not all), particularly rock and hip-hop. And while rock music itself is linked to whiteness, *Pariah* demonstrates that black (indie) rock exists and can be enjoyed communally by a predominantly black crowd. The film is also important in focusing on a female character and featuring music from female artists; as noted in the previous chapter, indie-rock has often privileged males over females. If it is difficult for white women to become indie-rock artists, it is even more so for women of colour: 'For black women rockers', Mahon has argued, 'the challenges increase exponentially. Their gender and race mark them as doubly outside of rock 'n' roll's white male club' (Mahon 2012: 208). While the film does not limit itself to indie-rock, it does of course feature a Tamar-kali live performance, during which black females both perform and enjoy energetic rock sounds. Yet it explores other modes of female, black indie music, and in this sense can be considered – through its carefully curated soundtrack – to intervene in broadening conceptions of indie music. It therefore chimes with Berlatsky's arguments about needing to redefine our ideas around indie if we are to move beyond its predominant whiteness.

If black indie music is to become more fully encouraged and recognised, then there needs to be greater acknowledgment and discussion of black indie-rock on the one hand, and more openness to other modes of independent black music as 'indie' on the other. *Pariah* is a film that points towards a more black-centric approach to indie, demonstrating examples of black indie-rock alongside a range of other black indie music. Such a shift can only happen if cognitive ideas of indie are modified, which requires structural change across indie music institutions – such as music publications, record labels, music clubs – that are far more open to, and supportive of, black participants. As indie label manager Matthew James-Wilson (2020) has stated, 'once the indie industry confronts its complacency in upholding racist traditions, it can create a more equal future for everyone'.

Notes

Sections of this chapter were originally published as '"Everything About Being Indie is All Tied to Not Being Black": Indie Music, Race and Identity in *Medicine for Melancholy* and *Pariah*' in *Music, Sound, and the Moving Image* 16.2 (2022), published by Liverpool University Press.

1. The composed score, while perhaps less likely to spark external associations in the same manner as widely known pre-existing songs, can still do so through generic/stylistic resemblances to other music. Of course, many film soundtracks actually combine composed scores and compiled songs.
2. The script lists some slightly different artists than those mentioned within this dialogue. I have not ascertained the exact reason for this, but in the script there is a clearer sense that Alike's listed artists are broadly related to alternative modes of hip-hop (more political and 'progressive' than the type of music played at the nightclub she frequents with Laura) and include The Roots, Black Star, Asheru, BlueBlack and Pharcyde.
3. It sounds as though they say Mahmabadia, which again is a play upon an actual artist name (like Trees being substituted for The Roots, Black Circle substituting for Black Star).
4. Allen does discuss another, earlier example of black bohemianism, *Love Jones* (Witcher, 1997), and refers to some other examples predating *Medicine for Melancholy*, including *She's Gotta Have It* (Lee, 1986) and *Slam* (Levin, 1998).

8 INDIE MUSIC, FILM AND RACE 2: *SORRY TO BOTHER YOU*

The previous chapter largely focused on modes of indie-rock music within African American filmmaking, highlighting how this unusual practice could delineate offbeat or eccentric black identities. *Pariah* also featured several other modes of black independent music, including soul, R&B and hip-hop, and therefore points towards how indie music might be considered differently, to be more inclusive of black modes of music. There have been some developments – such as the increased use of terms like alternative R&B and indie hip-hop – which indicate increased attention paid towards non-rock and *non-white* forms of indie and alternative music.

The annual music Afropunk Festival is representative of a broader acknowledgement of the idea of alternative black music. Initially the festival was mainly concerned with booking punk artists (it was founded by James Spooner and Matthew Morgan). The festival has, however, changed direction since its inception in 2005; in 2008 Spooner left, to be replaced by Jocelyn Cooper, who has steered it in a more commercial direction through forging many partnerships and expanding its musical palette. Originally free, Afropunk Festival started charging admission fees for the first time in 2015 and has grown significantly since its beginnings; while still held in Brooklyn, it has also held several other international Afropunk events in cities including Atlanta, Johannesburg, London and Paris. Rachel Lifter (2020: 109) has argued that whereas Afropunk Festival was originally based around a specific subculture – black punks – it is now more broadly addressing 'the other black experience'. The event now includes a range of different music, which still includes punk but also features hip-hop,

R&B and many other types of music. If the commercial imperatives of the organisers have nudged the festival into slightly more mainstream territory, the roster of artists does nevertheless indicate that the festival is now more interested in alternative and indie modes of various black music than in punk per se. As such, the festival can be considered a very visible, and increasingly international, event at which new, though still marginal, conceptions of indie music are being constructed. Lifter, who focuses primarily on indie fashions, has also argued that Afropunk Festival and its attendant coverage have led to 'Afro-diasporic blackness' being 'inserted into the visual imaginary of twenty-first century indie' (Lifter 2020: 105).

In this chapter I will focus on indie music in one film – *Sorry to Bother You* (Riley, 2018) – as this film features a range of indie hip-hop and electronic music and interrogates blackness in quite complex ways. The film is about Cassius (LeKeith Stanfield), who gets a job at a telesales company and works himself up the ranks; however, Cassius's rise in the company also leads to moral issues – when he gets promoted, he also gets shunned by his unionised friends. Eventually, Cassius joins a rebellion after being transformed into an equisapien, a consequence of being injected with a serum by the corporation Worryfree.

Like both *Medicine for Melancholy* and *Pariah*, *Sorry to Bother You* connects its music to alternative ideas of blackness, but it does so in a very different manner than those two films. Whereas they were both quite realist in tone, *Sorry to Bother You* is more surrealist, and can be considered an example of 'Afrosurrealism'. The notion of Afrosurrealism is often credited to Amira Baraka, who in a 1974 introduction to Henry Dumas's *Ark of Bones and Other Stories*, used the phrase 'Afrosurreal Expressionism' (Miller 2013: 114). For Francis Terri, the Afrosurreal is a continuation of surrealism, but whereas the surrealists in the earlier twentieth century often used blackness as a trope, Afosurrealism is black expression via surrealist aesthetics. Terri states that:

> European surrealism rebelliously embraced 'blackness' through a haze of obsessions and misunderstandings stirred up at viewing African or other diasporic masks and objects – and objectified people. Part of the work that Afrosurrealism does, alongside Afromodernism, is then to re-center blackness at the core of surrealism and modernism, not as catalytic matter but as the manifestations of black artists' own modalities. (Terri 2013: 100)

The film can also be connected to the idea of Afrofuturism, referring to science fiction which explores elements of black experience. As already noted, black representations have regularly been codified in rather reductive ways, with certain stereotypes and other recurrent tropes becoming linked to perceptions around blackness, perceptions that can and have become essentialised at times. Afrofuturism deviates from realist templates more readily associated with black cultural production, but its aesthetic avoidance of realism does not mean that it is merely escapist; rather, a great deal of Afrofuturist art concerns political issues and addresses the histories and current realities of black subjects. John Corbett (1994: 7) has asserted that Afrofuturist artists 'have constructed worlds of their own, futuristic environs that subtly signify on the marginalisation of black culture. These new discursive galaxies utilize a set of tropes and metaphors of space and alienation, linking their common diasporic African history to a notion of extraterrestriality'. Jazz musician and poet Sun Ra is often considered the chief pioneer of Afrofuturism, but Afrofuturism has also been evident in a range of other artists' work across different media: for example, Octavia E. Butler, Samuel Delaney and Funkadelic/Parliament have been considered seminal contributors to the development of Afrofutrist aesthetics. More recently there has been a growth in Afrofurist works – including the big-budget blockbuster *Black Panther* (Coogler, 2018) and the music of Janelle Monae – yet limited representations and perceptions of black culture are still in evidence.

There are undoubtedly some overlaps between Afrofuturism and Afrosurrealism, though Scot Miller stresses that Afrosurrealism is more concerned with the present than the future: 'Afro-Futurism is a diaspora intellectual and artistic movement that turns to science, technology, and science fiction to speculate on black possibilities in the future. Afrosurrealism is about the present' (Miller 2013: 114). While Miller touches on an important issue here, I am not sure that we can divide the two modes quite so easily. Many examples of Afrofuturism are concerned with the present and the future, as well as the past: Octavia E. Butler's *Kindred* (1979), for example, is a novel about time travel and has hence been connected to Afrofuturism, but it concerns time travel from the present to the past; Sun Ra's film *Space is the Place* (Corbett, 1974), meanwhile, is a key Afrofuturist text which addresses the past (Ancient Egypt, 1940s Chicago), the present (1970s Oklahoma) and the future (the Afro-space idyll). Despite its name, Afrofuturism generally refers to black science fiction, not all of which is set in the future. While *Sorry to Bother You* is more obviously an Afrosurrealist text, it can also be positioned as an Afrofuturist text in some ways through taking place in an alternate reality.

Music in *Sorry to Bother You*

Boots Riley, the director of *Sorry to Bother You*, is a member of the longstanding hip-hop group The Coup, who provide a substantial amount of the music for the film. Unlike *Medicine for Melancholy* and *Pariah*, the music in *Sorry to Bother You* is all newly produced for the film. Boots Riley has himself explained that the film consists of a 'soundtrack' and a 'score'. The Coup created the soundtrack, which is largely used diegetically, while Tune-Yards produced the score, which is used non-diegetically. Both acts have been considered indie: Tune-Yards are generally considered an indie band who create slightly experimental pop and record on long-standing indie label 4AD (now owned by the Beggars Group[1]); The Coup are a hip-hop/rap act, though they release records on independent labels and are often considered alternative hip-hop because of their eclectic influences and openly Marxist sympathies (which also place them in the 'conscious' hip-hop category). Both these acts have challenged generic boundaries in their work and their musical contributions reinforce some of the broader theoretical issues explored in the film, such as questioning cultural symbols and stereotypes, code switching, cultural appropriation and recontextualisation. The Coup's soundtrack is used rather sparsely in comparison to the Tune-Yards score, so I will largely focus on the latter in the following analysis, before turning attention to broader ways in which music informs the film.

The score by Tune-Yards features fewer vocals than their studio albums; whereas most Tune-Yards album tracks feature Merrill Garbus's sung vocals, the score for *Sorry to Bother You* only features her vocals occasionally and these tend to be non-lexical vocables rather than sung lyrics. The score also includes many repeated motifs across tracks; while this is common within film scoring, such elements are heightened in this instance, which reinforces other ways that the film interrogates fixed, essentialised concepts. Many tracks, for example, use elements from other songs and transform these through recontextualisation, which mirrors Cassius's progression as he transforms from an impecunious lost soul into a successful power marketer, before eventually transforming materially into an equisapien. One of the tracks on the score is called 'Transformative Experience' – which is first heard when Cassius gazes longingly at the gold elevator door which transports power callers upstairs.

As Cassius is the main character, much of the score links to his experiences, though Detroit (Tessa Thompson) also has music associated with her character to a lesser extent and it is worth noting the ways that these two characters are linked with specific segments of the score. Cassius is associated with a variety of different styles, whereas Detroit is linked to her theme or variations on it, which is indicative of their characters' identities more generally. Detroit is presented as a person who is more confident of who she is and what she wants to do than Cassius, illustrated in their first scene together in bed, when Cassius is neurotically fretting about death and at one point says: 'Okay, you've got your calling, your art means something, right? I'm just out here surviving, spinning around . . . '. Not only is Cassius poor, he is also adrift in the world and searching for purpose, and therefore ripe for transformation. His use of the term 'spinning around' is also telling, as Detroit literally does spin signs in the first part of the film, which again indicates their differences: she is more in control of her sense of self (the spinner), whereas he is not (the spun).

The varieties of music on the score associated with Cassius can very broadly be divided into the following: the minimal, deep bass sounds of 'STTS' and variations on it; the warped muzak of 'RegalView'; the harder hip-hop sounds of 'Money Money Money'; and the more airy, ambient tracks which often feature high-pitched, ethereal vocal textures. Some of these tracks, such as 'RegalView', function as unchanging leitmotifs: the track is used as a subtle underscore on several occasions when Cassius is at work. Most of the other leitmotifs, however, undergo variations of some kind when they reappear. 'STTS', for example, plays when Cassius gets a new job, and then when he is promoted. It then reappears in modified form (as 'Play My Clip') when Cassius exposes Worryfree's creation of equisapiens, in which the main synth melody is shifted to a higher octave, increased tempo and supplemented by further instrumental colour. The result is a deviation of 'STTS', indicative of Cassius's shift of allegiance and a growing moral awareness: if the previous instances of 'STTS' symbolised Cassius's career success, on this occasion it represents him rejecting compromised ideas of social progression in favour of a more moral – though economically precarious – position. The more delicate, ambient pieces are mainly associated with Cassius's desire to climb the ladder of career success, which involve mimicking whiteness. Many of these pieces are atmospheric and use elongated, ethereal vocal sounds; at times – in particular 'Steve Lift's Party' – they sound like stereotypical conceptions of heavenly music through calming textures and 'angelic' vocals. The film presents parallels between ideas of Heaven and career progression within a white world, which the score reinforces: the lift to the upstairs power callers' suite is gold and eyed desirously by Cassius prior to his entrance into this elite group. As with ideas around Heaven, there is an implication that American Dream-like notions of success are as illusory as religious ideas of Heaven, and both have been used to retain social hierarchies in different ways (the idea is that one should not complain about or question the dominant system one exists within, but should contribute to that system as effectively as possible in order to be rewarded; in the case of Heaven this is the reward that one only receives after death, while the American Dream tends to suppress issues related to race and class and exaggerate its achievability). In contrast, 'Money Money Money' – through its distorted, grainy beats and insistent bass groove – is a more earthy representation of material desire that runs through the film. It is the more materialist accompaniment to Cassius's desire for gain, whereas the ambient sounds represent the idealistic side to his aspirations, as well as the privileged upper echelons of the white elite.

Music associated with Detroit is less variable in nature than Cassius's; the music linked with her character – in particular 'SIGNS (Detroit's Theme)' – draws on (and refers to) various African singing traditions, which is appropriate as Detroit is also aligned with Africa in the film. The track is driven by vocal ululations, which are layered to create a kind of call-and-response effect; the track builds rhythmically through electronic percussion and steady bass notes, which are accompanied by chopped vocal snippets. That the most 'African' sounding piece is produced by a white indie band, as opposed to The Coup, links to two issues probed within the film: code-switching and the broader interrogation of cultural symbols. Riley draws attention to how both vocal and musical tropes are raced, which links to Jennifer Lynn Stoever's concept of the 'sonic color line'. Stoever (2016: 10–11) argues that sounds and the ways we are trained to listen to them are reflective of racial biases, that the 'sonic color line produces, codes, and polices racial difference through the ear, enabling us to hear race as well as see it'. Yet Stoever also draws attention to how raced sounds can be impersonated – she mentions the example of minstrelsy – which 'point to the instability of sound as a racial determinant and the possibility of crossing the racial color line' (Ibid.). By drawing attention to the mimicking of raced sounds, *Sorry to Bother You* highlights the socially constructed nature of seemingly natural sounds.

Code-switching is the process of adapting one's presentation to others according to context, and can include modifications in, for example, speech, appearance and behaviour. While people present themselves in modified ways according to context generally, code-switching is an intensified form of self-presentation particularly associated with minority groups who try to socially 'fit in'. African Americans, for example, will often modify their behaviour radically when attending job interviews in order to avoid being judged negatively (i.e. interviewers will often negatively perceive stereotypical attributes of black people, so black people may deliberately avoid conforming to such stereotypes). *Sorry to Bother You* overtly addresses code-switching through the 'white voice': for Cassius to progress at RegalView he must present himself as white, and this is most prominently manifested in his attempt to mimic white speech. Even Detroit, who is critical of Cassius's increased adoption of the white voice, uses a white voice when she speaks to white art dealers prior to and during her performance. There is an implication here that she might not be aware she is adopting it, as the process of code-switching is not always consciously registered; so commonly do African Americans have to adapt to white norms that many will not necessarily even be aware of doing so. To further emphasise code-switching, Detroit's art performance quotes from *The Last Dragon* (Schultz, 1985), a film about African Americans mimicking Chinese cultural forms, which draws attention to how code-switching does not always ape whiteness (even if this is by far its most dominant mode).

The Tune-Yards' music is heavily influenced by some forms of African music, most notably Congolese pop.[2] It is notable, also, that Garbus attended an anti-racist workshop and immersed herself in anti-racist literature following the release of the Tune-Yards' third album *Nikki-Nack* (2014), which Stephanie

Phillips (2021: 82) has argued was 'one example of a white musician attempting to understand how clearly to make out the line between cultural appreciation and appropriation'. While Garbus had drawn on many forms of music from other parts of the world, she claimed that she had not really confronted issues of whiteness and privilege in her music (Powers 2018). Her growing awareness of the politics of cross-ethnic and racial influences, and the desire to confront difficult questions of oneself, fits the broader philosophical thrust of *Sorry to Bother You*. The Tune-Yards' connections with African music relate to Riley's broader interrogation of cultural symbols, especially racial ones. If a white band can produce 'African-sounding' music, this draws attention to the ways that 'Africa' exists as a sometimes-reductive cultural signifier.

In her discussion of Afropunk Festival, Rachel Lifter noted how Gene Zipporah wrote an online critique of participants at the festival 'appropriating' African clothing and tribal marks. Zipporah argued:

> White people appropriate *Black culture*. Words such as *fancy dress*, *mockery* and *profiteering* are thrown around quite freely, but no one seems to realize that this selfsame violation is committed against us Africans – all under the guise of tribal fashion and connection to *The Motherland*. (Quoted in Lifter 2020: 122)

Lifter stresses that such critiques were rare, but these comments do point towards awareness of how African Americans might draw loosely on ideas of a motherland in exotic ways. I have already noted how Detroit's performance references African Americans 'appropriating' style from East Asian culture via the quotes from *The Last Dragon*. Detroit uses Africa within her artistic production to comment on black oppression and exploitation, but there is no evidence pointing to whether Detroit has a significant understanding of a complex, diverse continent consisting of numerous countries and cultures. While she is presented in a largely positive manner, Riley nevertheless points to her contradictions; Cassius, for example, critiques her art because while it addresses black radicalism, it is ultimately addressed to rich white people. Detroit uses Africa as a symbol to create art addressing issues of exploitation and black oppression, but her somewhat exoticised notion of Africa is ultimately in the service of rich white people and in no sense addresses concrete practices of exploitation.

The Coup's music has also challenged generic and other racially codified expectations. They are generally considered as a hip-hop act, though they released their 2006 album *Pick a Bigger Weapon* on the independent label Epitaph, which is mainly associated with punk music. The Coup also tend to mix things up in terms of their eclectic, generically diverse influences, which are inflected through a politically-oriented, intellectually curious stance.

Despite the serious intent behind their music, their sound is often energetic, danceable and upbeat. One notable influence on their music and approach is worth mentioning in terms of its broader philosophical import: Parliament/Funkadelic.[3] George Clinton sought to break down barriers between different musical forms, combining the physical appeal of dancing with a ceaseless intellectual curiosity that was often expressed comically. In the late 1970s, for example, when rock music had become increasingly perceived as a white mode of music, Funkadelic were recording 'Who Says a Funk Band Can't Play Rock'. For Clinton and his revolving cast of allies, rules such as this were arbitrary and malleable rather than solid and fixed.

The Coup's music combines appeals to the intellect and the body, recalling again George Clinton's frequent emphasis on how dancing can loosen the body and help one to 'dance your way out of your constrictions'.[4] While Clinton generally used the body and the mind as lyrically separate units, he also was challenging overly strict mind-body dualisms. Such dualistic separations between mind and body had fed into an intellectual perception of dance music as brainless and mechanistic in some quarters. As African Americans were often engaged in producing forms of dance music, such dismissals often reflected underlying racial prejudices. In the inter-war period, for example, moral concerns were often raised by whites concerning African Americans congregating at music venues. A particular concern was how energetic dancing could break down inhibitions and lead to social disorder, a phenomenon expertly satirised by Ishmael Reed in his 1972 novel *Mumbo Jumbo*, which depicts the hysteria around 'Jes Grew', a kind of epidemic originating in New Orleans in the 1920s that takes hold of subjects and causes them to dance recklessly, love jazz and appreciate African American culture more fully. For Reed and Clinton, dancing offers the chance to transcend the here-and-now, including the dominant structural and discursive limitations which constrain African American experience. Dancing is, therefore, not merely functional escapism, but also a means of liberating both the body and the mind, which are of course inextricably connected. In a similar manner, The Coup's music has always attempted to meld the mental and physical through producing danceable, Marxist-informed hip-hop music.

Hip-Hop, Recontextualisation and Anti-Essentialism

Hip-hop music feeds into the film on a broader, intellectual level through ideas of recontextualisation. Sampling other records, for example, while not exclusive to hip-hop, is a practice connected heavily to hip-hop production. Sampling allows producers to rip fragments of recordings from their original frameworks and to place them within a new context, transforming them in the process. *Sorry to Bother You* includes scenes which stress the importance of context in the function and reception of cultural production, not just through sonic sampling but also through other forms of appropriation and recontextualisation. Tricia Rose (1994: 83) has noted how 'hip hop has always been articulated via commodities and engaged in the revision of meanings attached to them. Conversely, hip hop signs and meanings are converted and behaviours relabelled by dominant institutions.' In *Sorry to Bother You*, such processes are also evident in the ways other cultural signs are caught within processes of recoding and transformation.

A particularly salient example of recontextualisation occurs through the modification of a billboard advertisement promoting Worryfree. We first encounter this advert in the street, revealed to us in full as the camera moves beyond Detroit's earrings. The image then transforms via a simple dissolve into a modified, hacked version of the poster, perpetrated by the Left Eye group. This deformation of the image is a typical piece of adbusting, as exemplified by the *Adbusters* organisation and other agents involved in culture jamming, the process of 'talking back' to the corporate dominance of public space, usually through undermining the original message and highlighting less pleasant realities underpinning corporate capitalism. In this specific example, the Left Eye group changes the meaning of the advert through modifying the text and elements of the image. This results in a shift from a much more passive, comfortable image to a more active, militant one: the main way this is achieved is through erasing the sofa that the man is sitting on and replacing it with a wicker chair, while the soda in his hands is replaced by a rifle and spear. The image now immediately recalls Eldritch Cleaver's iconic photo of Huey Newton taken in 1967, and therefore the militancy of the Black Panther Party. This image had also been drawn on for the cover of Funkadelic's 1979 album *Uncle Jam Wants You*, further drawing attention to transformation and recontextualisation, as well as Clinton's broader influence.

The message also shifts from the security of getting a job at Worryfree and providing for your child – which uses a stereotypical image of a lazy black man – to freedom, which has been graffitied over the Worryfree logo. The man is now transformed into a symbol of militancy and defiance. It is also relevant that the original advertisement is shot at night, and the modified ad at day, which implies that the latter is a more enlightened perspective in that it offers alternative messages to many advertisements, which tend to reinforce the status quo and encourage passive acceptance of it. Yet Riley also points to the limitations of culture jamming through showing another transformation of the advertisement later in the film. When Cassius visits Worryfree CEO Steve Lift's party, there is a shot of the culture jammed advertisement on Lift's wall. This is another process of transformation, except that in this instance the image has not been further altered in any major way. It has, however, been recontextualised, and through this transformation in setting, Riley seems to be stressing

Figure 8.1 and 8.2 *Sorry to Bother You*: Worryfree's billboard advertisement becomes transformed through the Left Eye Group's adbusting

how such cultural signs are malleable and subject to appropriation. In this instance, a political intervention in the form of culture jamming has been taken out of the public sphere and placed within a luxury mansion – itself sealed off from public space within a gated community – of a rich CEO. This points to the problems confronting both culture jammers and artists more generally: if they challenge dominant institutions and values, such challenges can be neutralised partly through being appropriated by those that they challenge. In the case of the culture jammed advertisement, Lift has merely taken the image and literally domesticated it. It has transformed from a political slogan (a spur to action) into a bourgeois status symbol (whose residual political message can nonetheless help to confer on its owner an 'edgy' status), demonstrating how radical cultural interventions can become easily co-opted.[5]

The many routes through which sampled material – whether sonic, visual or otherwise – can be appropriated, recontextualised and transformed, further leads to a questioning of any transhistorical and essential meanings and an attack on reductive assumptions. This process links to theoretical work on cultural subversion, in particular the theories of Antonio Gramsci and the subcultural theorist Dick Hebdige, both of whom were influenced by Marxist thought but placed more importance on culture than did Marx. Gramsci is best known for his influential theory of hegemony: broadly stated, this refers to the ways in which dominant social structures use their power via culture to propagate ideas and values, as opposed to physical policing through force and coercion. Ideas which are propagated culturally are ideological, but their ideological function is often concealed and adopted by many people as 'common sense'. Culture is thus positioned as a crucially important field through which ideas can be contested and fought over, and Gramsci stressed the need for counter-hegemonic ideas to be disseminated. Hebdige draws significantly on Gramsci's work and combines this with a semiotic approach to probe different subcultures – such as punk – and the ways they have often used commodities to signify rebellion, endowing them with 'implicitly oppositional meanings' (Hebdige 1979: 16). Hebdige claims that dominant political orders are never fixed; there is always room for opposition, even if the dominance of cultural and political life by the ruling order makes such opposition difficult. According to Hebdige (1979: 16–17):

> The symbiosis in which ideology and social order, production and reproduction, are linked is then neither fixed nor guaranteed. It can be prised open. The consensus can be fractured, challenged, overruled, and resistance to the groups in dominance cannot always be lightly dismissed or automatically incorporated.

Through symbolic means, subcultures can draw attention to the ideological underpinnings of supposedly 'natural' signs and recode them to create alternative significations which can sometimes attract the ire of those wedded to the status quo. Such subversive tactics, however, can also be incorporated back into dominant culture through reporting, labelling, framing and, on a more stylistic level, by incorporating styles of subcultures into the fashion industry. While Hebdige does stress how this is a continual process, he nonetheless tends towards the pessimistic in his conclusions, noting that the stylistic challenge of subcultures inevitably becomes incorporated, and that 'as soon as the original innovations which signify "subculture" are translated into commodities and made generally available, they become "frozen"' (1979: 96).

This pessimistic conclusion is undoubtedly linked to how Hebdige focuses primarily on style. The problem with the symbolic contestation of subcultures, he implies, is that they are too focused on stylistic disruption. Boots Riley would probably counter that cultural/symbolic subversion is important, but that such activities need to be combined with more direct political actions so that a constant challenge is built across different fields. The power of the ruling elite – economic, institutional and cultural – means that this is an incredibly difficult task, but not an impossibility. *Sorry to Bother You* supplements its continual play with, and questioning of, cultural symbols with direct political action, including the forming of a union, and culminates in an insurrection by the equisapiens. Riley here confronts how subversive activity can be tamed through incorporation and appropriation, but suggests that there is still potential for further transformation: the chain does not end there, but is potentially endless. If we revisit the culture jammed advertisement in *Sorry to Bother You*, one could consider the chain by which it becomes advertisement, subvertisement, then fine art as indicative of the ways in which processes of appropriation and control over signs are always being contested. That the film only shows three stages of this image being transformed perhaps implies that battles for control over the power to signify are inevitably weighted towards those in power, but the questioning, open-ended approach of Riley and his team also emphasises that power is never guaranteed. The ending of the film, which concludes as Cassius and the other equisapiens storm the gated apartment of Lift, both reaffirms this idea of conflict being open-ended – perhaps endless – as well as emphasising the necessity of combining political culture with political activism.

One particularly prominent 'sign' interrogated within the film is blackness itself. Obviously, to call blackness merely a sign risks causing offence through its gross reduction of a complex category. And yet Riley certainly does interrogate it as a sign in one respect; in fact, he seems to be critical of how the complexity and diversity of black lived experiences can be – and often are – reduced to a few essential attributes (reduced, that is, to convenient cultural symbols). This can manifest itself in racist terms, as when white people stereotype blacks for certain traits and attributes (e.g. having a more natural sense of rhythm than white people). In *Sorry to Bother You* such stereotypical reduction is evident when Steve Lift states to Cassius 'I want to hear about some of that Oakland gangster shit, man', and then asks him to rap. When Cassius replies that he can't rap, the other guests at the party – who have surrounded Cassius as though he is a party act – repeatedly chant 'rap, rap, rap'. The awkward, halting response from Cassius fails to conform to anyone's idea of good rapping, however, which highlights the absurdity of such reductionist and racist assumptions. Out of desperation, Cassius starts repeating the phrase 'Nigger shit, nigger shit', which the guests then repeat in an enthusiastic manner. This scene demonstrates how black people can be put in limited boxes via prevalent stereotypes, in this case blacks being considered rappers; and it also demonstrates how for many white people, while such stereotypes can be entertaining, they are only so when packaged as a performance. For, while Cassius is urged to act out prominent symbols of 'blackness' when entertaining Lift and his guests, in his general exchanges with Lift, he talks to him – as he is advised to – in his 'white voice'. The implication is that black people should try to act like white people as much as possible to get on in the (capitalist) world, apart from when they are entertaining. Cassius's status at the party as a figure of entertainment is reinforced when he spots several party guests watching YouTube footage of him being hit at the strike.

It is not, however, merely white people who are guilty of such stereotypical reductionism. While differently pitched, there is also an earlier discussion about blackness between Cassius, Detroit, Salvador and Squeeze, during which Salvador questions Cassius's 'blackness'; Cassius in reply claims 'I'm black', which Salvador mocks with 'you're like Lionel Ritchie black'. This shows how ingrained ideas around blackness aren't merely employed by whites but also infuse how black people think about themselves. It again relates to questions around racial identity noted by Gilroy, who believes it is important to 'recognize the anachronistic condition of the idea of "race" as a basis upon which human beings are distinguished and ranked' (Gilroy 2005: 37). As previously mentioned, Gilroy is very aware how various types of racism are enacted in everyday life and calls for these to be confronted. Yet he warns against depending on naturalist racial categories to do so, for these are themselves derived from colonialist ways of thinking. As such, he contends that race 'should be approached as an afterimage – a lingering effect of looking too casually into the damaging glare emanating from colonial conflicts at home and abroad' (Ibid.). The constant probing of racial, and other, categories in *Sorry to Bother You* connects to the very problems that Gilroy is discussing: to examine the ways in which racial categories are often used in everyday discourse and confront problematic, essentialist perceptions. It is relevant, then, that this discussion between Cassius, Detroit and Salvador also touches on other issues around essentialist perceptions. A notable point of discussion is when Cassius describes how he likes his spaghetti with sauce, which is not only a custom that Salvador considers 'white' but which also leads to a consideration of the origins of pasta. At one point Cassius mentions how pasta is Italian, before Detroit asserts that pasta is Chinese. This conversation again reflects on the issue of essentialised thinking and its limitations. Of course, many people think of pasta as being Italian, though if we explore the history of pasta, things are a little more complicated. Historical evidence does not offer any straightforward answers as to the origins of pasta, but it is widely considered to have been introduced into Italy from the Middle East, where it was further adapted. Detroit's comment about it being Chinese relates to some theories around pasta developing from noodles introduced to Italy by Marco Polo, though such viewpoints have largely been debunked. The fact that this topic of discussion follows on from Cassius's blackness being questioned is important, as it further draws attention to the complexities of origins (and by extension the 'nature' of things), and how categories can become codified in ways that simplify their underlying reality. This does not negate the importance of being black, particularly within societies where such a designation often leads to prejudice, repression and violence, but it does seem to warn against essentialised notions of blackness. Conversely, excessive code-switching is also posited as problematic: it may benefit an individual in some cases, but it does not challenge systemic prejudices against minorities; further, code-switching can take a cognitive toll on an individual through continually suppressing elements of their cultural identity.

The idea of Cassius 'selling out' is not merely related to race, but also to class. In fact, it is Cassius's betrayal of his fellow striking workers that is positioned as most problematic in the film, which is not entirely surprising considering Boots Riley's commitment to Communism and his background in political activism. There is also a difference in the film between the discussion of race and the class-based strike activities: racial discussions are largely abstract, whereas the class elements unfurl around particular, concrete events. The specificity of context is important, even within a film that avoids a realist aesthetic. The filming location is crucial in this regard: Oakland is a concrete location that Riley has lived within for the majority of his life, and it is also where the Black Panthers were established. Through emphasising the concrete and the contextual, Riley implies that any abstract ideas and categories – including but certainly not limited to blackness – need to be related to specific instances to avoid over-generalised, and often simplified, modes of perception.

As noted in relation to the culture jamming elements of the film, context – and history – are positioned as crucial filters affecting the meanings of various signs. If, for example, the same action or object can signify differently across variable contexts, and discrete objects (and people) can change and transform, then essentialism(s) must be questioned. This applies to the ways in which some music tracks are employed in the film as well. An example is the use of The Coup's 'OYAHYTT', which is used on more than one occasion. The track is upbeat and contains a catchy, snappy chorus, but its sprightly sonic qualities seem at odds with the visual action it matches with on its initial appearance. It accompanies Cassius when he is driving to work on his first day, but the energy of the music is contrasted with the lethargic, down-at-heel nature of Cassius's demeanour: he is comically cramped in his clapped-out car when he is driving to work, with his string-pulled windshield wiper adding an absurdist twist to the shot, and when he arrives at work his posture is exaggeratedly hunched. This is a deliberate moment of counterpoint music, where the qualities of the soundtrack seem out of kilter with the tone of the image. In this scene, music represents upbeat emotions related to getting a new job (Cassius is, after all, desperate to get money to pay off his many debts), but

Cassius's deflated posture indicates that the job might not be something to celebrate; we can understand this as a deliberate juxtaposition of sounds and images to indicate how this moment, in one sense, represents Cassius becoming entrapped within an oppressive system (and there are allusions to prisons at other points in the film, such as Worryfree's accommodation for its workers). The clash between the audio and visual energy, however, is further complicated by the lyrics of the track itself. The party-style atmosphere of the music is accompanied by militant lyrics, albeit rapped in a rhythmic style.

The lyrical militancy of the track may, for some viewers – as it did for me – only reveal itself after a few listens. As the lyrics are spat out rhythmically and use clipped language that is far from didactic in its allusiveness, they do not explicitly demand immediate attention. However, once one listens closely, such militancy becomes more evident through lyrical references to rage and combativeness. If Cassius's mien is on the depressive side, and the music on the celebratory, the lyrics add an aggressive dimension to the scene, though rage here is directed at corporations and therefore related to the broader anti-capitalist thrust of the film. Other lyrics also connect to themes and moments within the film: 'Nigga shit', for example, is repeated by Cassius later in the film, and 'Gimme that change' relates to his need for money and his more acquisitive characteristics.

The next time the track plays in the film it is once again used to accompany Cassius, but in a very different situation. While the first instance occurs when Cassius is feeling deflated (following a period of unemployment and with no seeming direction), the second instance appears after he has adopted a white voice for his telesales work and is starting to do well at his job. As opposed to the first time the track is played, in this scene the lively, colourful music matches the emotional tone of the visual actions, a briskly paced montage of Cassius

Figure 8.3 *Sorry to Bother You*: Cassius celebrates his telesales successes

celebrating his sales successes at different instances. Overtly, 'OYAHYTT' is more conventionally matched with the visual track, but this matching does not extend to the lyrical content of the track, whose militancy lends a critical dimension to the montage and points towards the alternative path of protest that Cassius will ultimately be drawn into.

The divergent moods and meanings evoked through the placement of 'OYAHYTT' at different points in the film again draws attention to how social and cultural signs do not have fixed meanings and highlights the importance of context in their signification and reception. The difficulty of fixing meaning is also raised in relation to specific objects and beings: the fact that the lyrics and musical qualities of 'OYAHYTT' seem at odds with each other indicates how single objects themselves might not have a clear, coherent identity, and as such can signify differently regardless of the contexts that they circulate within. This seems to apply not only to cultural objects but to people as well: earlier in the film Cassius is driven by economic gain – initially borne out of the need to survive but eventually becoming an end in itself – only to transform into a union protestor due to peer pressure and the growing realisation of Worryfree's exploitative practices. This draws attention to how human beings are themselves far from coherent in the ways that they think and act, subject as they are to multiple appeals and ties throughout their lifetimes.

Black Indie

The music in *Sorry to Bother You* features both white and black artists who can be considered indie: both Tune-Yards and The Coup release records on independent labels, and both attempt to create music that offers something different from 'typical' mainstream music: The Coup are associated with a more conscious, political approach than is standard, while Tune-Yards experiment with indie-pop conventions. As noted, however, it is still more likely for a white band working within rock, and sometimes pop, frameworks to be classified more regularly as indie, despite a growth of attention paid towards indie and/or alternative modes of music primarily associated with blackness. I will discuss the example of hip-hop and rap music here in a bit more detail, as this is the mode of black music that is most frequently discussed in such terms. As mentioned in the previous chapter, indie hip-hop, as well as other similar designations such as underground and alternative hip-hop, is now commonly used.

Indie hip-hop generally indicates independently released hip-hop music, as noted by Vito, but it can also be used to refer more to an alternative status of hip-hop artists, so I will use indie and alternative as largely synonymous in the following discussions. Alternative hip-hop tends to be used more frequently, so it is necessary to outline the general contours of this category. The category indicates differences from more dominant and mainstream modes of hip-hop, which can shift over time. In the late 1980s and early 1990s, for example, artists affiliated with Native Tongues were often considered alternative due to their difference from the majority of rap and hip-hop music: artists such as De La Soul and A Tribe Called Quest were perceived as less militant, more jazz-influenced and more positive than many hip-hop artists; they also drew on hippy influences and merged these with a more Afrocentric outlook. As such, they have also been considered as key to the emergence of alternative hip-hop, including 'conscious' hip-hop, which addresses social and political issues and is often included in discussions of alternative hip-hop. The main ways that conscious hip-hop is differentiated from 'mainstream' examples is lyrically; while this was the case with Native Tongues, the idea of conscious hip-hop became applied more frequently in the 1990s as hip-hop became more mainstream and gangsta rap became dominant.

Alternative hip-hop can refer to artists whose sound is considered non-conventional, often through experimentation or innovation, and can also be linked to production: as with lo-fi traditions in indie-rock, there is a swathe of rap music which is characterised by lo-fi production. Sensational is a rapper who recorded in the late 1990s and early 2000s with very low budgets; for his first album *Loaded with Power* (1997) he recorded vocals into headphones, which introduced an oddness to the sound (added to his already unusually croaky delivery). Lo-fi production might mesh with experimentation, as it did in the work of alternative rappers such as Company Flow and MF DOOM. Unusual instrumentation, vocal style or lyrical content can position hip-hop acts within the alternative category. More recently, JPEGMafia has regularly been discussed as an example of alternative hip-hop due to his sonic experimentation. One feature of JPEGMafia's music is his wildly diverse influences, and many hip-hop artists who engage in musical cross-pollination are also positioned as alternative, including Saul Williams, who draws on rock and spoken word poetry (and has collaborated with diverse artists including Trent Reznor, The Mars Volta and The Kills).

While not all independent hip-hop labels release music that can be considered alternative, there is a strong connection between independent labels and alternative styles. Historically, many independent labels have been associated with more left-field examples of hip-hop, including Anticon, Definitive Jux, Stones Throw and Wordsound. Alternative hip-hop artists might have their status strengthened by releasing on labels that are more associated with other modes of music: I have already mentioned that The Coup released a record on Epitaph; Shabbazz Palaces are also notable in this regard, having released most of their records on Sub Pop (they were the first hip-hop act to be released on the label); also significant is Flying Lotus, who releases records on British electronic indie label Warp.

If we do include alternative modes of hip-hop within discussions of 'indie music', then it becomes easier to identify indie music in African American independent films. I do not have the space to exhaustively discuss examples, but I will mention some films in this final section. An earlier example is *Slam* (Levin, 1998), which though helmed by a white director, focuses chiefly on black protagonists and features black music: the film not only stars Saul Williams as a slam poet but features a large number of tracks by experimental hip-hop musician DJ Spooky. *Crooked* (Fernando, 2002) is an example of a micro-budget hip-hop film but is notable as it was produced by an independent hip-hop label, Wordsound. Shot with hand-held digital cameras, guerrilla style, the film featured several alternative hip-hop artists both in the film and on its soundtrack (also released on Wordsound), including Antipop Consortium, Prince Paul, Sensational and Spectre. *Dope* (Famuyiwa, 2015) is another film which can be aligned with 'alt-black' or 'black indie' music. The film's main protagonist Malcolm (Shameik Moore) is a 'black nerd', and his otherness is again linked to music amongst other factors. Malcolm listens mainly to old school hip-hop, expressing a preference for classic 1990s hip-hop as opposed to more contemporary fare. In some ways the film can be linked to broader retro-trends within indie music cultures, as discussed in Chapter 4. Malcolm's otherness also extends to his musical band, Awreeoh, who perform indie-rock-style music (written by Pharrell Williams). Malcolm's otherness is expressed musically in two broad ways: by his tastes for older hip-hop and his preferences for music more associated with whiteness; there is even a narrated section which stresses that Malcolm and his friends are 'always getting ridiculed by their peers because they're into white shit', which includes being into music acts such as TV on the Radio and Trash Talk. The director of *Dope*, Rick Famuyiwa, had previously included several alt-hip-hop and R&B

Figure 8.4 *Dope*: a list of 'white shit'

tracks in an earlier film, *Brown Sugar* (2002), by artists such as Erykah Badu, Bahamadia, Mos Def and The Roots. Famuyiwa also often includes music artists in his films: Mos Def and Queen Latifah appeared in *Brown Sugar*, which also featured cameos from De La Soul and The Roots amongst others; A$AP Rocky, Vince Staples and Zoë Kravitz appeared in *Dope*. Another example of black filmmaking that can be linked to indie is Flying Lotus's own low-budget, surrealist production *Kuso* (2017), which he scored himself. In this film, Lotus's skewed, experimental hip-hop meshes with its outré aesthetics, including icky body horror and a fragmented narrative.

R&B is another musical mode primarily associated with black artists and which has had some examples categorised as alternative and indie. While not positioned as indie and/or alternative to quite the same degree as hip-hop, it is nevertheless discussed in such ways on occasions. As with hip-hop, indie/alternative R&B can refer to any R&B music released on an independent label, but more commonly refers to R&B music that is considered different from more mainstream examples of the genre, often through musical experimentation and innovation. One of the first examples of alternative R&B to be heavily discussed is 'neo-soul'. Emerging in the late 1980s/early 1990s, some artists associated with the label include D'Angelo, Erykah Badu and Lauren Hill. More recently, artists who have been dubbed alternative R&B and/or indie R&B include Blood Orange, Kelela, L'Rain, Miguel, Frank Ocean, Solange and FKA Twigs. Neo-soul, alternative R&B and indie R&B are contested terms; some artists reject the label, but others are more accepting of such categories. Miguel, for example, has commented that he is comfortable with the term 'indie R&B' because it 'insinuates a higher art. Or a deeper or somehow more artistic delivery of rhythm and blues music' (Jonze 2013).

It is more difficult to name film soundtracks dominated by alternative modes of R&B than by hip-hop. There has, nevertheless, been an increase in the licensing of alt-R&B music in films and television programmes over the past decade, so it is likely to become an increasingly important resource for filmmakers. *Queen and Slim* (Matsoukas, 2019) is a relatively recent film which does employ a number of alt-R&B tracks by artists such as Bilal, Blood Orange and Solange, alongside other musical styles including hip-hop, jazz and more mainstream soul. Ava DuVernay's early features, particularly *Middle of Nowhere* (2012), also feature much independent music, largely from black artists. While the choice of artists may have been partially influenced by limited budgets, *Middle of Nowhere* features some selections that can be considered alternative hip-hop and R&B, by artists such as Goapele, The Nonce and Oddisee. While the music in these films does not link conceptually to content in the ways that it does in many films mentioned, the often spacious, reflective tracks that DuVernay uses do nevertheless chime with the films' subtle, yet powerful, depictions of characters subject to emotionally testing experiences.

Conclusion

In this and the previous chapter, I have largely focused on examining indie music in selected African American films. The films were examined because they contain artists and tracks that conform to more dominant modes of indie, generally linked to whiteness: *Medicine for Melancholy* contains mostly white indie-rock music; *Pariah* features a broader range of music by black artists, though some of this music is rock music; while *Sorry to Bother You* features a score by a recognised white indie band, even though Tune-Yards' music does play around with sonic colour codes. *Pariah* – through its other modes of black independent music – and *Sorry to Bother You* – through The Coup's soundtrack – also feature other modes of music that can be considered indie. As argued, if we extend our notions of indie to be more accepting of music often coded as black, then black indie music becomes identifiable in more African American independent films. But is this expansion of indie music desirable? In the conclusion to the previous chapter I argued that such developments could lead positively to less racially prejudiced conceptions of indie music, but here I will briefly outline two theoretical objections to expanding conceptions of indie music in this manner. The first is more abstract and conceptual; the second is concerned with race.

Firstly, as indie music is already a very broad concept, it might be argued that a racially expanded understanding of the term will broaden its connotations even further, therefore lessening its value as a descriptive category. There is certainly some truth to this argument, but the term is already very broad and does not contain great descriptive value in and of itself; as mentioned in the Introduction, it is also used in inconsistent ways by different constituencies. In some ways, its vague nature makes it an ideal term to use in marketing and, to a lesser extent, criticism; more specific categories – e.g. musical subgenres often connected to indie music – can be used if one wants to be more precise. I would therefore argue that indie is necessarily a broad term, one which can be more fully understood through attending to its employment in specific discursive contexts. As noted in the Introduction, two prominent yet distinct ways that indie has been used are in a purely institutional sense (as a diminutive of independent) and in aesthetic/generic ways (as a broad type of music, usually considered to be slightly alternative to more conventional or mainstream examples). Yet these do not exhaust its connotations: indie can, of course, connote ethical/political positions, and it can often refer to a combination of ethical, aesthetic and institutional factors, while its aesthetic qualities have been complicated further through historical shifts in musical styles. In this regard, I would not consider the extension of indie in ways that refer more commonly to 'black' styles of music to be problematic; as mentioned, this has already happened to an extent even if it is still currently a marginal way of understanding indie.

A second possible objection is that this expansion of indie music is problematic in the sense of trying to align black cultural production with whiteness. This is a thorny issue, but I would argue that such dismissals can problematically reproduce limits on black expression, which the films discussed tend to critique in their different ways. Consequently, both black music artists creating music more traditionally considered to be 'white' (indie-rock in particular) *and* those artists creating alternative modes of types of music traditionally encoded as 'black' – particularly if releasing on independent labels – should be positioned as indie, which will help to address indie music's broader race issues *and* hopefully permit black music artists to be able to more freely express themselves without overly worrying that they are sufficiently 'black'.

Notes

1. Beggars Group is an independent British company which owns or partly-owns a number of independent labels including 4AD, Matador and Rough Trade. It has long been involved in promoting and distributing independent records.
2. Garbus herself had studied in Kenya and was exposed to many forms of African music there, and also studied for a period whilst in Haiti; Haitian percussion music is another global form she has drawn inspiration from.
3. The two bands are usually considered together, as they were both organised by George Clinton and overlapped to a significant extent, even if Funkadelic were – at least initially – more rock-influenced and tended to avoid the prominent horns that were a frequent staple of Parliament's recordings.
4. From 'One Nation Under a Groove' (1978).
5. This is perhaps also a commentary on how some political graffiti work has been celebrated and valued by dominant artistic institutions, leading to absurd prices being paid for it.

9. CONCLUSION

Interconnections between indie film and indie music have accelerated because of the increased use of 'indie' as a broad music and film descriptor within the US, the continued commercialisation of the indie film and music spheres and the growing importance of niche cultures. This is the case across a range of different types of indie productions, but it applies particularly to the higher end of such filmmaking, including 'indie' films released by studio divisions or indie films which contain funding and distribution from studios; it is often within such filmmaking that the presence of indie music tends to be signalled most prominently. Matthew Nicholls has argued that music tends to be foregrounded within American independent films in noticeable ways, and that it is often important for viewers to be aware of the music, which can then cement a film's indie status:

> Not only is the audibility or aesthetic quality of the music important, but the choices are too; in a sense, musical selections (particularly obscure or nonmainstream choices) can become important distinctions that contribute toward a film's indie authenticity. (Nicholls 2011: 34)

In the films I have analysed closely, music can be used both very noticeably *and* in more subtle ways, but I would certainly agree with Nicholls that its use can often strengthen the indie identity of a film: Nicholls (2011: 115) has mentioned how several independent films placed indie music within their trailers, a tactic which underpins an indie status. In studio-backed 'indie' films there is a greater tendency for indie music to be highlighted as part of a self-conscious indie aesthetic. As noted, however, if a film is perceived as trying too hard to come across as indie, then it might be considered inauthentic by some. So, while indie music can bolster a film's indie credentials, such an outcome cannot be guaranteed.

Authenticity is often highly valued within indie cultures, but there is no consensus on how films or music can be considered authentic or not. Such judgements will depend on specific audiences' broader values and tastes. Whether accepted as authentic or not, indie music – often alongside other indie markers – is frequently employed in films and has the potential to lead to a general perception of such films as non-mainstream, including films released by studios. Indie is a broad term which can imply very low-budget filmmaking and higher-end, yet still relatively niche-oriented productions; or wildly experimental, personally released records and major company releases by artists who are well-known but still retain 'indie cred'. It needs to be stressed that the 'mainstream' tends to be imaginarily constructed and can therefore be conceived differently by people. To take a hypothetical example: studio-backed specialist 'indie' films might be accepted as indie by some, but rejected by others, dependent on their broader tastes and cultural experiences: indie does not mean the same thing to all people but can exist in a variety of guises. Its broadness presents difficulties defining the concept, but within the industry this can be useful in the sense that it indicates broad-yet-still niche values that can help to target disparate audiences seeking to engage with something a bit 'different' from typical Hollywood fare. In this book I have attempted to strike a balance between the broad ways in which indie music functions and analysis of more specific iterations. The discursive employment of indie as a music and film concept has increased since the 1980s, and indie music has been recognised by people in the film industry as a valuable element which has the potential to attract audiences.

New modes of distributing and exhibiting films offer alternative routes for independent filmmakers to get their films seen and generate revenue. But, as Sarah Sinwell (2020: 77) has pointed out, while DIY production and self-distribution in the indie world 'have become political and ideological tools that support the antimainstream values associated with independent film at the margins . . . these distribution and exhibition models are also dependent on the corporate structures of organisations like YouTube, Google . . .'. A similar situation exists in the music world; Hesmondhalgh and Meier (2015: 102) have argued that digital technologies do not necessarily offer musicians greater freedoms from corporate control, claiming that they 'have failed to offer a sustainable and meaningful institutional alternative to corporate capitalism (in its cultural-industry and IT forms)'. In some ways, despite dramatic technological shifts, the struggles of attaining independence are still as difficult, and riven with contradictions, as they were in the 1990s.

Due to the 'corporatisation of indie media' (Sinwell 2020: 109), some critics have questioned the relevance of the concept. Alex Ogg (2009: 571) has written that the 'concept of indie has become almost meaningless beyond branding'. Kaya Oakes (2009: 207) has argued that the term originally referred to independence but 'when it's applied to rock bands recording for major labels, cars manufactured in factories, iPods, or six-hundred-dollar purses . . . it really has lost its meaning'. Such opinions are understandable, but while the branding of indie has certainly expanded in recent years, it is not a concept that can be purely reduced to branding. Ogg and Oakes both highlight the huge amount of 'indie' media being released by major companies as one of the main reasons it has become emptied of meaning. Even if indie was nothing more than a brand – which I don't think it is – then the question of how a category devoid of meaning can be branded needs to be addressed. Oakes's argument also contains occasional inconsistencies. She outlines her understanding of indie as 'philosophical' – encompassing an anti-corporate ethos and a commitment to DIY production – and bemoans how indie is now more frequently understood as a 'genre' (xii) or a branded 'aesthetic' (195). But her own discussion of indie music betrays aesthetic and generic preferences for some music over others: she mostly discusses white indie-rock, but if she had adhered more rigorously to her own definitions, she would have explored a greater variety of musical forms. At one stage, she discusses how many of her students do not listen to indie-rock, noting that 'many prefer hip-hop', without mentioning how much hip-hop is independently released. This demonstrates how difficult it can be to discuss indie in a straightforward manner due to the variable ways it can be understood, such as philosophically, industrially or aesthetically.

Indie music is now arguably even more difficult to define than it was in the 1980s, because so many forms have been discussed as indie over its history, and because of the often vague and sometimes inconsistent ways it is employed. I do personally have some issues with the increased use of the term indie to apply to so many different artists and cultural artefacts, especially if these emanate from corporations. I think it would be preferable if we used the term to refer to independently produced and distributed culture. Yet there are two issues with such a recommendation: firstly, there are often cases where the independent status of cultural artefacts is not straightforward, such as productions that involve both independent and non-independent companies; secondly, the term will undoubtedly continue to be employed frequently, so it is more sensible to both track the ways that it has been/is being used, and to attempt to intervene in debates about its meanings. If, as I think is desirable, there is a shift towards conceiving of indie more in an adjectival sense than as a noun, then the racial biases intertwined with dominant conceptions of indie music might be challenged (though this would need to be supported by broader, systemic changes). As indicated in Chapter 8, this has gained traction in many quarters, though indie music more broadly is still currently associated with whiteness.

In this book I have explored some prominent ways in which indie music has been used, and how particular indie music cultures have been represented, across a range of American indie films since the 1980s. By focusing on selected case studies, I have been able to examine the specificity of indie music's functions within selected films but have also sought to outline some broader historical developments and issues. My selective focus has resulted in some interactions between indie music cultures and American indie film only being briefly touched upon or overlooked. I have noted indie music documentaries on occasion but have mainly focused on fiction feature films; while I have previously written about some indie music documentaries (Sexton 2014), this is an area of filmmaking that is still growing and which has been stimulated by the increased affordability of filmmaking, the expansion of funding revenues (particularly crowdfunding, or what Geoff King [2013: 89] has described as 'do-it-with-others') and screening venues (both concrete and virtual). Documentaries on specific music artists have the benefit of appealing primarily to an existing fan base, though they will often seek additional viewers, and are worthy of further scrutiny. There has also been a rise in music artists creating their own specialist films, which once again will often primarily appeal to existing fans of said artists. I have already mentioned Flying Lotus's *Kuso* (2017), but we can also add other examples, including The Flaming Lips' *Christmas on Mars* (Coyne, Beesley and Salisbury, 2008) and Animal Collective's *Oddsac* (Perez, 2010), both low-budget, experimental films; more recently, St Vincent has co-written with Carrie Brownstein a self-reflective meta-documentary, *The Nowhere In* (Benz, 2021). Indie musicians have also been involved increasingly in scoring films; though I have explored a few scores within this book, this is another area that warrants further exploration. Examples of indie musicians moving into film scoring, including for American independent productions, include Belle and Sebastian, Dean & Britta, Explosions in the Sky, Grizzly Bear, Clint Mansell, Sun City Girls, Tamar-kali, Josephine Wiggs and David Winigo.

The interrelations between music video direction and feature film direction is another avenue worthy of further research. Many music video directors move into film directing, and several independent filmmakers have directed indie music videos. A significant number of directors fit such a mould, including Sofia Coppola, Jonathan Dayton and Valerie Farris, Sam Fleischner, Steve Hanft, Todd Haynes, Spike Jonze, Mike Mills, Phil Morrison, Danny Perez, Boots Riley, Floria Sigismondi and Edgar Wright. Some of these directors work with low budgets, such as Hanft and Perez, who I have already written on (see Sexton 2019), but others like Coppola and Wright work on larger budgeted, studio-backed indies. Many indie music artists were originally sceptical of the music video. It was often considered inauthentic in the 1980s and many bands did not even make music videos at first; when they did so, their videos were often very low-budget, lo-fi and would frequently avoid focusing on singers and musicians in performance (if they did include performances, these were more likely to feature live concert footage as opposed to lip-synching in a studio). This began to alter in the 1990s: it became more difficult to shun the music video because of financial pressures to make them and due to the increasing centrality of video within music culture (see Holt 2011). This indicates how indie music has become increasingly embedded within audio-visual media. Further studies could investigate the heightened visualisation of indie music, and the relations between directors of indie music videos and their feature filmmaking.

Other related research areas deserving of further investigation include actors, directors and other personnel who work in both film and music. I have covered this to an extent through examining how real musicians often appeared in and sometimes contributed music to films about music scenes, which often worked to enhance the authenticity of a film. There are many other strands that can be explored, such as actors who are also indie musicians, including Zooey Deschanel, Vincent Gallo, Caleb Landry Jones, Will Oldham and Jason Schwartzman; as well as directors who have also been in indie bands, such as Steve Hanft, Mike Mills and Miranda July. Finally, future studies could investigate indie music's intersections not just with film, but also with other media. There are now many 'indie' cultural sectors, including video games, publishing, design and television. Newman (2011) and Oakes (2009) have both analysed broader indie cultures to an extent, though such intersections are arguably worthy of more detailed scrutiny. Indie television in particular is a growing research area (e.g. Christian 2015); I noted in Chapter 2 that some reporters stressed the growth of indie music in American television during the mid-2000s, and this is a subject that warrants further research, including a consideration of how film and television have been transformed by online distribution and exhibition (see King 2013; Sinwell 2020). Online developments have led to changes in how people engage with films. Multiple screens and devices can now be used to access content across platforms, and clips related to films are often shared on social media sites and video hosting services. As music clips – particularly music videos – are popular on many such platforms, music's role in the exposure of film assumes even more importance. Trailers have long since employed music, but they are now accompanied by the sharing of film clips that are musically-dominated, and which sometimes – as Vernallis (2013: 3–4) has argued – might 'be placed on YouTube and inadvertently experienced as music videos'.[1] Indie music is certainly not the only type of music being used in such ways, but it is nevertheless an increasingly important mode recognised as such by many industry figures and audiences, even if their understandings of the convoluted concept might differ.

NOTE

1. Vernallis cites examples from *Scott Pilgrim Versus the World* (Wright, 2010), *Southland Tales* (Kelly, 2006) and *Across the Universe* (Taymor, 2007). These films contain music video-style segments that she sees as particularly influenced by music video, and which might be mistaken for music videos if watched out of context. Interestingly, the two former films use a lot of music which would be classed as indie.

BIBLIOGRAPHY

Abraham, Amelia (2015), 'Films for Outsiders: An Interview with Gregg Araki', *Vice*, 20 March, <http://www.vice.com/en_uk/article/yvxmxv/gregg-araki> (last accessed 5 April 2022).

Allen, Reniqua (2013), 'From Love to Melancholy: The Evolution of the Black Bohemian Identity in Black Indie Love Films from Gen-X to Gen-Y', *Journal of Black Studies* 44.5: 508–28.

Anderson, Tim (2013a), 'Lost in Translation: Popular Music, Adolescence, and the Melodramatic Mode of Sofia Coppola', in Arved Ashby (ed.), *Popular Music and the New Auteur: Visionary Filmmakers After MTV* (New York: Oxford University Press), pp. 63–83.

Anderson, Tim (2013b), 'From Background Music to Above-the-Line Actor: The Rise of the Music Supervisor in Converging Televisual Environments', *Journal of Popular Music Studies* 25.3: 371–88.

Anon. (1984), 'Profile of Yank Indie Product is Tall in Fest's Official Sections', *Variety*, 15 Feb, p. 43.

Anon. (2011), 'Interview with Dee Rees – Writer and Director of Pariah', *Women and Hollywood*, 29 December, <https://womenandhollywood.com/interview-with-dee-rees-writer-and-director-of-pariah-8b695975e106> (last accessed 5 April 2022).

Ashby, Arved (ed.) (2013), *Popular Music and the New Auteur: Visionary Filmmakers after MTV* (New York: Oxford University Press).

Atwood, Brett (1994), 'Indie Film Soundtracks Help Expose Modern Rock Acts', *Billboard*, 8 October, p. 32.

Azerrad, Michael (2001), *Our Band Could be Your Life: Scenes from the American Indie Underground 1981–1991* (New York: Back Bay Books).

Babbit, Jamie (2007), 'From the Director', *Itty Titty Bitty Committee Press Kit*, <www.power-up.net/ittybitty/press/ITTY-PressKit.pdf> (last accessed 5 April 2022).

Backman Rogers, Anna (2019), *Sofia Coppola: The Politics of Visual Pleasure* (New York and Oxford: Berghahn Books).

Bannister, Matthew (2006a), *White Boys, White Noise: Masculinities and 1980s Indie Guitar Rock* (Aldershot: Ashgate).

Bannister, Matthew (2006b), '"Loaded": Indie Guitar Rock, Canonism, White Masculinities', *Popular Music* 25.1: 77–95.

Barton-Fumo, Margaret (2013), 'Fighting for Their Right to Party: Roger Corman's The Wild Angels', *Senses of Cinema*, 67,<https://www.sensesofcinema.com/2013/cteq/fighting-for-their-right-to-party-roger-cormans-the-wild-angels> (last accessed 5 April 2022).

Baumgarten, Marjorie (2005), 'Mysterious Skin (review)', *The Austin Chronicle*, 1 July, https://www.austinchronicle.com/events/film/2005-07-01/276777 (last accessed 5 April 2022).

Belsito, Peter (2001), 'Jim Jarmusch', in Ludvig Huertzberg (ed.), *Jim Jarmusch: Interviews* (Jackson: University Press of Mississippi) pp. 21–47 (Originally published in Belsito, Peter (1985), *Notes from the Pop Underground* (San Francisco: Last Gasp).).

Berlatsky, Noah (2015), 'Why "Indie" Music is so Unbearably White', *The New Republic*, 2 April, <https://newrepublic.com/article/121437/why-indie-music-so-unbearably-white> (last accessed 5 April 2022).

Butler, Susan (2009), 'Movie Soundtracks: Needing to Know the Score', *Music Week*, 15 August, p. 12.

Cherkis, Jason (2015), 'The Lost Girls' *The Huffington Post*, 9 July, <https://highline.huffingtonpost.com/articles/en/the-lost-girls> (last accessed 5 April 2022).

Christian, Aymar Jean (2015), 'Indie TV: Innovation in Series Development', in James Bennett and Niki Strange (eds), *Media Independence: Working with Freedom or Working for Free?* (London and New York: Routledge), pp. 159–81.

Clayton, Jace (2010), 'Vampires of Lima', in Mark Greif, Kathleen Ross and Dayna Tortorici (eds), *What Was the Hipster? A Sociological Investigation* (New York: HarperCollins eBooks), pp. 45–52.

Cook, Pam (2009), 'Portrait of a Lady: Sofia Coppola', *Sight and Sound* 16.11: 36–40.

Corbett, John (1994), 'Brothers from Another Planet: The Space Madness of Lee "Scratch" Perry, Sun Ra, and George Clinton', in John Corbett, *Extended Play: Sounding Off from John Cage to Dr. Funkenstein* (Durham and London: Duke University Press), pp. 7–24.

Crisafulli, Chuck (2003), 'Composers Praise Indies Small Films Offer "Wonderful Work"', *Hollywood Reporter*, 21 Nov 2003, retrieved from LexisNexis Academic Database.

Crisafulli, Chuck (2007), 'Sounds Like Indie Spirit,' *hollywoodreporter.com*, 17 April, <https://www.hollywoodreporter.com/business/business-news/sounds-like-indie-spirit-134226/#!> (last accessed 5 April 2022).

Davis, Aeron (2013), *Promotional Cultures: The Rise and Spread of Advertising, Public Relations, Marketing and Branding* (Cambridge: Polity).

Debord, Guy (1995 [1967]), *The Society of the Spectacle*, trans. Donald Nicholson-Smith (New York: Zone Books).

DeClue, Jennifer (2018), 'The Circuitous Route of Presenting Black Butch: The Travels of Dee Rees's *Pariah*', in Yvonne Welbon and Alexandra Juhasz (eds), *Sisters in the Life: A History of Out African American Lesbian Media-Making* (Durham: Duke University Press), pp. 225–48.

Downes, Julia (2012), 'The Expansion of Punk Rock: Riot Grrrl Challenges to Gender Power Relations in British Indie Music Subcultures', *Women's Studies: An Interdisciplinary Journal* 41.2: 204–37.

Dubowksy, Jack Curtis (2014), 'Musical Cachet in New Queer Cinema', *Music, Sound and the Moving Image* 8.1: 25–56.

Duncombe, Stephen (2008), *Notes from Underground: Zines and the Politics of Alternative Culture*, 2nd edition (Bloomington: Microcosm Press).

Egan, Kate and Sarah Thomas (2013), 'Introduction: Star-Making, Cult-Making and Forms of Authenticity', in Kate Egan and Sarah Thomas (eds), *Cult Film Stardom* (Basingstoke: Palgrave Macmillan) pp. 1–20.

Evans, Greg (1994), 'Miramax taps Kimball for new music VP post', *Daily Variety*, 14 September, p. 15.

Fisher, Mark (2014), *Ghosts of My Life: Writings on Depression, Hauntology and Lost Futures* (London: Zero).

Flowers, Jonathan Charles (2018), 'How is it Okay to be a Black Nerd?', in Kathryn E. Lane (ed.), *Age of the Geek: Depictions of Nerds and Geeks in Popular Culture* (London: Palgrave MacMillan), pp. 169–92.

Fonarow, Wendy (2006), *Empire of Dirt: The Aesthetics and Rituals of British Indie Music* (Middletown: Wesleyan University Press).

Francis, Terri (2013), 'Introduction: The No-Theory Chant of Afrosurrealism', *Black Camera* 5.3: 95–112.

Frere-Jones, Sasha (2007), 'A Paler Shade of White', *The New Yorker*, 15 October, <https://www.newyorker.com/magazine/2007/10/22/a-paler-shade-of-white> (last accessed 5 April 2022).

Friedman, Wayne (2010), 'Social Media Gains Virility', *Variety*, 5 October, p. 9.

Frith, Simon (1996), *Performing Rites: On the Value of Popular Music* (Oxford: Oxford University Press).

Frith, Simon (2016), 'Music and Identity', in Simon Frith, *Taking Popular Music Seriously: Selected Essays* (Oxon and New York: Routledge), pp. 293–312.

Gallo, Phil (2003), 'Tracking the Indies: Yetnikoff, McKnight to Specialize in Pic Music', *Daily Variety*, 22 October, p. 18.

Garwood, Ian (2016), 'Vinyl Noise and Narrative in CD-Era Indiewood', in Liz Greene and Danijela Kulezic-Wilson (eds), *The Palgrave Handbook of Sound Design and Music in Screen Media: Integrated Soundtracks* (London: Palgrave Macmillan), pp. 245–60.

Gillespie, Michael Boyce (2016), *Film Blackness: American Cinema and the Idea of Black Film* (New York: Columbia University Press).

Gilroy, Paul (2005), *Postcolonial Melancholia* (New York: Columbia University Press).

Gorbman, Claudia (2007), 'Auteur Music', in Daniel Goldmark, Lawrence Kramer and Richard Leppert (eds), *Beyond the Soundtrack: Representing Music in Cinema* (Los Angeles: University of California Press), pp. 149–62.

Gottlieb, Joanne and Gayle Wald (1994), 'Smells Like Teen Spirit: Riot Grrrls, Revolution and Women in Independent Rock', in Tricia Rose and Andrew Ross (eds), *Microphone Fiends: Youth Music and Youth Culture* (London and New York: Routledge), pp. 250–74.
Gray, Jonathan (2010), *Show Sold Separately: Promos, Spoilers and Other Media Paratexts* (New York: New York University Press).
Greif, Mark (2010), 'Positions', In Mark Greif, Kathleen Ross and Dayna Tortorici (eds), *What Was the Hipster? A Sociological Investigation* (New York: HarperCollins eBooks), pp. 20–9.
Grodal, Torben (1997), *Moving Pictures: A New Theory of Film Genres, Feelings, and Cognition* (Oxford: Oxford University Press).
Handyside, Fiona (2017), *Sofia Coppola: A Cinema of Girlhood* (London: IB Tauris).
Hanson, Peter (2002), *The Cinema of Generation X* (eBook) (Jefferson, North Carolina and London: McFarland).
Haring, Bruce (1992), 'Pied Piper of Grunge', *Daily Variety*, 14 Sept, p. 11.
Harris, Brandon (2011), 'Out in the Neighborhood: Dee Rees on Her Directorial Debut, Pariah', *Filmmaker Magazine*, 8 Nov, <https://filmmakermagazine.com/34803-out-in-the-neighborhood-dee-rees-pariah/#.XxGFHB3TU1g> (last accessed 5 April 2022).
Hart, Kylo-Patrick R. (2003), 'Auteur/Bricoleur/Provocateur: Gregg Araki and Post-punk Style in *The Doom Generation*', *Journal of Film and Video* 55.1: 30–8.
Hebdige, Dick (1979), *Subculture: The Meaning of Style* (London and New York: Routledge).
Hesmondhalgh, David (1999), 'Indie: the Institutional Politics and Aesthetics of a Popular Music Genre', *Cultural Studies* 13.1: 34–61.
Hesmondhalgh, David and Leslie M. Meier (2015), 'Popular Music, Independence and the Concept of the Alternative in Contemporary Capitalism', in James Bennett and Niki Strange (eds), *Media Independence: Working with Freedom or Working for Free?* (London and New York: Routledge), pp. 94–116.
Hibbett, Ryan (2005), 'What is Indie Rock?', *Popular Music and Society* 28.1: 55–77.
Holt, Fabian (2011), 'Is Music Becoming More Visual? Online Video Content in the Music Industry', *Visual Studies* 26.1: 50–61.
Houston, Taylor Martin (2012), 'The Homosocial Construction of Alternative Masculinities: Men in Indie Rock Bands', *The Journal of Men's Studies* 20.2: 158–75.
Howard, Yetta (2017), 'The Queerness of Industrial Music', *Social Text* 35.4: 33–51.
Howells, Thomas (2013), *Late Century Dream: Movements in the US Indie Underground* (London: Black Dog Publishing).
Iampolski, Mikhail (1998), *The Memory of Tiresias: Intertextuality and Film*, trans. Harsha Ram (Berkeley and Los Angeles: University of California Press).
James-Wilson, Matthew (2020), 'What it's Like to be Black in Indie Music', *Pitchfork*, 28 September, <https://pitchfork.com/features/article/what-its-like-to-be-black-in-indie-music> (last accessed 5 April 2022).
Jarnow, Jesse (2012), *Big Day Coming: Yo La Tengo and the Rise of Indie Rock* (New York: Gotham Books).
Jones, Chris (2004), 'Air: Talkie Walkie Review', *BBC Music*, <https://www.bbc.co.uk/music/reviews/32rg> (last accessed 5 April 2022).

Jonze, Tim (2013). 'Miguel: The Slow-Burn Success of a New R&B Superstar', *The Guardian*, 9 February, <https://www.theguardian.com/music/2013/feb/09/miguel-kaleidoscope-dream> (last accessed 5 April 2022).

Kang, Nancy (2016), 'Audre's Daughter: Black Lesbian Steganography in Dee Rees' *Pariah* and Audre Lorde's *Zami: A New Spelling of My Name*', *Journal of Lesbian Studies* 20.2: 266–97.

Kassabian, Anahid (2001), *Hearing Film: Tracking Identifications in Contemporary Hollywood Film Music* (London and New York: Routledge).

Katz, Richard (1998), 'IFX Rides Indie Music Biz', *Daily Variety*, 7 October, p. 20.

Kearney, Mary Celeste (1997), 'The Missing Links: Riot Grrrl – Feminism – Lesbian Culture!', in Sheila Whiteley (ed.), *Sexing the Groove: Popular Music and Gender* (Abingdon: Routledge), pp. 207–29.

Keenan, Elizabeth K. (2021), 'Riot Grrrl: Nostalgia and Historiography', in George McKay and Gina Arnold (eds), *The Oxford Handbook of Punk Rock* (Oxford: Oxford University Press). Online publication, DOI: 10.1093/oxfordhb/9780190859565.001.0001

Keightley, Keir (2001), 'Reconsidering Rock', in Simon Frith, Will Straw and John Street (eds), *The Cambridge Companion to Pop and Rock* (Cambridge: Cambridge University Press), pp. 287–368.

Kennedy, Todd (2010), 'Off with Hollywood's Head: Sofia Coppola as Feminine Auteur', *Film Criticism* 35.1: 37–59.

Kerrigan, Finola (2017), 'Marketing American Indie in the Shadow of Hollywood', in Geoff King (ed.), *A Companion to American Indie Film* (Malden: Wiley Blackwell), pp. 181–206.

King, Geoff (2013), *Indie 2.0: Change and Continuity in Contemporary Indie Film* (London: I. B. Tauris).

King, Geoff (ed.), (2017), *A Companion to American Indie Film* (Malden: Wiley Blackwell).

Klady, Leonard (1998), 'Shadrach Preem to Open L.A. Indie Fest', *Daily Variety*, 17 March, p. 4.

Klein, Bethany, Leslie M. Meier and Devon Powers (2016), 'Selling Out: Musicians, Autonomy, and Compromise in the Digital Age', *Popular Music and Society* 40.2: 222–38.

Klein, Naomi (2000), *No Logo: No Space, No Choice, No Jobs* (London: Flamingo).

Koresky, Michael (2005), 'Mysterious Skin (review)', *Film Comment*, May–June, pp. 73–4.

Kruse, Holly (2003), *Site and Sound: Understanding Independent Music Scenes* (New York: Peter Lang).

Laing, Dave (2015), *One Chord Wonders: Power and Meaning in Punk Rock* (Oakland: PM Press). Originally published by Open University Press, 1985.

Leonard, Marion (1997), '"Rebel Girl, You Are the Queen of My World": Feminism, "Subculture" and Grrrl Power', in Sheila Whiteley (ed.), *Sexing the Groove: Popular Music and Gender* (Abingdon: Routledge), pp. 230–55.

Lewandowski, Natalie (2010), 'Understanding Creative Roles in Entertainment: The Music Supervisor as Case Study', *Continuum: Journal of Media & Cultural Studies* 24.6: 865–75.

Lifter, Rachel (2020), *Fashioning Indie: Popular Fashion, Music and Gender* (London: Bloomsbury).

Lim, Dennis (2009), 'Examining Race and a Future Beyond it', *The New York Times*, 21 January, <https://www.nytimes.com/2009/01/25/movies/25denn.html?_r=0> (last accessed 5 April 2022).

London, Jeffrey (2017), 'Portland Oregon, Music Scenes, and Change: A Cultural Approach to Collective Strategies of Empowerment', *City & Community* 16.1: 47–65.

Lorde, Audre (2007), 'The Transformation of Silence into Language and Action', in Audre Lorde, *Sister Outsider: Essays and Speeches* (New York: Crossing Press).

Lorde, Audre (2018), *Zami: A New Spelling of My Name* (London: Penguin).

Lyons, James (2004), *Selling Seattle: Representing Contemporary America* (London: Wallflower Press).

McGuigan, Jim (2009), *Cool Capitalism* (London: Pluto Press).

MacLeod, Dewar (2020), *Making the Scene in the Garden State: Popular Music in New Jersey from Edison to Springsteen and Beyond* (New Brunswick: Rutgers University Press).

Mahon, Maureen (2004), *Right to Rock: The Black Rock Coalition and the Cultural Politics of Race* (Durham and London: Duke University Press).

Maly, Ico and Piia Varis (2016), 'The 21st-Century Hipster: On Micro-Populations in Times of Superdiversity', *European Journal of Cultural Studies* 19.6: 637–53.

Marcus, Greil (2001), *Lipstick Traces: A Secret History of the Twentieth Century* (London: Faber and Faber). Originally published by Secker and Warburg, 1989.

Marcus, Sara (2010), *Girls to the Front: The Story of the RIOT GRRRL Revolution* (New York: HarperCollins).

Miller, D. Scot (2013), 'Afrosurreal Manifesto: Black is the New Black – a 21st Century Manifesto', *Black Camera* 5.1: 113–17.

Moore, Ryan (2010), *Sells Like Teen Spirit: Music, Youth Culture and Social Crisis* (New York: New York University Press).

Moran, James M. (1996), 'Gregg Araki: Guerilla Film-Maker for a Queer Generation', *Film Quarterly* 55.1: 18–26.

Newman, Michael Z. (2011), *Indie: An American Film Culture* (New York: Columbia University Press).

Newman, Michael Z. (2017), 'Indie Film as Indie Culture', in Geoff King (ed.), *A Companion to American Indie Film* (Malden: Wiley Blackwell), pp. 25–41.

Nicholls, Matthew William (2011), *Interactions Between Contemporary American Independent Cinema and Popular Music Culture* (PhD Thesis: University of Southampton).

Oakes, Kaya (2009), *Slanted and Enchanted: The Evolution of Indie Culture* (New York: Holt).

Ogg, Alex (2009), *Independence Days: The Story of UK Independent Record Labels* (London: Cherry Red Books).

O'Meara, Jennifer (2015), 'Character as DJ: *Melomamia* and Diegetically Controlled Music', *The New Soundtrack* 5.2: 133–51.

O'Neill, Phelim (2011), 'Gregg Araki's Films are Giving the US a Crash Course in Shoegazing', *The Guardian*, 6 August, <https://www.theguardian.com/film/2011/aug/06/gregg-araki-kaboom-shoegazing> (last accessed 5 April 2022).

Ortner, Sherry B. (2015), *Not Hollywood: Independent Film at the Twilight of the American Dream* (Durham: Duke University Press).
Perren, Alisa (2012), *Indie, Inc. Miramax and the Transformation of Hollywood in the 1990s* (Austin: University of Texas Press).
Phillips, Stephanie (2021), *Why Solange Matters* (London: Faber & Faber).
Powers, Ann (2018), 'Tune-Yards' Merrill Garbus Pierces Her Own Privilege', *NPR Music*, 19 January, <https://www.npr.org/sections/allsongs/2018/01/19/578822264/tune-yards-merrill-garbus-pierces-her-own-privilege> (last accessed 5 April 2022).
Pribram, E. Deidre (2001), *Cinema & Culture: Independent Film in the United States, 1980–2001* (New York: Peter Lang).
Raha, Maria (2005), *Cinderella's Big Score: Women of the Punk and Indie Underground* (Berkeley: Seal Press).
Reed, S. Alexander (2013), *Assimilate: A Critical History of Industrial Music* (Oxford and New York: Oxford University Press).
Regev, Motti (2013), *Pop-Rock Music: Aesthetic Cosmopolitanism in Late Modernity* (Cambridge and Malden: Polity Press).
Reynolds, Simon (2007), 'Madchester Versus Dreampop', in Simon Reynolds, *Bring the Noise: 20 Years of Writing About Rock and Hip-Hop* (London: Faber and Faber), pp. 120–3. Article originally published in *Village Voice*, November 1990.
Reynolds, Simon (2012), *Retromania: Pop's Addiction to its Own Past* (London: Faber and Faber).
Rich, B. Ruby (1992), 'New Queer Cinema', *Sight & Sound* 2.5: 30–4.
Rich, B. Ruby (2013), *New Queer Cinema: The Director's Cut* (Durham and London: Duke University Press).
Richardson, Mark (2003), 'Various Artists, Lost in Translation (review)', *Pitchfork*, 1 October, <https://pitchfork.com/reviews/albums/7714-lost-in-translation> (last accessed 5 April 2022).
Roberts, Randall (2015), 'Former Runaways Members React to Kim Fowley Rape Allegations', *Los Angeles Times*, 14 July, <https://www.latimes.com/entertainment/music/posts/la-et-ms-runaways-members-kim-fowley-rape-allegations-20150713-story.html> (last accessed 5 April 2022).
Rose, Tricia (1994), 'A Style Nobody Can Deal With: Politics, Style and the Postindustrial City in Hip Hop', in Tricia Rose and Andrew Ross (eds), *Microphone Fiends: Youth Music and Youth Culture* (New York and London: Routledge), pp. 71–88.
Royster, Francesca T. (2012), *Sounding Like a No-No: Queer Sounds and Eccentric Acts in the Post-Soul Era* (Ann Arbor: University of Michigan Press).
Rusty, Brandon (2014), 'Fans Demand an Apology from Kathleen Hanna in Toronto Julie Ruin Concert Banner Drop', *Chart Attack*, 7 April, <https://www.chartattack.com/julie-ruin-concert-banner-drop> (last accessed 5 April 2022).
Sahim, Sarah (2015), 'The Unbearable Whiteness of Indie', *Pitchfork*, 25 March, <https://pitchfork.com/thepitch/710-the-unbearable-whiteness-of-indie> (last accessed 5 April 2022).
Seidelman, Susan (2018), 'Director's Commentary', *Smithereens* (New York: Criterion Collection). Commentary originally recorded for Shout! Factory, 2004.
Sexton, Jamie (2012), 'Weird Britain in Exile: Ghost Box, Hauntology and Alternative Heritage', *Popular Music and Society* 35.4: 561–84.

Sexton, Jamie (2014), 'Lo-Fi Excavations: Surveying the Indie-Rock Documentary', in Holly Rogers (ed.), *Music and Sound in Nonfiction Film* (London: Routledge), pp. 156–70.

Sexton, Jamie (2015), 'Creeping Decay: Cult Soundtracks, Residual Media, and Digital Technologies', *New Review of Film and Television Studies* 13.1: 12–30.

Sexton, Jamie (2019), 'Low Budget Audio-visual Aesthetics in Indie Music Video and Feature Filmmaking: The Works of Steve Hanft and Danny Perez', in Lori Burns and Stan Hawkins (eds), *The Bloomsbury Handbook to Popular Music Video Analysis* (New York and London: Bloomsbury), pp. 27–46.

Shady, Justin (2010), 'Establishing Hipster Cred on an Indie Budget', *Variety*, 10 June, A8.

Shank, Barry (1994), *Dissonant Identities: The Rock 'n' Roll Scene in Austin, Texas* (Hanover: Wesleyan University Press).

Smaill, Belinda (2013), 'Sofia Coppola', *Feminist Media Studies* 13.1: 148–62.

Smith, Jeff (2001), 'Taking Music Supervisors Seriously', in Philip Brophy (ed.), *Cinesonic: Experiencing the Soundtrack* (North Ryde NSW, Australia: Southwest Press), 125–46.

Spiers, Emily (2015), '"Killing Ourselves is Not Subversive": Riot Grrrl from Zine to Screen and the Commodification of Female Transgression', *Women: A Cultural Review* 26.1–2: 1–21.

Stern, Marlow (2017), 'Sofia Coppola Discusses "Lost in Translation" on its 10th Anniversary', *Daily Beast*, 2 September, <https://www.thedailybeast.com/sofia-coppola-discusses-lost-in-translation-on-its-10th-anniversary> (last accessed 5 April 2022).

Stoever, Jennifer Lynn (2016), *The Sonic Color Line: Race and the Cultural Politics of Listening* (New York: New York University Press).

Strachan, Robert (2007), 'Micro-independent Record Labels in the UK: Discourse, DIY Cultural Production and the Music Industry', *European Journal of Cultural Studies* 10.2: 245–65.

Taylor, Leila (2019), *Darkly: Black History and America's Gothic Soul* (London: Repeater Books).

Thornton, Sarah (1995), *Club Cultures: Music, Media and Subcultural Capital* (Cambridge: Polity).

Tompkins, Joseph (2009), 'What's the Deal with Soundtrack Albums?: Metal Music and the Customized Aesthetics of Contemporary Horror', *Cinema Journal* 49.1: 65–81.

Tzioumakis, Yannis (2011a), 'Academic Discourses and American Independent Cinema: In Search of a Field of Studies. Part 1: From the Beginnings to the 1980s', *New Review of Film and Television Studies* 11.2: 105–31.

Tzioumakis, Yannis (2011b), 'Academic Discourses and American Independent Cinema: in Search of a Field of Studies. Part 2: From the 1990s to Date', *New Review of Film and Television Studies* 11.3: 311–40.

Tzioumakis, Yannis (2012), *Hollywood's Indies: Classics Divisions, Specialty Labels and the American Market* (Edinburgh: Edinburgh University Press).

Vernallis, Carol (2013), *Unruly Media: YouTube, Music Video, and the New Digital Cinema* (New York: Oxford University Press).

Vesey, Alyx (2009), 'Alexandra Patsavas: Music Supervisor', *Feminist Music Geek*, 19 December, <https://feministmusicgeek.wordpress.com/2009/12/18/alexandra-patsavas-music-supervisor> (last accessed 5 April 2022).

Vito, Christopher (2019), *The Value of Independent Hip-Hop in the Post-Golden Era: Hip-Hop's Rebels* (Cham: Palgrave Pivot).
Walker, Michael (1992), 'Chronicling the Post-Baby Boom Generation', *The New York Times*, 6 September, Section 2, p. 7.
Weaver, Jimmy (2013), 'Making a Scene: The Female Punk Narrative in Lou Adler's *Ladies and Gentlemen, The Fabulous Stains* and Susan Seidelman's *Smithereens*', *Punk & Post-Punk* 2.2: 179–95.
Wierzbicki, James (ed.) (2012), *Music, Sound and Filmmakers: Sonic Style in Cinema* (New York: Routledge).
Woo, Benjamin, Jamie Rennie and Stuart R. Poyntz (2015), 'Scene Thinking: Introduction', *Cultural Studies* 29.3: 285–97.
Wyatt, Justin (1994), *High Concept: Movies and Marketing in Hollywood* (Austin: University of Texas Press).

INDEX

16Volt, 41, 42, 45
400 Blows, The, 89
4AD Records, 44, 45, 56n, 158, 175n
500 Days of Summer, 15
7 Year Bitch, 109

A&M Records, 8
A$AP Rocky, 173
Adam and the Ants, 76
adbusting, 163, 164
Adickdid, 118
Adler, Lou, 22, 83, 101
Afrofuturism, 156–7
Afro-Punk, 133
Afropunk Fest, 155, 156, 161,
Afrosurrealism, 156–7
Air, 60–7, 70, 78
Alice in Chains, 26–7, 108
alternative rock, 14, 24, 25, 34n, 58, 104–7, 134
Alvin, Dave, 23
ambient music, 51, 60, 67, 69, 71, 159
American Beauty, 62
Amps, The, 58–9, 79
Anders, Allison, 23–4, 36, 102, 118

Anderson, Tim, 31–2, 58–9
Anderson, Wes, 33
Answering Machine, The, 139
Anticon Records, 171
Aphex Twin, 48, 73
A. R. Kane, 45
Araki, Gregg, 15, 33, 35–56, 78, 79
Audio Dyslexia, 150
Auslander, Philip, 100
auteur music, 35–7
authenticity, 13–14, 32, 76, 82–4, 87, 92, 100–2, 109, 117, 120–1, 125, 176–7
Azerrad, Michael, 5, 106

Babbit, Jamie, 118, 122, 123, 127, 130n
Babes in Toyland, 109, 118
Backman-Rogers, Anna, 62
Bad Brains, 136
Badu, Erykah, 173
Bahamadia, 148, 173
Bannister, Matthew, 111
Baraka, Amira, 156
Barton-Fumo, Margaret, 96
Batchelor Party, 24

Baumgarten, Marjorie, 51
Beachwood Sparks, 1
Beatles, The, 80
Bed, Bath and Beyond, 58
Beggars Group, 158, 179n,
Beguiled, The, 79
Belle and Sebastien, 179
Berlatsky, Noah, 135–6, 153
Berman, Susan, 82–3, 103n
Berry, Chuck, 136
Bexton, Nathan, 50
Big Joanie, 133, 136
Bikini Kill, 23, 112, 118, 124, 129n
Bilal, 173
Black Flag, 21, 92
Black Lips, 1
Black Panther, 157
Black Panther Party, 163, 168
Black Rock Coalition, 133
Blank Generation (1980), 18
Blank Generation, The (1976), 18, 83, 91–2
Blasters, The, 23
Bling Ring, The, 58, 79
Blondie, 18, 20
Blood Orange, 173
Bloodcat Love, 139, 142
Blue Velvet, 62
Book of Life, 37
Borden, Lizzie, 123, 127
Border Radio, 23, 36, 102
Born in Flames, 123, 127
Bow Wow Wow, 76, 78
Bratmobile, 23, 112
Britpop, 49
Broken Social Scene, 1
Brooker, Benjamin, 136
Brown Sugar, 173
Brownstein, Carrie, 179
Budd, Harold, 51–2, 54
Burroughs, William, 38
But I'm a Cheerleader, 122
Butler, Octavia E., 157
Butthole Surfers, 36

Cale, John, 87
Canoe, 139
Canonero, Milena, 76
Carmellini, Beth, 117
Cartel, the (independent music distributor), 5, 7
Casiotone for the Painfully Alone, 142–3
Cave, Nick, 36
CBS Records, 4, 33
Changes, The, 76
Chemlab, 41
Cheriel, Nalina, 118
Chewing Pics, 150
chillwave, 3
Chiswick Records, 5
Cholodenko, Lisa, 33, 37
Chop Chop Records, 33
Chris & Cosey, 39, 41, 42
Chris D., 23
Christmas on Mars, 179
Circle Jerks, 21, 22, 92
Clarke, Larry, 33
Clash, The, 101, 102
Clayton, Jace, 139
Cleaver, Eldritch, 163
Clerks, 26–7, 28, 109
Clinton, George, 162, 163, 175n
Clockwork Orange, A, 94–5
Clueless, 59
Cobain, Kurt, 107, 129n
Cocaine Cowboys, 18
Cocker Spaniels, The, 136
Cocteau Twins, 45, 46, 51, 52, 55, 56n
code-switching, 158, 160, 168
Cohen, Linda, 33
Coil, 39, 56n
college rock, 5, 6
Colombier, Michel, 63
Columbia Pictures, 77
Commotion Records, 33
Company Flow, 171
Cook, Pam, 57
Cook, Paul, 23, 101
Coon, Caroline, 101
Cooper, Jocelyn, 155

Coppola, Sofia, 15, 37, 57–79, 179
Corbett, John, 157
Corman, Roger, 19, 20, 93, 96
costume drama, 73
Coup, The, 157–8, 160–2, 168, 170, 171, 174
Cramps, The, 18
Creation Records, 8, 66
Crooked, 172
Crowe, Cameron, 107
cult films/followings, 1, 21, 19, 23, 66, 72, 81, 91
cultural appropriation, 140, 158, 160–2
culture jamming, 163, 164, 168
Cure, The, 23
Curve, 53

D'Angelo, 173
Daft Punk, 49
dance music, 6, 7, 39, 49, 162
Davis, Aeron, 30
Davis, Angela, 124
Dazed and Confused, 37
De La Soul, 171, 173
Dead Can Dance, 42
Deal, Kim, 58
Dean & Britta, 179
Death Cab for Cutie, 33
Death in Vegas, 67, 68
Debord, Guy, 84–6
Decca Records, 4
Decline of Western Civilization, The, 18, 91–2, 98, 99, 101, 103n
DeClue, Jennifer, 152
Decolonise Fest, 133, 136
Definitive Jux Records, 171
Del-Byzanteens, The, 19
Delaney, Samuel, 157
Demme, Jonathan, 87, 103n
Devo, 20
DGC Records, 25
D.I, 92–3, 98
Dickless, 109
Diddley, Bo, 136
DiFranco, Ani, 111, 113, 118
Dinosaur Jr., 36

Disney, 11, 24
Divine Horsemen, 24
DIY, 4, 11, 17, 18, 33n, 36, 59, 75, 90, 109, 125, 132, 134, 177, 178
DJ Spooky, 172
Doe, John, 23–4
Doom Generation, The, 38, 46–50, 51
Dope, 172–3
Dowd, Nancy, 101
Down and Out with the Dolls, 118–22, 128
Down By Law, 19
Downes, Julia, 112
dream pop, 45–6, 48, 51, 54, 69, 71, 78
Drugstore Cowboy, 40
Dubowsky, Jack Curtis, 39–40
Dumas, Henry, 156
Duvall, James, 45, 46, 47
DuVernay, Ava, 173

Echo and the Bunnymen, 24, 34n, 39, 43
Eisenstein, Sergei, 35
electronic music, 9, 12, 49, 60–1, 74, 124, 135, 147, 156
EMI, 4, 8, 75
Empire Records, 114
Eno, Brian, 20
Epitaph Records, 161, 171
Erasers, The, 18
ESG, 87
Esquivel, Juan García, 61
Evil Stig, 118
Explosions in the Sky, 179

Factory Records, 8
Famuyiwa, Rick, 172–3
fanzines, 10, 81–2, 91, 92, 102, 106, 110, 111, 112, 119, 124
Fear No Evil, 24
Feelies, The, 82–3, 86–90, 103n
feminism, 58, 61, 112, 122–7
Ferrari, Marc, 29
FKA Twigs, 136, 173
Flaming Lips, The, 9, 56, 179
Flesh Eaters, The, 23, 24

Flying Lotus, 171, 173, 179
Focus Features, 11
Ford, John, 38
Foreigner, The, 18
Fox Searchlight Pictures, 11
Fraser, Elizabeth, 51–2
Free Kitten, 58, 59, 79n
Frenzy (1993), 124
Frere-Jones, Sasha, 134–5
Frith, Simon, 3, 149, 152
funk music, 87, 134
Funkadelic/Parliament, 157, 162, 163, 175n

Gainsbourg, Serge, 63
Gang of Four, 73–6
Garbus, Merrill, 158, 160–1, 175n
Garden State, 15
Garwood, Ian, 72
Gas Food Lodging, 36
Gatto, Dan, 51
Generation X, 26, 106, 108–9, 113–15
Germs, The, 92, 100
Gibson, Alex, 92, 100, 103n
Gillespie, Michael, 137, 140, 152
Gilmore, Craig, 38, 43
Gilroy, Paul, 143–4, 167
Girlfriends, 124
Gits, The, 118
Glass Eye, 36
Go Fish, 124
Go-Go's, The, 58
Goapele, 173
Godard, Jean-Luc, 35, 36, 44, 48, 49
Gorbman, Claudia, 35–6
Gordan, Benjie, 26
Gordon, Kim, 58
Gossip, The, 124
goth music, 55, 133
Gottlieb, Joanne, 59, 111
Graduate, The, 115
Gramsci, Antonio, 165
Gray, Jonathan, 65
Grease, 22
Great Outdoors, The, 37
Green on Red, 24, 36

Grey, Camila, 125
Grey's Anatomy, 33
Grizzly Bear, 179
Grodal, Torban, 55–6
grunge music, 3, 5, 14, 15, 24, 25–7, 82, 102, 104–18, 129n
Guerilla Girls, 123
Gun Club, The, 117
Guncrazy, 27
Guthrie, Robin, 51–4
Gypsophile, 142

Haas, Charles, 97
Hailey, Leisha, 118
Handyside, Fiona, 62, 73, 76
Hanft, Steve, 37, 179, 180
Hannah, Kathleen, 122, 124, 129n
Hanson, Peter, 115, 116
Hart, Kylo-Patrick R, 46–7
Hartley, Hal, 33, 37
Harvey, P. J., 37, 125
Heavens to Betsy, 112, 124
Hebdidge, Dick, 165
Heems, 135
Hell, Richard, 18, 20, 83–7
Hendrix, Jimi, 136
Hesmondhalgh, David, 3, 7, 8–9, 13, 177
Hibbett, Ryan, 3, 5
High, Joel C, 31
Hindi Gods, 118
hip-hop, 3, 47, 79, 132, 133, 142, 144, 147, 148, 153, 154n, 155–9, 161, 162–73, 178
hipsters/hipsterism, 137, 139–42, 144, 152
His Name is Alive, 44
Hitchcock, Alfred, 36, 62
HIV/AIDS, 38, 41, 42, 44
Hole, 109, 121–2
Hollywood (film industry), 10–11, 35, 40, 48, 77, 82–3, 88, 101, 108, 109, 152, 177
Holofcener, Nicole, 37
Houston, Taylor Martin, 111
Howard, Yetta, 39

Howells, Thomas, 81
Hughes, John, 24, 50, 103n,
Hunter, Tim, 97
Hut Records, 7
Hype!, 105–9, 115

Iampolski, Mikhail, 77
identification, 55–6, 143
IFC Channel, 28
indie-rock, 1, 10, 14, 24, 27, 28, 36, 37, 56, 61, 74, 78, 107, 108, 109, 111, 112, 114, 115, 117, 118, 122, 125, 128, 134, 135, 136, 154, 155, 171, 174, 175, 178
industrial music, 3, 4, 12, 37, 38–9, 41, 42, 44, 45, 48, 56n
Industrial Records, 38
Internet Movie Database (IMDb), 29, 72
I.R.S. Records, 8
Itty Bitty Titty Committee, The, 118, 122–8, 130n

JagJaguwar Records, 12
James-Wilson, Matthew, 154
jangle pop, 3, 5, 16n, 66
Jarmusch, Jim, 18–19, 33n
jazz, 19, 67, 79, 87, 142, 157, 162, 171, 173
Jenkins, Barry, 14, 133, 136, 140, 142, 143, 153
Jesus and Mary Chain, The, 24, 34n, 39, 44, 55, 67, 71
Jett, Joan, 118, 130n
Jingle Punks, 29
Johnston, Daniel, 27, 36
Jones, Steve, 23, 101
Jordan, Jeremy, 49
Joy Division, 39, 42
JPEGMafia, 171
Juned, 118
Juno, 15, 29

K Records, 7
Kaboom, 54
Kang, Nancy, 145, 151
Kassabian, Anahid, 65, 143

Kearney, Mary Celeste, 113, 128
Keenan, Elizabeth K., 113
Keightley, Keir, 10, 30
Kelela, 173
Kennedy, Todd, 57, 62
Kerrigan, Finola, 31
Khia, 144–5
Kids, 27
Kill Rock Stars, 125, 130n
Kills, The, 171
Kimball, Jeffrey, 26
King, Geoff, 10, 179, 180
Klein, Bethany, 14, 30
Klein, Naomi, 108, 116–17
KONK, 19
Koresky, Michael, 51
Korine, Harmony, 33
Kovács, András Bálint, 89
Král, Ivan, 18, 83
Kravitz, Zoë, 173
Kruse, Holly, 5, 7, 81
Kubrick, Stanley, 36, 94
Kuso, 173, 179

L Word, The, 124
L7, 118
Laderman, David, 84
Ladies and Gentlemen, The Fabulous Stains, 21–3, 83, 101
Laing, Dave, 4, 84
Land of the Loops, 59
Last Dragon, The, 160, 161
Le Tigre, 124, 129n
Lemmy, 119
Lemonheads, The, 33
Lent, Dean, 23
Leonard, Marion, 112
Lewandoski, Natalie, 31–2
Lick the Star, 58–60, 62, 78
Lifter, Rachel, 16n, 155–6, 161
Lil' Kim, 145
Linklater, Richard, 33, 36–7
Little Richard, 136
Living End, The, 38–44, 45, 49, 55
lo-fi production, 6, 38, 67, 138, 142, 153, 171, 180

Lollapalooza, 25, 56, 122
London, Jeffrey, 81
Long Weekend (O'Despair), The, 56n
Lorde, Audrey, 145, 151
Los Angeles Independent Film Festival, 28
Lost in Translation, 58, 66–72, 78
Lounge Lizards, The, 19
Love, Courtney, 121–2
Love Among Freaks, 26
Love and a .45, 27
Lowery, David, 28
Lunch, Lydia, 18
Lurie, John, 18–19
Lwin, Annabella, 76
Lyons, James, 106–7

McElrath, Jenni, 117
McGuigan, Jim, 116
McKnight, Tracy, 33
McLaren, Malcolm, 75–6, 84
MacLeod, Dewar, 81, 82
Mad Love, 27
Maddala, Vivek, 54
Madlib, 142
Madonna, 37, 81
Mahon, Maureen, 133, 136, 152, 153
Manning Jr, Roger J., 69
Mansell, Clint, 179
Marcus, Sarah, 112
Marie Antoinette, 58, 72–9
Mars, Thomas, 58
Mars Volta, The, 171
Martt, Mike, 117
Mascis, J., 36
MasterSource, 28
Matter of Degrees, A, 27, 33
MCA Records, 8
Meat Puppets, 36
Medicine for Melancholy, 14, 136–44, 152–3, 156, 157, 174
Medved, Michael, 48
Meier, Leslie M., 177
Melody Maker, 46, 106
Men in Orbit, 19
metal (music), 6, 26, 39, 41, 47, 65, 104

MF DOOM, 171
M.I.A., 135
Microsoft, 110, 111, 115, 129n
Middle of Nowhere, 173
Miguel, 173
Miller, Scot, 156, 157
Minaj, Nicki, 145
Ministry, 45
Miramax, 11, 24, 26
Mommy, 118
Monae, Janelle, 157
Moore, Ryan, 90–1, 106, 109, 110
Moore, Thurston, 58
Moose (band), 7, 46
Morgan, Matthew, 155
Morrissey, 43
Mos Def, 173
Mottola, Greg, 33
Moyle, Allan, 21, 22, 27, 101, 114
MTV, 25, 38, 54, 101
Murmurs, The, 118
music documentaries, 12, 18, 82, 83, 91–2, 102, 105–7, 133, 179
music scenes/subcultures, 2, 4, 12, 14, 18, 80–130, 133, 135, 165, 180
music supervisors, 25, 26, 31–3, 37, 58, 60, 66
My Bloody Valentine, 46, 66–7, 70
Mysterious Skin, 38, 51–4
Mystery Train, 19

National Organization for Women, 124
Native Tongues, 171
Need, The, 124
neo-soul, 132, 173
New Line Pictures, 11
New Musical Express, 5, 60, 72
New Order, 24, 73
New Queer Cinema, 38
new wave music, 18, 19, 38, 74, 87
New World Pictures, 19, 20, 93
New Yorker, The, 134
Newman, Michael, 2, 10–11, 13, 27, 31, 35, 83, 139, 180
Newton, Huey, 163
Nguyen, Mimi Thi, 128

niche cultures/ niche markets, 2, 10, 11, 22, 24–5, 27, 31–2, 56, 61, 72, 79, 81, 101, 102, 104, 106–7, 129n, 176
Nicholls, Matthew William, 16n, 176
Nick and Norah's Infinite Playlist, 29
Nine Inch Nails, 47
Nirvana, 5, 25, 27, 105, 106, 109, 129n
Nitecaps, The, 83, 87, 89
no wave music, 19, 103n
Nonce, The, 173
Now Apocalypse, 54
Nowhere In, The, 179
Nowhere, 49–50, 51
N.W.A., 47

O.C., The, 33
O'Meara, Jennifer, 42
Oakes, Kaya, 107, 178, 180
Ocean, Frank, 173
October Films, 11
Octopus Project, The, 139
Oddisee, 173
Oddsac, 179
On the Rocks, 79
Orde Records, 22
Ortner, Sherry B., 10
Over the Edge, 97

Pale Saints, The, 44
Paramount Pictures, 22, 65
paratexts, 65
Parents Music Resource Center (PMRC), 47
Pariah, 14, 133, 144–54, 155, 156, 157, 174
Party Animal, 24
Patsavas, Alexandra, 33
Pavitt, Bruce, 106
Peaches, 67, 124
Pearl Jam, 108
Pederson, Chris, 92
Perks of Being a Wallflower, The, 33
Permanent Vacation, 19
Perren, Alisa, 24, 109, 129n
Perrey & Kingsley, 61

Peterson, Kristine, 109, 117
Phillips, Stephanie, 133, 161
Phoenix, 58, 67, 79
Pink Floyd, 63, 103n
Pitchfork, 67, 72, 134
Pixies, 33
Plugz, The, 21
Poe, Amos, 18
Poison, 38
Poledouris, Zoë, 119
PolyGram Records, 4
Poneman, Jonathan, 106
Pop, Iggy, 21
Porches, 79
Poster, Randall, 33
POWER UP, 122, 130n
Poyntz Stuart R., 81
Presley, Elvis, 80
Pretty in Pink, 24
Pribram, E. Deidre, 83
promotional culture, 29–31
Psych-Out, 20
Psychic TV, 39, 56n
Pump Up the Volume, 27
punk music, 3–5, 7, 17–24, 26, 29, 33n, 58, 59, 75, 76–8, 80–103, 104, 111–13, 117, 124, 127–8, 133, 136, 148, 155, 156, 161
  hardcore punk, 20, 21, 23, 87, 90–100, 111, 112, 136
  post-punk, 4, 17, 18, 19, 22, 39, 73, 74, 76, 77, 78, 82, 87, 116

Quatro, Suzi, 23
Queen and Slim, 173
Queen Latifah, 173
queercore, 113, 124

R&B, 132, 133, 136, 144, 147, 148, 155, 156, 172, 173
race (and indie music), 127–8, 131–75
Radio Dept., 78
Radio Sloan, 124
Raha, Maria, 3, 111
Ramones, The, 18–20, 23
Ranaldo, Lee, 36

RCA Records, 4
Reagan, Ronald, 21, 90–1, 97
Reality Bites, 114
Rebel Without a Cause, 97
recontextualisation, 158, 162–4
Recording Industry Association of
    America (RIAA), 47
Red Five, 117
Red Hot Chili Peppers, 92
Red House Painters, 44
Red Italy, 19
Redd Kross, 58
Reed, Alexander S., 38–9
Reed, Ishmael, 162
Rees, Dee, 145, 148, 151
Regev, Motti, 16n, 132
reggae music, 87, 134
Reid, Jamie, 74, 75, 84
Reiter, Jill, 124
Reitzell, Brian, 33, 58, 60, 66, 67, 69
R.E.M., 6, 24,
Rennie, Jamie, 81
Repo Man, 20–2, 26
retro, 60–2, 78, 172
Reynolds, Simon, 67, 78
Reznor, Trent, 47, 171
Ride, 52, 53, 55
Riley, Boots, 156, 157, 160, 161, 163,
    165, 166, 168, 179
riot grrrl, 58–9, 101, 102, 104, 109,
    111, 112, 113, 118, 121–8,
    129n,130n
Robert Stigwood Organisation, 22
rock 'n' roll, 20, 80, 101, 136
Rock 'n' Roll High School, 19–20
Rock All Night, 20
rock music, 22, 23, 24, 25, 27, 45, 46,
    48, 58, 100, 101, 109, 118, 119,
    120, 121, 134, 136,147, 148, 150,
    153, 162, 170, 171, 174
Rocky Horror Picture Show, The, 22
Rolling Stones, The, 80
Rome '78, 19
Ronettes, The, 71
Roots, The, 154n, 173
Rose, Tricia, 163

Rotten, Johnny, 84, 103n
Rough Trade Records, 8, 16n, 175n
Ruby Rich, B., 38, 123, 126
Rundgren, Todd, 20

S.F.W., 27, 114
Sahim, Sarah, 134–5
St Vincent, 179
Santigold, 136
Saturday Night Fever, 22
Schemel, Patty, 125
Scott Pilgrim Versus the World, 1–2, 15,
    181n
Sebadoh, 27
Sedgwick, Edie, 60
Seidelman, Susan, 19, 22, 82–4, 86–8,
    103n
Sensational, 171, 172
Sex Pistols, 23, 74, 75, 84, 101–2
sex, lies and videotape, 24, 40
Shabazz Palaces, 171
Shadow of a Doubt, 62
Shake, Rattle and Rock, 20
Shank, Barry, 81
Shazam, 29
Shields, Kevin, 66–7, 70
Shivers, Coyote, 119
Shockoe Noise, 28
shoegaze, 37, 45, 46, 49, 51, 54
Sigur Rós, 52
Simonon, Paul, 101
Simple Men, 37
Singers and Players, 87
Singles,107–9
Siouxsie and the Banshees, 55, 76
situationism, 84
Slacker, 36, 37
slackers, 36, 106, 113, 114, 115
Slam, 154, 172
Slant 6, 124
Slaves to the Underground, 14,
    114–18
Sleater-Kinney, 118, 124, 125
Sloan, 60
Slowdive, 52
Slumber Party, 124

Smaill, Belinda, 57–8
Smashing Pumpkins, 108
Smiley Face, 38, 54
Smith, Jeff, 31, 108
Smith, Kevin, 26
Smith, Murray, 56
Smith, Patti, 18, 118
Smithereens, 18, 19, 21, 22, 82–90, 91, 92, 101, 102
Smiths, The, 5, 24, 39, 40
Solange, 173
Some Kind of Wonderful, 24
Somewhere, 79
Sonic Youth, 9, 19, 36, 37, 58
Sony Pictures Classics, 11
Sorry to Bother You, 133, 134, 155–70, 174
Soul Asylum, 26
soul music, 134, 140, 144, 148, 173
Soundgarden, 108
Source Records, 65
Space is the Place, 157
Spheeris, Penelope, 20, 82, 90–102
Splendor, 51, 55
Spooner, James, 133, 136, 155
Spotify, 29, 132
Squarepusher, 67
SST Records, 7
Staples, Vince, 173
Starr, Kinnie, 119
Stereolab, 61
Stiff Records, 5
Stiffed, 136
Stock, Aitken and Waterman, 6
Stoever, Jennifer Lynn, 160
Stones Throw Records, 171
Strachan, Robert, 8
Stranger than Paradise, 18, 19
Strutter, 24
Styrene, Poly, 136
Sub Pop (fanzine), 82
Sub Pop (record label), 7, 25, 26, 81, 105–6, 129n, 130m, 171
Suburbia, 20, 21, 82, 90–102, 103n
SubUrbia, 36
Subway Riders, 18

Sugar Town, 24
Suicidal Tendencies, 21
Sun City Girls, 179
Sun Ra, 157
Sundance film festival, 26
Superchunk, 36
Surviving Desire, 37
Swa, Sparla, 148, 150
Swoon, 38

Talking Heads, 18, 20, 23
Tamar-kali, 148, 149, 153, 179
taste cultures, 29–31, 129n
Taylor, John, 97, 103n
Taylor, Leila, 133
Team Dresch, 118, 124
Teen Angels, The, 118
teen movies, 24, 33, 50, 54
Television (band), 18
television (medium), 17, 25, 29, 31–3, 37, 46, 48, 50, 54, 82, 102, 116, 173, 180
Tellier, Sébastien, 67
Terri, Frances, 156
This is How the World Ends, 54
This Mortal Coil, 44
Three Bewildered People in the Night, 56n
Throbbing Gristle, 38, 39, 56n
Throwing Muses, 33
Tiger Trap, 125
Times Square, 21–3, 101
Tompkins, Joseph, 65
Totally Fucked Up, 44–6, 47, 48, 49, 56
Touch and Go Records, 7
Trash Talk,
Travis, Abby, 118
Tribe Called Quest, A, 171
Troche, Rose, 124
True, Everett, 106, 129n
T.S.O.L (True Sound of Liberty), 92, 94
Tucker, Corin, 124
Tune-Yards, 158–61, 170, 174
Turner Broadcasting System, 11, 16n

TV on the Radio, 136, 139, 172
Twin/Tone Records, 7
Tzioumakis, Yannis, 10, 11, 25

Uh Huh Her, 118, 125
Underground USA, 19
Universal Music Group (UMG), 16n, 28, 130n
Universal Pictures, 2, 20, 25
Unmade Beds, 18
Unrest, 45

Vandals, The, 96, 99
Vannier, Jean-Claude, 63
Variety (film), 18, 19
Velvet Monkeys, The, 36
Verve, The, 7, 49
Vesey, Alyx, 33
video games, 16n, 17, 29, 31, 47–8, 116, 180
Violators, The, 92
Virgin Records, 7, 65
Virgin Suicides, The, 58, 60–6, 67, 68
Vito, Christopher, 132, 170
Vivre sa Vie, 44
Voss, Kurt, 23–4, 102, 118

Waits, Tom, 141
Walston, Wayne, 92
Walt Mink, 58
Warhol, Andy, 18
Warner Bros., 16n, 20, 107, 130n, 132
Warp Records, 171

Watermelon Woman, The, 124
Wax Trax! Records, 7, 39, 56n
WEA Records, 4
Weaver, Jimmy, 82–4
Weill, Claudia, 124
Westerberg, Paul, 108
Westwood, Vivienne, 75–6
White Bird in a Blizzard, 38, 54, 55
White Denim, 139
White Stripes, 58
Wiggs, Josephine, 179
Wild Angels, The, 20, 96–7
Wild in the Streets, 20
Williams, Pharrell, 172
Williams, Saul, 171–2
Wilson, Kaia, 118
Wingate, Dick, 108
Winnigo, David, 179
Wolfgang Press, The, 44
Woo, Benjamin, 81
Woodshock, 36
Wordsound Records, 171–2
Wu-Tang Clan, 132
Wyatt, Justin, 80, 108

X (band), 92
X-Ray Spex, 136

Yesterday's New Quintet, 141–2
Yetnikoff, Walter, 33
Yo La Tengo, 37

Zapata, Mia, 118
Zipporah, Gene, 161

EU Authorised Representative:
Easy Access System Europe Mustamäe tee 50, 10621 Tallinn, Estonia
gpsr.requests@easproject.com

Printed and bound by CPI Group (UK) Ltd, Croydon, CR0 4YY
24/02/2026
02059271-0007